COLOR FOR THE ELECTRONIC AGE

Jan V. White

COLOR FOR THE ELECTRONIC AGE

A Xerox Press Book
Watson-Guptill Publications/New York

First published in 1990 in New York by Watson-Guptill Publications,
a division of Billboard Publications, Inc.,
1515 Broadway, New York, N.Y. 10036

Library of Congress Cataloging-in-Publication Data

White, Jan V., 1928–
Color for the electronic age / Jan V. White.
p. cm.
"A Xerox Press Book."
Includes bibliographical references.
ISBN 0–8230–0732–4
1. Desktop publishing. 2. Electronic publishing. 3. Color—printing—Data processing. I. Title.
Z286.D47W49 1990
686.2′254466—dc20 89–77555
CIP

Distributed in the United Kingdom by Phaidon Press Ltd.,
Littlegate House, St. Ebbe's St., Oxford

Distributed in Europe, the Far East, Southeast and Central Asia,
and South America by Rotovision S.A.,
9 Route Suisse, CH-1295 Mies, Switzerland.

Manufactured in Singapore

First printing, 1990

1 2 3 4 5 6 7 8 9 10/95 94 93 92 91 90

Contents

Preface

Words are usually considered the language of communication. But this is far too narrow and constricting. Communication in print and in presentations is as much a visual process as it is a verbal one. Even the simplest word-ideas need to be translated into type in order to be transmitted to the reader. Type is words made visible. It is impossible to separate thoughts-in-words from typography. Type can help or hinder the deciphering and comprehension of those thoughts. It follows, therefore, that typography is a form of communication in itself. You could even call it a dialect of the language of communication.

All the other means by which we communicate in print or visual presentations are also dialects. Pictures are a dialect that speaks to the emotions. Infographics are a dialect that explains facts by verbal/visual means. Charts and graphs are a dialect that renders statistics readily comprehensible. So, too, is color a dialect whose object is thought to be embellishment and decoration. It is the purpose of this book to show how color can be more than that.

There are many excellent books on color, but, to my knowledge, this is the first attempt at treating it as a *dialect of functional communication*. The idea had been mulling for a long time, and I merely needed a chance to make it happen. Such an opportunity arose when Richard M. Lunde, David Kwiatkouski, and Carmen Y. Howes of the Xerox Corporation approached me with their need—a study of color as *value-added*. This, surely, is just another way of saying functional communication. Xerox Press under Ken Felderstein's inspiring leadership made the project possible. It only took a year's work and thirty-eight years' preparation.

I asked my friend Rohn Engh, head of Photo Source International, whether he knew where I could find photographs that I could use as examples, realizing that I was intending to do them violence by showing them in a variety of mechanically produced versions. He understood both the need and the danger, yet offered his own for the experiment. I hope he will not be mad at me. They are credited where they occur. Blame my own questionable photographic skills for the uncredited ones.

The most difficult color manipulations as well as a number of the chart and graph variations were produced by COLORTEC of Norwalk, Connecticut. My thanks to Misty Gruber, Steve Abramson, and Dave Zwang for their vital help. Thanks also to Carl Rosen for his sensitive editing.

I believe myself to be mild and even-tempered. Perhaps sweet-natured would be more apt as description. I have always thought that the placid manatee and I float in tranquility. Nonetheless, my sons tell me that I am a bear with a tiger's claws and a camel's ill temper when I am working on a book. I simply cannot understand why they say such a thing. Yet when Toby, Alex, Gregory, and Christopher agree, there must be something to it, and when Caroline, my daughter-in-law, gently concurs, my delusions evaporate. Therefore, to redress the ills I have visited upon her, I dedicate this book to my long-suffering Clare.

1. INTRODUCTION

Contrary to what we hear, this is not the Age of Information. It would be more accurate to call it the Age of Information Chaos. How much better, were it the Age of Knowledge.

How to turn information into knowledge? Well, color can help if it is used intelligently. It is only a detail, true, yet its importance is growing, for technology is making color available in printed media at an ever-increasing rate and at an ever-decreasing cost. Therefore, this book is about how:

Color can help give visual order to information chaos.

Please note that I said, "color can *help*." Color cannot do it alone. It is merely one of the means at our disposal. It is a technique, a tool, a language. Color is one part of a coordinated effort to communicate in print. Added to typography (as tone of voice), infographics, charts, graphs, symbolism, and verbal/visual presentation, it is one of the means to an end: comprehension; knowledge.

Color should not be used just because it is available. Potentially, it can do more than merely make reports, letters, and charts eye-catching. We must be discriminating and avoid acting like children with a new box of crayons. Color should not be used to dazzle but to enlighten and thus to add value.

Color can sharpen the delivery of a message. Color can code elements, so their ranking and relationships are more easily comprehended. Organized information is always more easily assimilated than disorganized information. Further, color coding helps people to remember information longer.

Color can increase the velocity of comprehension. By using it effectively, the producer (writer, editor, designer, publisher) has done much of the work of analyzing for the viewer/reader.

Color can help to establish identity and character. Color produces strong associations and is vividly remembered. Consistency in hue, applied with discipline, is a vital element in building both recognition and character within a document and in a series of related documents. It is a vital factor in defining corporate identity.

Color can enliven the product. Color applied with taste and care can beautify. It is more valuable, though, when used to bring out inherent beauty than when it is a cosmetic added to the surface.

This book is not about using color to make pages pretty.

Not that there is anything wrong with prettiness. Certainly, nobody is advocating ugliness. In some situations, prettiness is the desired goal. And, without question, prettiness charms the viewer, sets a pleasant mood, and often makes the product look nicer. Such a quality can indeed make the product more valuable.

Unfortunately, color is too often mistaken for decoration. Dressing up the page too often camouflages the underlying message. It might appear pretty, but such beauty is indeed skin-deep and too often merely phony.

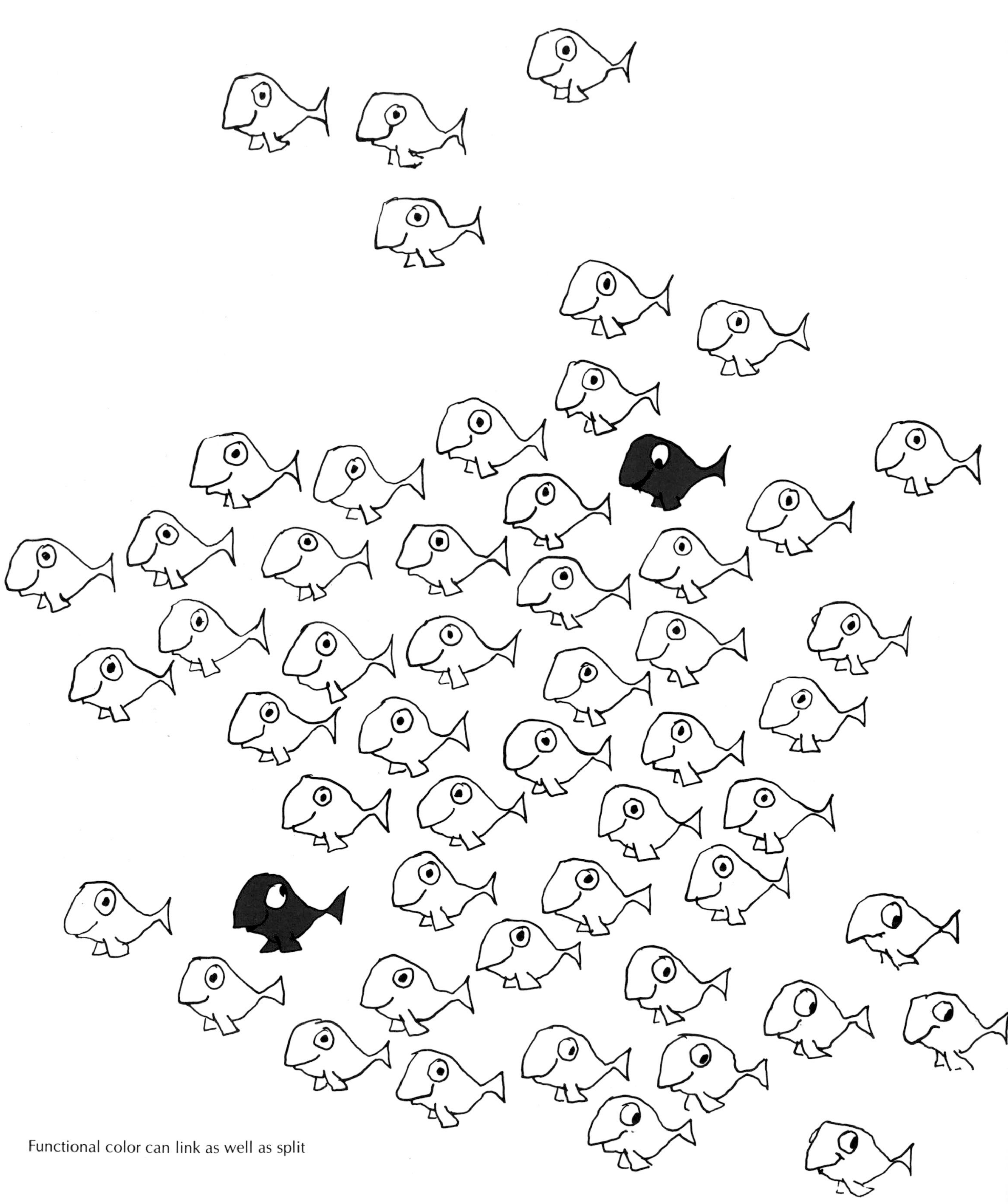

Functional color can link as well as split

This book is about the functional use of color. It is about color as a tool: how it can be used to focus attention, explain relationships, analyze data; how it can help the viewer/reader understand information faster and more vividly; and how it can make printed matter easier to absorb, helping turn information into knowledge. This is value worth adding. Prettiness is a side issue, a by-product, a lagniappe.

Personal idiosyncrasies also affect our choices and reactions. The editor of the first magazine I worked on loved blue. Guess what color I had to use any time a second color became available? (He also wore brown shoes with blue suits. This was in the 1950s, when Doing Your Own Thing had not yet been invented.) Such subjective attitudes should remain personal and should never be allowed to impinge on professional decision making. Color in a publication context is a medium of communication to be chosen and used with deliberation, not emotion.

Though color is a universal language that speaks to the emotions, we speak it both instinctively and culturally. Our responses are based on training and environment, which is why color is a complex subject that must be approached with respect and concern. Many studies have been done on color topics ranging from the physics of light to the use of color in psychological therapy, but this is not one of them. This book does not pretend to be a scientific treatise. It approaches the use of color from a strictly practical angle, based on common sense and accumulated experience.

The introduction thus plunges right into generally accepted tips or insights on color itself. Then follows the application of color in the product as a whole: in words; in pictures; in illustrations; and in charts and graphs.

Because so much color material is produced as business documentation, where hard copy is blended with overhead presentations, color on the screen is discussed in chapter 3. There are some fundamental differences between color in print and on screen that must be understood.

In all cases, however, color is thought of as a material assigned to fulfill specific tasks. Using color to fulfill a wider purpose brings the highest return on the investment in color capability.

2. THE BASICS

How color is used and how people see it

You probably learned to think about colors from paints. At school you found that a dollop of red added to a brushful of blue makes purple and red mixed with a glob of yellow makes orange. At least that is what it looked like on the painting you proudly brought home.

There is nothing wrong with this view of color. It is perfectly logical and valid. It is the Brewster, Prang, or color wheel theory of color. It is based on three primary colors: red, yellow, and blue.

A secondary color results from mixing two of the primary colors in equal amounts: red plus yellow makes orange; yellow plus blue makes green; blue plus red makes purple.

A tertiary color is created by combining one primary color with one secondary color: red plus orange makes red-orange; orange plus yellow makes yellow-orange; yellow plus green makes yellow-green; green plus blue makes blue-green; blue plus purple makes blue-purple; purple plus red makes red-purple. When these colors are placed around a wheel, a sequence is derived that follows the sequence of colors seen in a rainbow.

Combining these twelve colors in various proportions and adding black or white allows an unlimited palette to be devised.

This, however, is a piece of background knowledge that you might as well shelve, unless you intend to paint. It is mentioned here simply because it is something almost everyone knows. Yet it is likely to confuse you, because it has little to do with color as used on the printed page or on the screen. "Shelving it" is perhaps the wrong phrase. Things on shelves are too visible. It might be better to store everything that you learned about color at school in a safe-deposit box, lock it up, and lose the key. You will still be able to get at it when you need it, if you pay the bank the cost of a new key.

It is vital that you understand the terminology

The following terms refer to color, whether in print or on the screen. The terms are the same whether produced traditionally or electronically.

Hue: The name of a color, such as brown, blue, green. People can distinguish thousands of subtle variations. We pick colors on the basis of hue because we "like them." Hue, however, is less important than value and chroma in handling color well.

Value: The darkness or lightness of a hue.

Shade is the darkness of a hue produced by adding black.

Tint is the lightness of a hue produced by adding white.

Hues—even the pure ones—vary widely in value. Yellow is very light, violet is very dark. Successful color relationships depend more on the careful handling of values than of hues.

Chroma: The intensity or vividness of a color, its brightness or dullness. The brighter it is, the more "saturated" it is said to be. The strongest chroma is very colorful. The weakest chroma looks like a neutral gray.

(*Hue*, *value*, and *chroma* are terms used in the Munsell system. See page 189.)

Visibility: The purer the hue, the more visible it is both at a distance and, in terms of noticeability, close up. The subtler the value in shade or tint, the more difficult it is to discern.

Contrast: The greater the contrast, the stronger the visibility. Black on yellow and black on white are the strongest contrasts.

Here is the color wheel, which is in general use. There are all sorts of variations worked out for measuring scientific balances of color depending on whether it is studied as light waves, pigments in suspension, or what have you. The color wheel is the practical compromise we work with in the less-than-precise world of print and presentation.

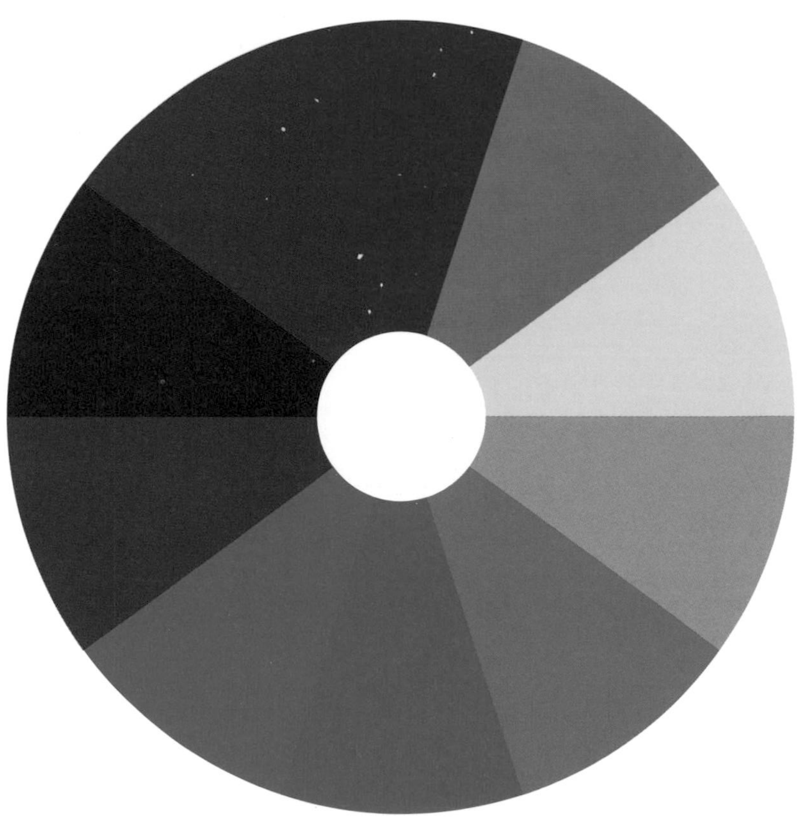

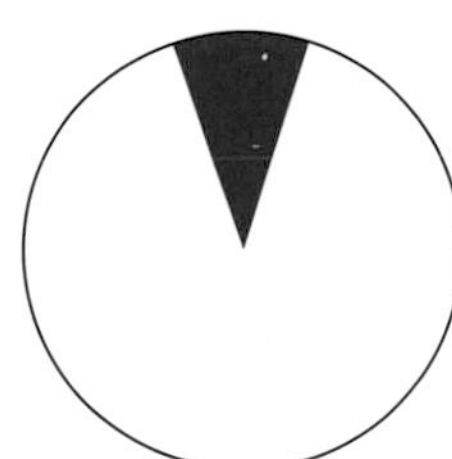

Monochromatic color schemes use one basic hue to give unity to the product. Variations in lightness or darkness are used, but essentially these are red or green color schemes.

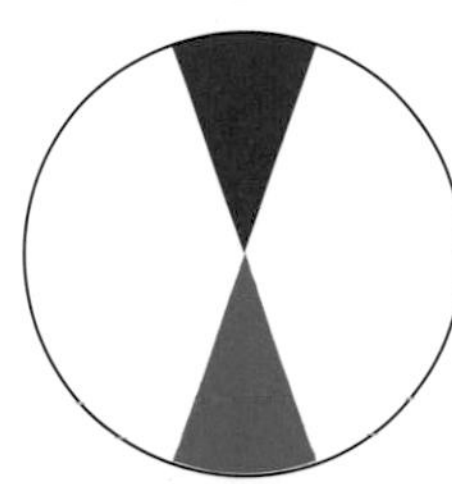

Complementary color schemes use hues that lie directly opposite each other on the color wheel. (They are called complementary because they contain all the colors of the spectrum between them.) It is usually wise to use the quiet color as the dominant color and the brighter color as an accent.

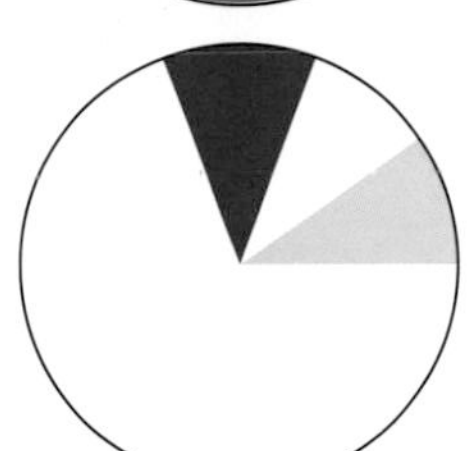

Analogous color schemes use hues that lie close together on the color wheel. Since the colors are related, they are harmonious. Nonetheless, one color should be picked as the dominant color with the others supporting it.

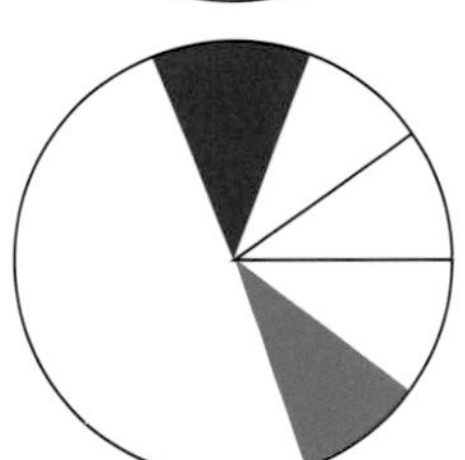

Contrasting color schemes use hues that have three colors between them on the color wheel. Though they are called contrasting, they need not clash or create unpleasant combinations. The brightest colors should be used as an accent to a design, the less bright ones as background.

Achromatic color schemes use no colored hues (achromatic means without color). These schemes are based entirely on black, white, and grays.

Black-plus color schemes use a palette limited to grays plus one hue. Grays blend with any color. Bright colors go well with light gray, pale ones with dark gray, dull colors go well with black. Contrast is the key to balance.

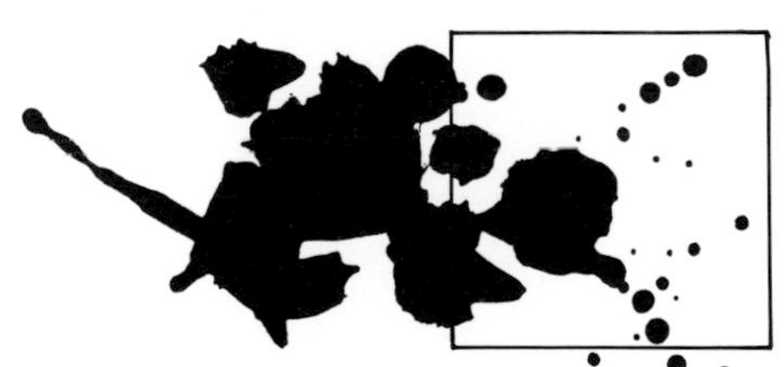

And white is a color. So is black.

It is vital that you understand the magic and trickery of color. Color is always seen in its surroundings. What it is near and how much of it there is affects how it looks.

No book on color would be complete without showing some of the psychological tricks that colors play on perception. Since this is a book on the practical aspects of using color, these apparent magic tricks must be seen as characteristics of the material merely to be aware of. They are traps to watch out for.

A brilliant, pure color on a background of its own shade appears very different from the same color seen against a background of its complementary.

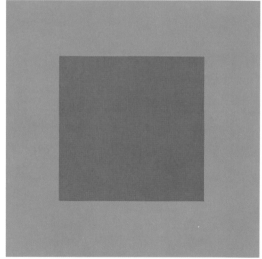

The blue-gray in the left panel is seen against a dark color. It therefore appears lighter than the one in the right-hand panel, whose border is paler. Yet the blue-gray is the same in both.

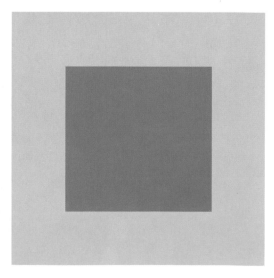

Much of the success of using color depends on proportion and relationships. The large area of darker background makes the little yellow square jump off the page. Reverse the colors, and the contrast is much less successful. Change the proportions, and there is hardly any motion.

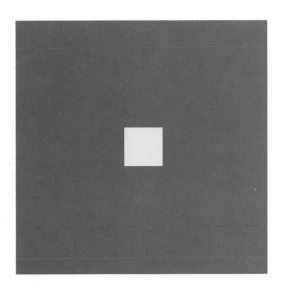

The illusion of size is affected by a color's strength. In both of these squares, the red overpowers the black. This is why the inner red square looks larger than the black one. They are, of course, both the same size.

When pure complementary colors are placed next to each other, they have an upsetting effect on the color receptors in the human eye, and visual vibration ensues. Purple and green clash. They can be brought into harmony by mixing a little of each with the other.

When two contrasting colors abut, they appear to intensify along the edge where they meet. The phenomenon of "simultaneous contrast" was already studied by Leonardo da Vinci. It is no esoteric trick, but a disturbing effect to be guarded against. Running a sliver of white (or black) to separate two colors placed next to each other gets rid of the problem.

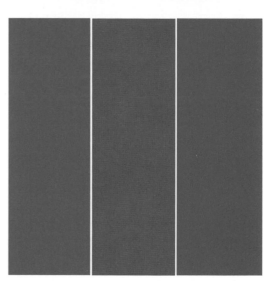

The illusion of depth and layering on the surface of the paper depends on color. The line of white type seems to advance, especially in contrast to a line of black type, which seems to recede.

A LINE OF WHITE TYPE SEEMS TO ADVANCE ON THE RIGHT BACKGROUND

WHEN CONTRASTED TO A LINE OF BLACK ON THE SAME BACKGROUND

Whatever color you may choose to use, you must apply it so that it works for you: It should make sense, clarify ideas, and add value to what you show and tell.

First, analyze the information to find how color can be used to code it; for instance, if there are tasks the viewer is to perform, make them vivid with color.

Anything on a page that is not ordinary black-on-white text is looked at first. A picture is inevitably the first element to attract the eye; color is likely to be the next. Therefore, it is logical to assign color to the most important information, so it is sure to be noticed. It will probably motivate the reader to penetrate deeper into the text.

The importance brought into evidence by color is also a cogent rationale for running the item larger, bolder. This not only increases the tone of voice, with which you are shouting, "Hey, look at me," but also makes the color element more legible. Color contrasts less with white paper than black does. To compensate for the decreased contrast, increase the inked area by size.

Draw attention by using colors that have high-value and high-chroma—bright ones. Common-sense places for using such colors are danger signals, reminders, on-screen cursors, and similar elements. Bright red seems to be most successful, perhaps, because it is an established signal in American culture. But avoid confusing the viewer by reducing the brightness of those bright elements with a background that is too colorful. You should neither pull your punches nor create competition for them. Decide what is vitally important, then let it stand out that way. Plan the hierarchy of brightness so that it becomes a clear language. Be consistent with it, so that it can perform its intended function.

Viewers sense color relationships very clearly. Be consistent in the use of color groupings. Do not use colors denoting commands in one chapter to denote menu choices in another. It only confuses.

When color coding is established, use the same colors throughout the product and during the entire life cycle of the information unit.

It is confusing to change colors from one technique to another; for example, hard-copy printout as compared to slides; on-screen as compared to traditional offset; overheads as compared to architectural signage. Coordination of means demands coordination of hues. You must plan carefully to ensure their similarity.

Do not confuse the viewer/reader with too many color codes. Under normal conditions, two colors in addition to black are easily understood and remembered. As the number of colors increases, the work's effectiveness decreases, because it requires effort to remember so many different colors.

To ensure understanding under all conditions, duplicate color coding with coded shape. Such redundancy makes the original intelligible when it is translated into other media or even into black-and-white copies. A distinct—albeit minor—advantage of color/shape redundancy is that it helps those with color-impaired vision. Further, if documents are likely to be examined under less-than-ideal lighting conditions, paralleling colors with typographic variations as well as icons helps overcome the lack of contrast and makes the ideas clear. So, if you make a bar red, give it a scraggly outline and texture as well. If the main graph line is in blue, make it fatter than the others so that it stands out by shape as well as hue.

Color has characteristics you need to be aware of. You must get past "liking" a certain hue, if you are to control color and use it cleverly for a certain purpose.

Color is a language like any other, requiring both a provider and a recipient, a speaker and a hearer, an informer and an interpreter. Your understanding has to be on the same wavelength (pun intended) as that of your viewer.

In a publication on computers, a picture of an elephant may be incongruous and startling (even if it illustrates a story on memory, which is a cliché). It would be so common in a natural-history magazine that few would pay it much attention (unless it is remarkable for a specific reason).

Here are some observations for you to consider. Some may be appropriate to your needs, others less so. Never mind. They are cited with one purpose only: to make you aware that color used functionally in print or in presentations is not an artistic, subjective, or intuitive medium but one that must be controlled intellectually.

Black is a color, and is so white. They can be used actively as part of a color scheme, not merely to organize and propel information.

White space is a vital element on a page. It gives both pattern and clarity. Moats between elements on a page identify related groupings of images and words. Manipulating white space yields varieties of character for your product. Its generous use gives your product a feeling of elegance and value. By contrast, its tightness gives your product a feeling of value by making it look fully packed. White space must not be seen merely as a neutral background, lying fallow. Used deliberately, it makes colors work better in all respects.

Color can help communicate nuances of meaning. Like type, color can scream as well as whisper. If it screams too loudly, the subtleties of meaning are swamped by the visual noise.

Use bright colors in small areas, pale or dull colors in large areas.

Warm colors are brighter, more dynamic, more active, and thus more "attractive" than cool colors. They are used at their best in small areas contrasted to cool backgrounds.

Warm colors appear closer to the viewer than cool ones. Therefore, canny users of color assign red, yellow, or orange to elements that are supposed to be in the foreground. They assign blue, green, or violet to objects in the background. If elements in the foreground are intended to overlap those in the background, the effect of depth and separation is emphasized by the right use of color, and understanding is thus enhanced.

Light or pale colors tend to make an object appear larger than it is. Dark colors make it appear smaller. Therefore, canny users of color assign pastel tints of yellow, white, or red to expand the elements they need to make important. They play down others by hiding them in shades of blue, gray, brown, or purple.

Maximum visibility is a characteristic of yellow. Next in visibility come orange, vermilion (an orange-red), and yellow-green. These are precisely the colors of the blaring, aggressive, fluorescent paints you see on posters. They work.

Bright colors are in vogue. Colorfulness in itself is fashionable. It is thought to appeal to the young. It so happens that oldsters, whose physical ability to distinguish colors is less acute, also derive value from the trend. The question remains, Which color combinations appeal to all segments of the public?

By contrast, "hospital green" is fast going out of style. It had originally been chosen not only as being restful and relaxing but also because it makes people look healthier, since it is a good background to skin colors. (The fact that it is the complementary color to that of blood and thus ideal in operating rooms is somewhat grisly. Surgeons like it.) As anything else made common by overuse, its physiological virtues have been undercut by negative psychological undertones: hospital green is now synonymous with institutions and is therefore being covered over with more domestic hues.

Eight percent of men and 1 percent of women are color-impaired. Green and red are the usual problem colors. It is wise to use them only in their midrange values, where they are good and strong and therefore more likely to be distinguished. Blue, incidentally, is the universally recognizable color.

Color does not add much colorfulness to a page unless it is used strongly. A little blue dot or a purple rule do not add all that much (unless they are very carefully composed). It is wiser to be a bit more generous than this. If such generosity also supports meaning, then even a comparatively small area of color can pack a punch. But if the color area is hardly visible, you are wasting its potential.

Light blue does not photocopy well. There is even a nonreproducing blue that does not show up in the camera used in the traditional offset-printing processes. Avoid using pale blue on such pieces as forms, which will probably be reproduced by photocopying.

Color does not just look nice. It also has cultural connotations. You must bear them in mind when picking the colors you intend to use.

Picking colors is both personal and impersonal. On the one hand, you reveal your own personality by the colors you choose for your own wardrobe. It says something about you. On the other hand, such individual taste should play little or no part in your deliberate decisions affecting the professional work you perform.

Is it possible to divorce personal preference from professional demands? Probably not completely. Individual and accultured connotations are too deeply rooted. It is vital to realize, however, that what one person interprets one way may be interpreted by another very differently. The sign of mourning in Western cultures is black. It is white in China. Which is right?

So which is the *right* color for an application? It is impossible to say, because the choice depends on the applications as well as the audience for whom the message is intended.

Perhaps we are asking the wrong questions. Instead, it would be better to become aware of how people react to various colors, how they interpret them, and how popular some colors are as compared to others. Then a color choice can be made based on some degree of reason and confidence rather than personal "liking." It is a fact, though, that people judge value by first-glance emotion. Their initial reaction to an object is a response strongly based on its color.

Innumerable surveys have been made, and studying and understanding reaction to color is an important science, because purveyors of goods and services rely on these reactions to succeed in the marketplace. There are some useful pointers, for instance:

Sugar is never packaged in green, because green carries connotations of sourness. It is packaged in blue, because blue is a color we associate with sweetness.

"Green is a deadly color for theater posters. We never use it unless we're doing an Irish show. It has been tested as a very unappealing color to people in the street. A big favorite is red and there's a great feeling for red and black together," says Frank Verlizzo, designer for Serino/Coyne, a theatrical advertising agency (*Sky*, November 1988).

Black on yellow was selected most frequently as most legible, though yellow was less popular with respondents than red, blue, and green, in a survey of political posters taken by W. Gary Howard of the University of West Florida, Pensacola. (It is probably the ease of legibility of yellow on black that accounts for yellow's preference. Black on blue and red with green were the combinations found to be least legible and least liked.)

Blue was the overwhelming favorite as a color in the same survey. The tests also proved that its popularity was not based on political symbolism, where blue is the color of conservatism. Blue connotes calm, authority, respect; sky, water, cold. Blue means reliability and corporate strength to financial people, but it means death to doctors and cooling water to people working around nuclear reactors.

Warm colors represent action, closeness; leisure activity, recreation, fun.

Cool colors represent status, remoteness, background information; tragic or romantic situations, efficiency, work.

Bright hues, especially warm ones like yellow and orange, are active and seem to help mental activity. They are also seen as being cheerful. This is why they are gaining favor in schools. (Dull, cool colors have the opposite effect and create quiet and a relaxing mood.)

Simple colors are preferred by the lower socioeconomic strata, whereas the upper crust prefer dirty off-colors.

High chroma colors represent tension, melodrama, comedy.

Gray is neutral, a fine background, and its subtlety makes it symbolic of success. But those who prefer bright colors find it boring.

Red connotes stop, danger, fire, heat.

Yellow connotes caution, slow, testing. It is the most visible of all colors, so a lot of it makes people jittery and nervous.

Orange is informal, cheerful, liked (though not necessarily preferred) by one and all.

Green connotes OK, go, all-clear, nature, safety, security.

Brown is informal and not a power color for men's or women's suits.

Black is associated with witchcraft, but is also seen as powerful, sophisticated, and authoritarian.

White connotes refinement, purity, honesty. (*Candidus* in Latin means both "white" and "honest." Romans nominated for office wore the *toga candida* [white toga], as a symbol of their probity; hence the word *candidate*.)*

*For an exhaustive collection of color meanings see Henry Dreyfuss, *The Symbol Sourcebook* (New York: Van Nostrand Reinhold, 1984).

Some colors carry symbolism that is generally understood. Some comes from the way the color is used, some from the way it is referred to in speech.

International signage is establishing a universally understood system of traffic symbols. We are all being taught an accultured response to them. Traffic signals changing from green to amber to red means "yes, wait, no" or "go, slow, stop." There is good reason to expand the application of these universally understood symbols to nontraffic situations. To make stopping visually active, run it in red—in whatever context it may be. The color will positively reinforce the thought. To emphasize the acceptability of an action, run it in green. Green subliminally connotes safety to proceed.

Red road signs means NO.

Blue road signs mean OK.

Red overrules blue.

Green is the symbol for health services.

Yellow means warning.

Black is plain information.

Warmth is red, coldness is blue. Hence the design of the dashboard symbol for the car heater.

A carpet would not be festive or be perceived as honoring a very important person were it not red.

Colors played an important part in medieval heraldry. The palette was restricted to available materials. Each color (tincture) had its symbolic meaning. *Blazon* is the language used to describe the "accidents," which were the colors, furs, and metals that composed the heraldic shield. A complex symbolic, systematized language of shape, color, and meaning was developed over the years. Like corporate identity programs, it was strictly codified and enforced. Here are the nine colors with their heraldic names, meanings, and conventional black-and-white representations (tricking).

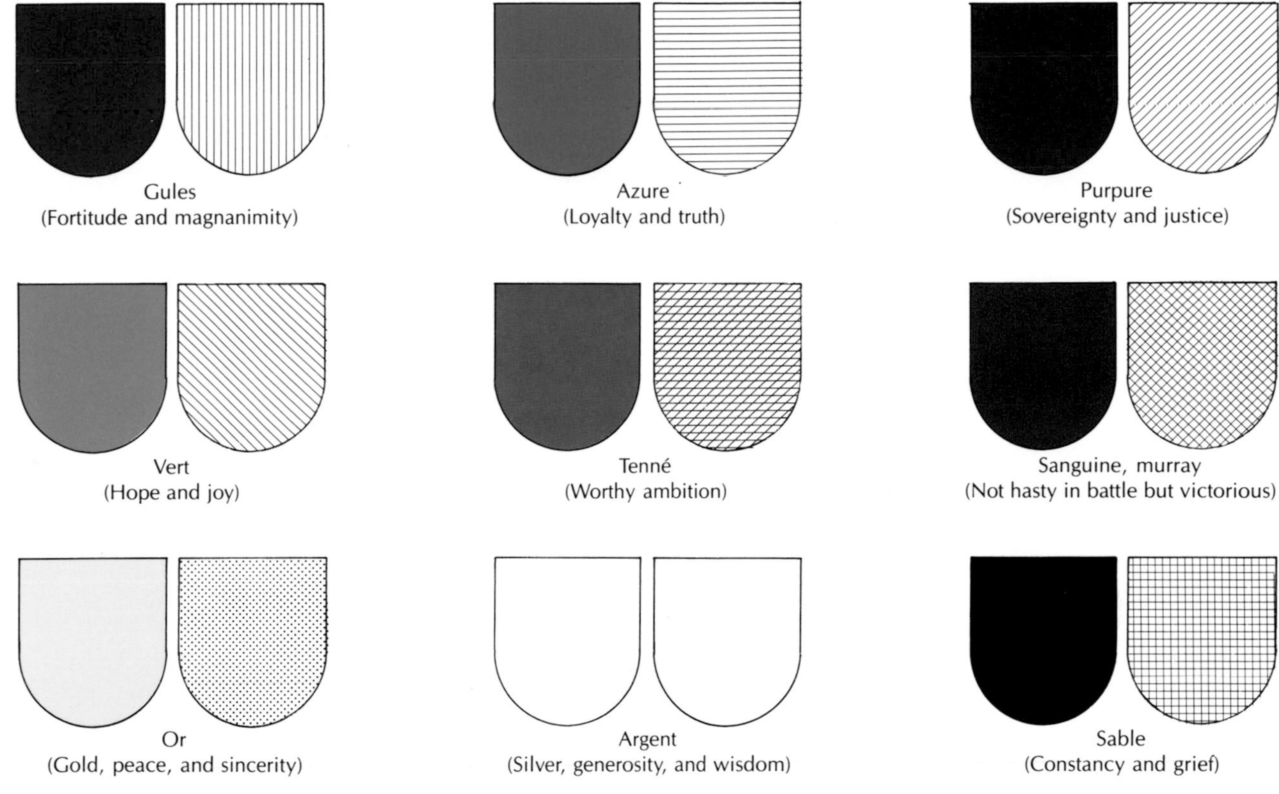

Like colors, shapes had their symbolic meanings. It might be wise to avoid using some of the following "abatements dishonorable" on a coat of arms, for reasons stated.

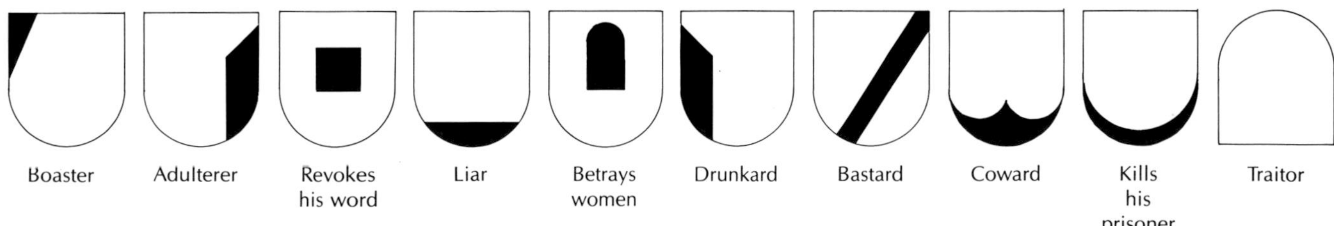

The ancient Greek king would not be kingly, were his robe not purple

A zebra is black and white. So is a penguin. Present them in hues, and you create a startling, attention-getting paradox.

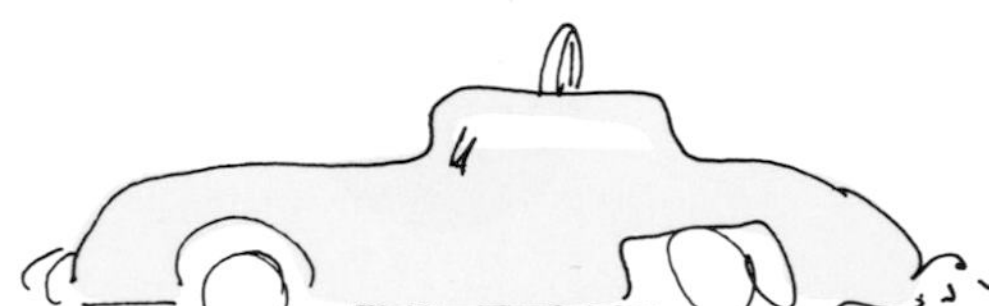

Taxicabs are most taxicabbish when they are yellow. (Originally the color was picked to make them visible. It worked.)

Christmas is green and red.

Halloween is orange and black.

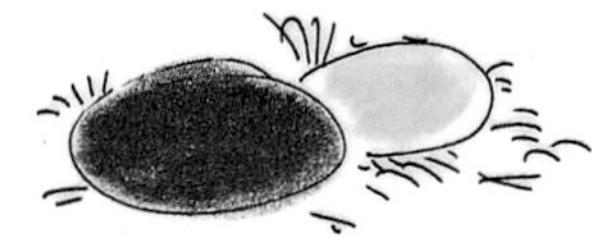

Easter is purple and yellow.

St. Valentine's Day is red and pink.

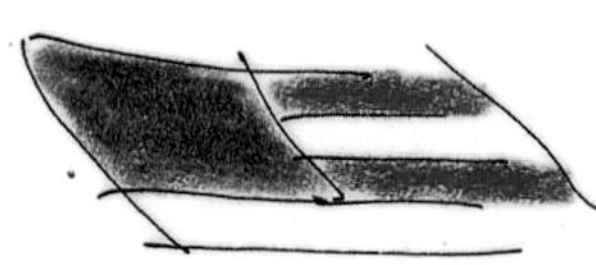

The Fourth of July is red, white, and blue.

Blue = cold

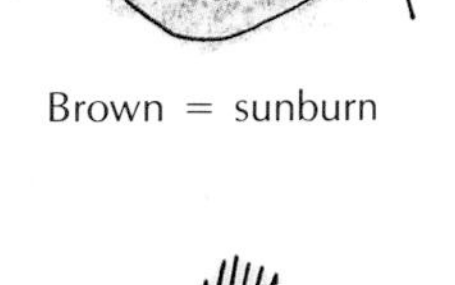

Brown = sunburn

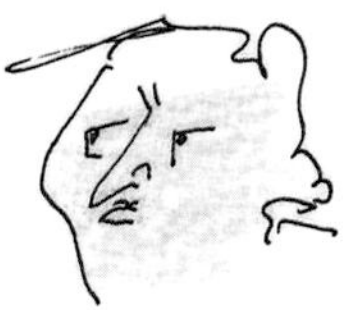

Green = envy, illness

Red = embarrassment

Purple = rage

Yellow = jaundice

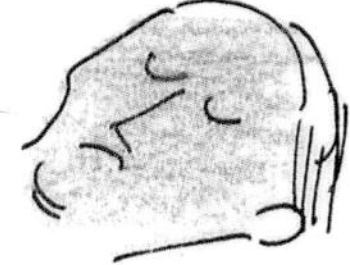

Gray = death

Pink = health

The expression of a human face, coupled with its appropriate color, is a form of cartooning that is clearly understood.

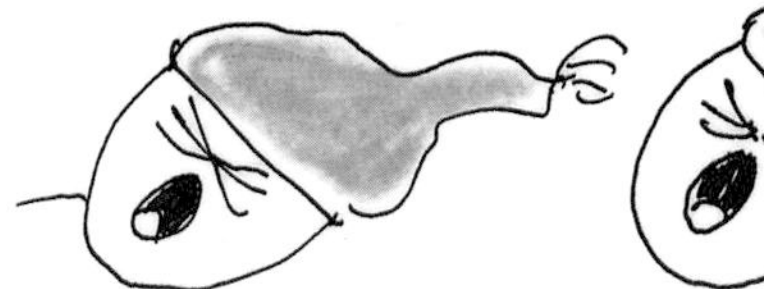

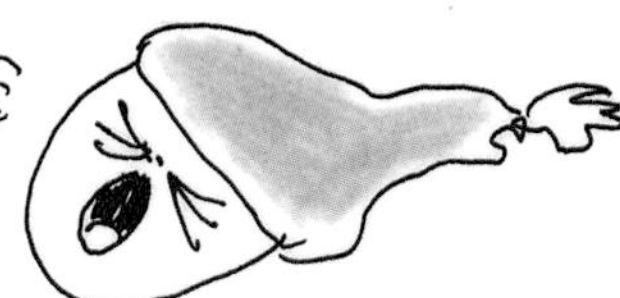

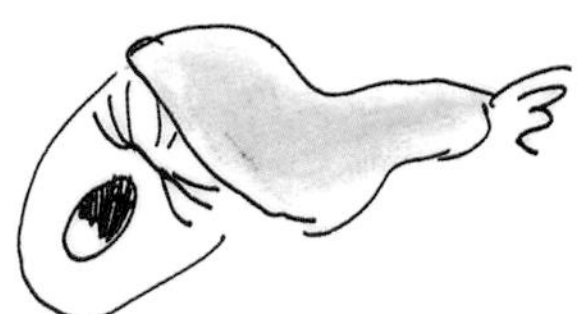

Baby boys are blue, and baby girls are pink. Presents bought before babies are born must be neutral: pale yellow or white—or there will be trouble.

When a color has implications that everyone is likely to understand, it can help to reinforce an idea. The route to comprehension is shortened. Many of these understandings originate in common speech, which alludes to color in terms that are meaningful, even if they are not to be taken literally. To be "in the red" is very different from being "in the black." (Yes, these phrases have clear origins: They come from the colors of ink used in ledger books.) How about being "in the pink"? Or "blue-sky"? Never mind their origins. They are idioms.

When is an idiom a cliché? A good question. Idioms become clichés when they are overused or applied without imagination. Nonetheless, their underlying message is commonly understood. This is why, perhaps, a cliché is sometimes precisely what may be needed to catapult an obvious point off the page into the viewer's mind. When a cliché is used in a fresh way, it rises to being an idiom. General speech—both verbal and visual—is thus enriched.

Every human activity, profession, and interest has its own specialized jargon. Use them all as potential idea-accelerators, but only when you can be reasonably certain that your visual shorthand will be understood by the audience.

It is vital that you understand the technical difference between four-color process and two-color printing—whether produced traditionally or electronically.

Four-color-process colors are used in printing to simulate any and all other colors. The four colors (black, process yellow, process blue [cyan], and process red [magenta]) have been developed to complement and balance each other. They are printed separately and on top of each other in varying proportions. The resultant variety of colors is created by the variety of proportions of the four process colors combined with the whiteness of the paper.

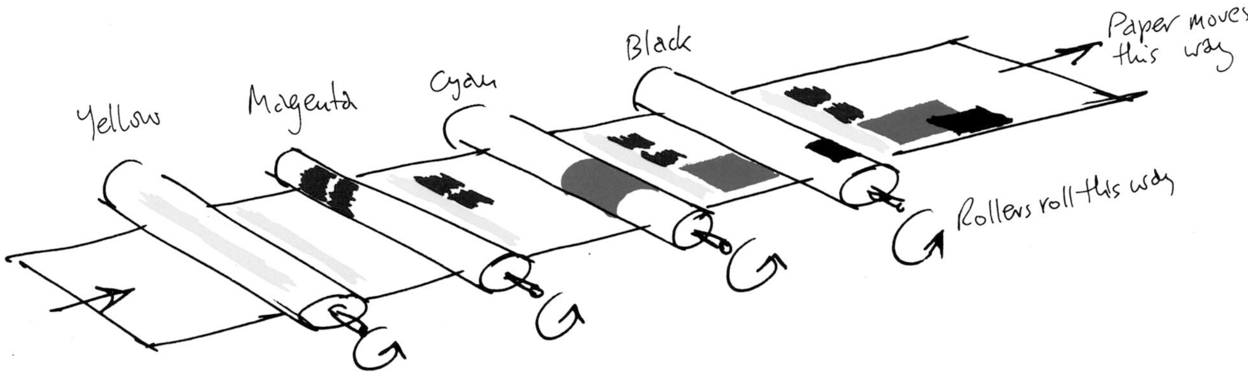

The paper is touched four times, once by each of the four process colors. (A press is considerably more complicated than this diagram.)

Individually, the four colors are not very handsome. The magenta looks brashly pink when screened down from its solid state. The yellow is invisible on white paper except in large panels, where it looks crude and vulgar. The cyan is a pale turquoise and the only color that can be used successfully by itself. This is done so often that it looks common and cheap. It is surprising that such unlikely hues added together can form the visual miracles that they do. The operative words are "added together." Individually they are unhappy. In combination they can sing with joy.

In pictures: Just as a normal black-and-white halftone is photographed through a grid of fine lines to convert its continuous tone into an array of dots of various sizes to make it printable, so is an original color photograph converted into dots. It is, however, a little more complicated because the original must be "separated" into four separate plates, one for each of the four process colors. The tiny dots meld in the eye and produce, as faithfully as possible, an illusion of the color values of the "continuous tone" originals.

In panels: Color in flat areas can vary from "solid," that, is 100 percent of the ink, to none, zero percent. Mechanical screens normally vary the density in increments of 10 percent steps, though 5 percent are also available. Even greater flexibility is available in electronic technology. Superimposing screens of various percentages in various combinations of the four process colors can simulate any color you wish—in flat areas. (To avoid muddy colors, it is best not to let the sum of all the percentages exceed 240.)

If you are unfamiliar with this material, it can sound confusing. Take heart and look at page 72. It will begin to make sense when you see some examples.

Second, matched, or mixed colors differ from process colors in that they are "real" rather than simulated. Think of them as ready-made tubes of ink of a specific hue: dark red, light pink, olive green.

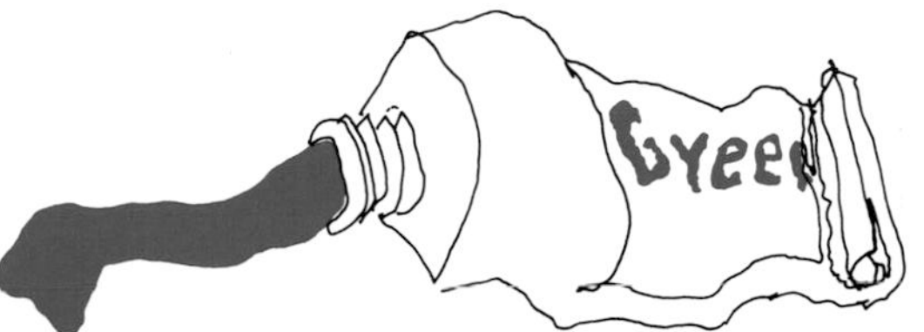

They are used solid or in screened form in panels or any other way on the page you wish (except in photographs, unless you are being very courageous and tricky). The printer can buy them by swatch or number from ink manufacturers, if they are standard hues. If they are unusual, the printer can mix them for you the same way that paint stores produce the color you want for your walls—with a splash of this and a squeeze of that. The paint store follows formulas produced by the manufacturer, and their result is visible on the paint chips. There are many ink manufacturers who produce their own ink-colors palettes. The Pantone® Matching System,* however, is universally known and used as a basis for choosing and specifying the colors of matched inks (see page 191). These are the "PMS colors."

If you choose a specific color in the PMS system, it can be printed one of two ways:

1. As a matched ink
   (if you have a two-color press, one cylinder of the press is used for black, the other one for the color of your choice).
2. As a simulation by means of the process colors
   (if you have a four-color press, one cylinder is used for each of the four process colors, and the black carries the black segment of the process colors as well as the type).

Four-color-process printing is, clearly, more expensive than two-color printing. So is the prepress preparation of material.

*Pantone, Inc.'s check-standard trademark for color reproduction and color reproduction materials.

3. PRESENTATIONS AND PUBLICATIONS

Using color for continuity and identity

Presentations with slides and overheads are identical to printed publications in one major respect: They are both constructed as streams of information. The streams flow as sequences of impressions, slide after slide, overhead after overhead, page after page. They stop and go very much like filmstrips. The audience, whether viewers/*listeners* or viewers/*readers*, needs time to absorb the information. Presentations are controlled by the speaker, so the audiences are forced to begin at the beginning. Printed pieces have the advantage of accessibility anywhere. The rate of speed in which each impression is revealed is controlled by the speaker in the case of the presentation and by the individual viewer/reader in the case of printed matter.

The repetitive characteristic presentations and print share is an area where color can be exploited to add a dimension of recognition, clarity, and ease of interpretation. This demands that the presentation planner and editor/designer take a long view of their product, as the individual units of which the product is assembled are not isolated units but a flow, a continuum, a series.

It matters little how many pages there are or how many visuals make up a presentation. The principle of continuity is as valid for a six hundred-page manual as it is for a four-page brochure, a newsletter, or a complex book, a short slide show or an in-depth lecture on an abstruse subject requiring dozens of overheads. Since they are all constructed of segments, color can be used to make that construction clear. If the segments have subsets, color can separate them from the matrix in which they occur. Color can help to codify the ideas in the presentations or publications in various ways. It can also unify them and give them a character of their own. Or it can relate them clearly within a corporate identity.

There are two fundamental requirements for using color cleverly in an overall context.

1. Remember that it is the patterning itself—the regular recurrence of colors applied to repetitive elements—that creates a dependable effect. Once you have developed your system, stick to it. You weaken it whenever you depart from it. Reserve such departures for situations where emphasis is justified.
2. Make the system as simple as possible. The simpler, the better. Not only do people understand and remember a technique more easily if it is simple, but simplicity usually results in elegance. To achieve simplicity requires much thought, and deep analysis usually gets rid of jarring or obscure complexities. The resulting impression should be so obvious that any keys or instructions on "how to use this document" would be foolish. Unfortunately, such obviousness is hard to attain.

Presentations are visual impressions flashed on a screen in sequence. Color must be planned to reinforce relationships, patterning, and continuity.

The purpose of presentations is to explain, to sway, to persuade. Graphics are used to prove points. They might well be called "decision-support graphics" in corporate use. Translation of data into graphics can make information easier to understand, if the visuals are accompanied by good verbal explanation. (This is no different from graphics in print, which also require good titles and captions or legends.)

The presentation is a flowing sequence of impressions that must be carefully planned and coordinated to prevent confusion. Since it is controlled by the presenter, the viewer/listener is denied the time to study at his or her own pace. Therefore, each item must be clear, and the relationships of item to item must make sense. No extraneous detail or irrational change should disturb the logic of the flow. Most important, the visuals must agree with the speaker's words. The wording should not be identical, because the audience will read at a different pace than the speaker, creating confusion and destroying concentration. The thrust and meaning of the visuals, however, should complement the speaker's verbal explanation.

Here are ten principles for the use of color in slides or overheads that respond to the peculiar requirements of verbal-visual presentations before audiences. Of course, they are not *rules*. There are no such things. There is no right way or wrong way that can be proved or quantified. There is only an effective or ineffective way based on common sense and experience.

1. Use color to make the best of the physical situation in which the presentation will be viewed.

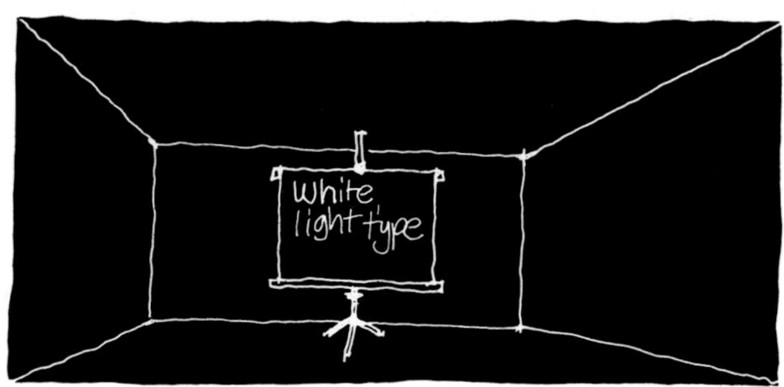

In dark viewing situations, use dark backgrounds for your slides. Make the text, small shapes, and thin linework very light. White, yellow, or red show up best and therefore read best when they are seen against a dark background. Blue, green, dark red, brown, and gray are good background colors for slides.

In light viewing situations, use light backgrounds for your overheads. Black, dark blue, or brown read best against a light background. Be sure to make your text, small shapes, and thin linework very dark so that they show up. White, pale green, pale blue, and light yellow are good backgrounds for overheads.

2. Use color to explain, never just to decorate. Do not make something pretty for the sake of prettiness or because color is available. Instead, lead the eye to the significant elements by emphasizing and highlighting with color.

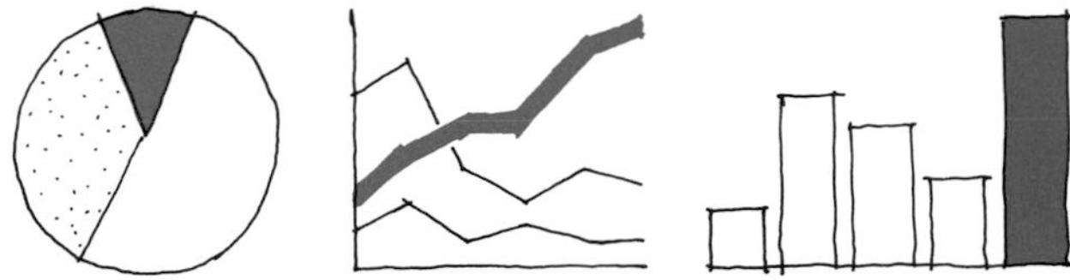

3. Use color to emphasize a single point per visual: one pie-chart segment, one trend line, one row of figures, one verbal point, one bar or column. Avoid showing two sets of data on one visual, unless the comparison itself is the point.

4. Use color to make the emphasized elements more vivid. Make the backgrounds of slides dark. Since white or yellow shine out from a dark background most dramatically, reserve these colors for the most important words or items. Color the normal material blue or green. Use red very sparingly and only in small areas.

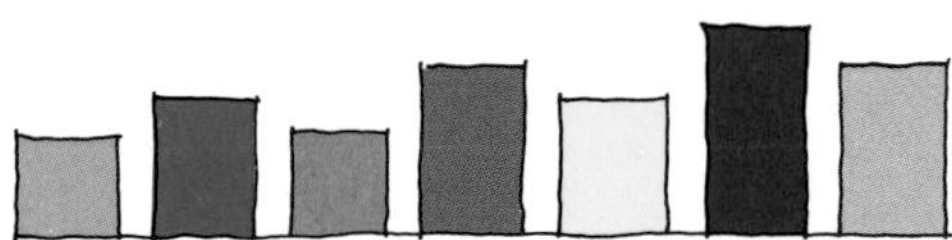

5. Use color to prioritize information. Audiences will look at the brightest area first. Control their response by putting the most important material in the brightest colors.

6. Use color to make the new points in a slide presentation stand out. Assign the most vivid color to the fresh data. The contrast of the vivid and the subdued makes the proposal stand out and appear that much more weighty. By the same token, dull colors can be used to play down information that is undesirable, negative, or unimportant.

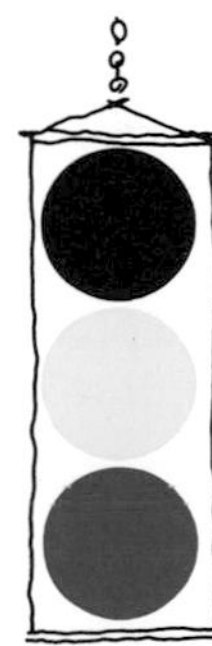

7. Use color to symbolize. The most obvious symbols: red for danger, green for go, amber for caution.

8. Use color to identify a recurring theme; for instance, identify new data in an insurance contract as distinct from the boilerplate. Distinguish one set of elements from another, such as the current situation versus the projected results in a business analysis.

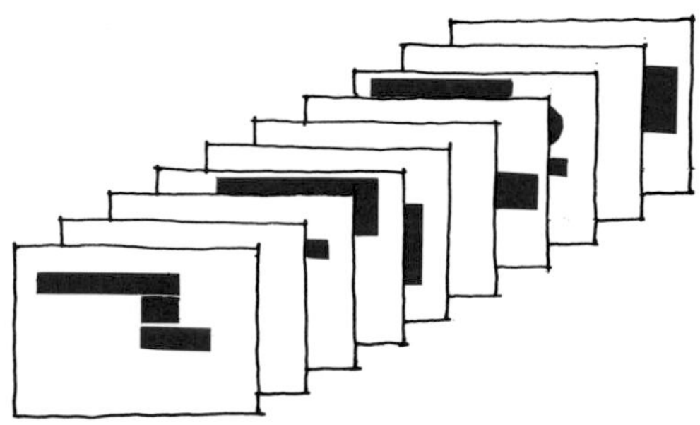

9. Use color so that its implications help the audience to sort out the material. By assigning orange to positive attributes, for instance, every time orange appears on the screen, the audience will immediately interpret the item as "good news." It takes no more than two or three repetitions of such color assignment for the audience to catch on, especially if its first appearance is dramatic and pointed out by the speaker.

10. Use color sequencing to build the presentation to a climax. Start with a cool green, then progress from cooler to warmer until you end up with a hot brilliant orange. Or start with a dark shade and progress from darker to lighter until you end up with pure white.

Though slides are presented in sequence over time, they can—and must—be planned like print, in space. Work on them as a series from left to right. (See page 78 for color sequencing destined for print. It is identical to color sequencing destined for projected visuals.)

Here are eight practical suggestions on planning programs that might prove helpful:

1. Perhaps it might be well to remember the technique proved so efficacious in television: The normal half-hour TV program attempts to make no more than three main points. The full-hour program makes five. Keeping the project simple in content as well as look (that is, color) is always efficacious.

2. Interspersing text slides among pictorial ones is often confusing. The viewer who has become accustomed to seeing visual symbols, and therefore expects to see them, is startled and brought short by the necessity of reading messages while simultaneously listening to similar substance spoken by the narrator. Too often the parallel processes cancel each other out, and the viewer/listener tunes out and concentrates on such extraneous visual details, as the dot on the *i* that is missing on the screen. In mixed shows, therefore, as many thoughts as possible should be turned into graphic form. Textual slides should be kept to a minimum. Those that are used should consist of "illustrative" words rather than summaries of the presenter's speech. Wherever possible, tie the text slides to the pictorial slides with a common color.

3. Start with a colorful title visual. Use clip art if necessary. Follow the opener with an agenda visual that shows the key steps in the presentation. Wind up with a conclusion visual that lists action items or recommendations. Assign a color to them that will tie them together and make them unique by comparison to the rest of the show.

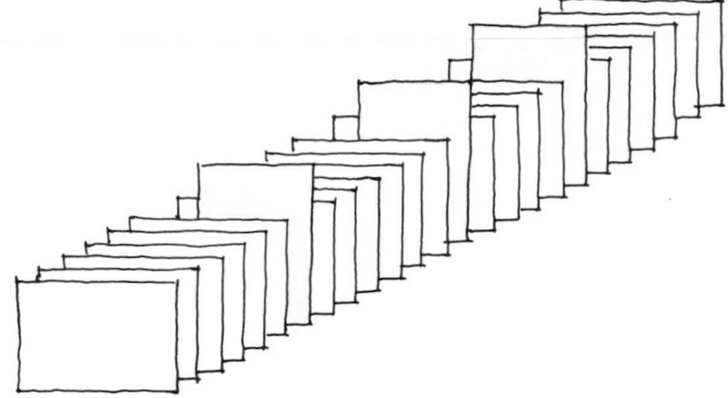

4. Keep the same format throughout so that the audience gets used to looking at a predictable arrangement. Avoid mixing vertical and horizontal slides—unless the verticals are strategically inserted as deliberate breaks. Their change of direction could be emphasized with a change of color.

5. Many canny presenters never put their conclusions on the last slide. Instead, they pose a concluding question such as, What are the three points . . .? The presenter then summarizes each point, drawing on audience participation, if possible. The conclusions are spelled out, of course, in the hard-copy handouts. What an aid to remembering it would be if the printed pieces matched the color on-screen.

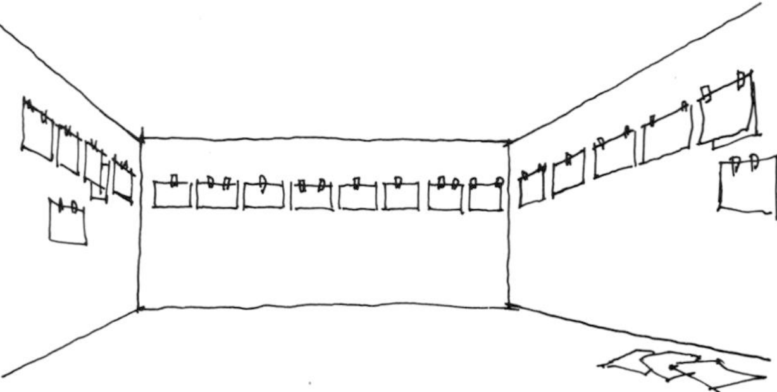

6. In preparing the presentation, make hard-copy printouts of each visual, and hang them around the room in sequence, from left to right. This is the only way that you can examine them to discover anomalies in layout sequencing. Seeing them all at once reveals situations that call for improvement of sequencing, patterning, presentation, and color.

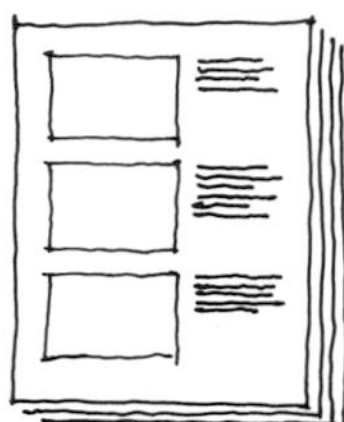

7. Make miniatures of the hard copies, reducing them to a size that will allow three images to be placed vertically down the left-hand side of an 8½-x-11-inch page. A 3-inch-wide image is about right. Write the accompanying text alongside each on the right.

8. To foster greater audience intimacy, when the group is small enough, switch from the screen to a flip charts or chalkboard wherever it makes sense. The screen—whether used for slides or overheads—has an authoritarian distance, whereas flip charts or chalkboards are an extension of the personality of the speaker. Use colored chalk or markers that follow the color scheme established in the slides or overheads.

Here are five general thoughts on the arrangement of slides themselves:

1. Limit each visual to the essentials. Simplify and edit out everything that is not vital. Avoid showing supporting information. Perhaps a handout distributed after the presentation could contain the background research. A useful rule of thumb: no more than six words per line, six lines per visual, or two illustrations per visual. . .and only one thought in bright color.

2. Use simple typefaces in large sizes. It is the message that matters, so avoid interposing fancy type between the thought and its reader.

3. Leave generous space around the outer edges of the visual, especially if the center is very colorful.

4. People start reading in the top-left corner, then follow diagonally down to the lower-right corner. Arrange material to follow this basic pattern. A bright color up there could be a good way to attract the eye to that starting point.

5. Place the most important information at the top, because that is where people tend to read first (use the brightest color for it, too). Few scan the bottom of a page or slide first. Place the most positive copy in the top-left corner. The expected, traditional, static, dignified way of putting a title in the middle is analogous to the placement of a newspaper logo on the front page. It sits there

like a bump on a log. Many newspapers use a trick whenever they want to gain our attention: they put the headline above the logo, up in that top-left corner. Should the kernel of the information—the benefit to the viewer—be written as a lead-in to the title and placed up there? Or should the title itself be flush left in that corner for maximally active participation in catapulting information off the screen into the viewer's mind? (Besides, at the top it is less likely to be hidden by the shadow of some especially tall head sitting between the projector and the screen.)

Publications are constructed of pages, revealed as a succession of impressions. Color strengthens the product by controlling continuity, sequencing, pacing, and unity.

A single color used throughout a publication provides continuity, unity, and character. Consistency gives the product identity. In a broader context, it helps to build a corporate identity: think of the images, such as the IBM blue, that immediately come to mind.

Where color is used more decoratively than informatively, standardize the use as well as the hues on a product level, in order to embellish the entire product. See beyond the confines of a single page to the product as a whole. Seldom is the need to think broadly more important than in this regard. The temptation to "play" with colors can be overwhelming. We have all been told that "variety keeps the viewer interested." As a result, we are often trapped into using red on one page, green on the next, and yellow on the third. We think that variety is a good thing. Besides, if it is available, why not use it? Unfortunately, indiscriminate mixing of colors creates a visual babel, even worse than that created by an indiscriminate mixing of various typefaces. (This is a characteristic of much contemporary electronically produced publishing. It is not a failing of the technology, but of its users. The temptation of the available riches is irresistible. Professionalism developed over time will take care of the problem—we hope.)

It is better to pick a single color and apply it to all the repetitive signaling devices. Standardize harmonious colors for the nameplate (logo), indexes, table of contents, column tags, or department headings, as well as all the other repetitive signage that the piece may need. The color will not merely unify the publication, but it will also strengthen its overall image. Besides, you can use different colors for the illustrations or other events in the sequence of pages, wherever this might be appropriate. They will fall into place in the overall context in which they are viewed.

One more reason not to change colors, where consistency would pay off better, is that the complexity of too many colors causes confusion. It has been found that people can distinguish—and easily remember—four colors, if those colors are broadly different from each other. This has been found to be an optimal number. Realism, aesthetics, or function, of course, may demand more. But these should be the exceptions rather than the rule. Four colors is the optimal practical maximum.

Use color as a distinguishing characteristic

On any page of a document or printed publication there are elements that refer to the document rather than to the subject it contains. What they are can vary from product to product. Recognizing them for what they are is simple when you take the long view.

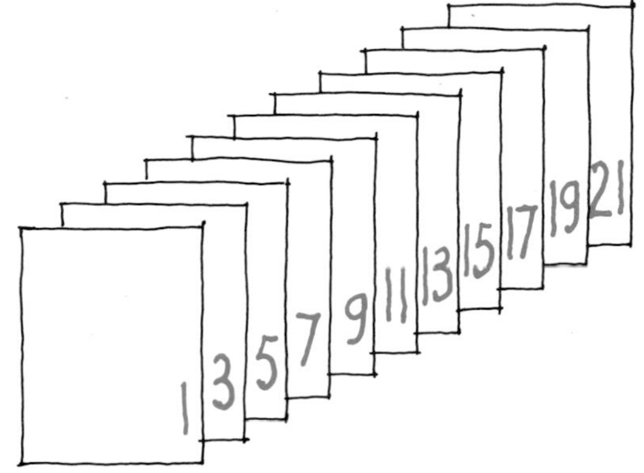

The most obvious examples are folios: page numbers. Few publications do without them. They appear on every page. They are independent of the content, relating only to the publications as a whole. They are usually set in small type to separate them from the visual texture of the rest of the material on the page. Think how much clearer such differentiation would be if they were in color. Imagine what would happen if for some reason it became advisable to play them up. Perhaps their decorative quality could be exploited and they could be set much larger. In an enormous size, they could be run in a gentle mauve. The product's character would change completely, enriched by a feature that is normally not noticed. Yet the text on the page could perfectly well remain boringly normal, ten-point Times Roman type in two 20-pica columns. The page numbers are independent of the text. They belong to the vehicle, not the substance it carries.

You have to decide whether you want to use this device in the first place. If you do, you commit yourself to a discipline that can prove burdensome. Yet you cannot afford to do things by halves. Sticking to the rules you make for yourself here and there, wherever it happens

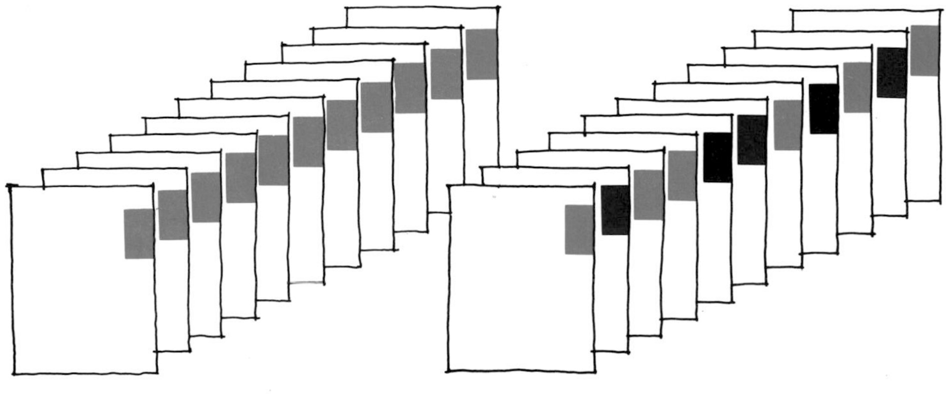

to be convenient, and departing from them where it is a nuisance is worse than doing nothing at all: it muddles the user. Besides, it looks shoddy.

What is the most important commitment as far as color is concerned? If you want your device to be a strong visual identifier, it must appear "different." If it is not different enough, it will not stand out well enough, thus failing to achieve what you intended it to. In short, it demands to have a color reserved for its own special use. Therefore, if you assign purple to your device, you cannot use purple anywhere else, lest you dilute the trademark quality of your device, whose singular visual characteristic is its purpleness.

Anything that repeats is potentially character-yielding material. Page numbering has already been cited. Other areas include:

Headers and footers (often called *running heads* and *running feet* in the book-publishing trade, *continued lines* in magazines, and *jump lines* in newspaper parlance). They are convenience signals. They are like whispered instructions to the reader. If the publication needs a lot of such instructions, it is helpful to signal their presence by making them different from the bulk of the material. Not only will they be found more conveniently, but the ease with which they can be found will be appreciated as a helpful service. And in purely visual terms, the page will appear more interesting at first glance. It will be less dauntingly, monotonously gray.

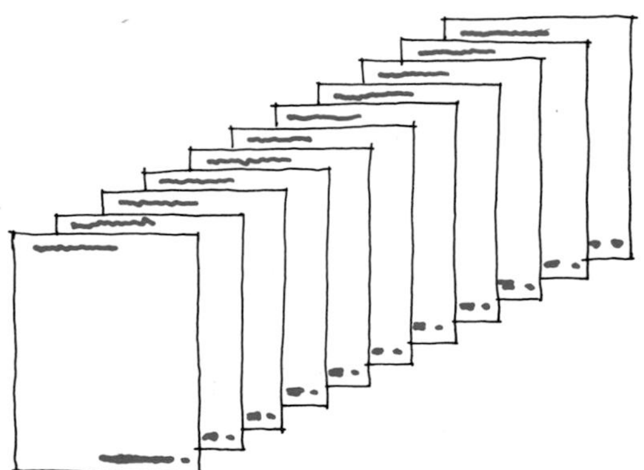

True, the page will look busier and spottier. This is a characteristic that some people find offensive, because simplicity, purity, and plainness have been touted as aesthetically positive values. Philosophically, this is absolutely so. But we do not face philosophical dilemmas. We face practical ones. Resolving this dilemma is not a question of aesthetics but of efficient function. If spottiness improves the publication's usability for the reader, then it is fulfilling its function more effectively. Spottiness makes it a better publication. Reason enough to go ahead and use color for spots. Yet, as in all things, restraint must be used, or the plethora of colored spots will become self-defeating. Measles is not a good thing for the patient's health or looks.

Frames and backgrounds for boxes and panels. Assume that you are preparing a publication illustrated with numerous charts and diagrams. Expand the idea from just one document and imagine that this publication is a monthly magazine and that its field is crowded with competitors. How can you make it stand out from the crowd—without investing a penny more? By consistent application of color. Make all the backgrounds of the diagrams the same hue. This way you create a unified image, recognizable as the "green book" or the "orange book." Obviously the hue you pick has to be dignified and

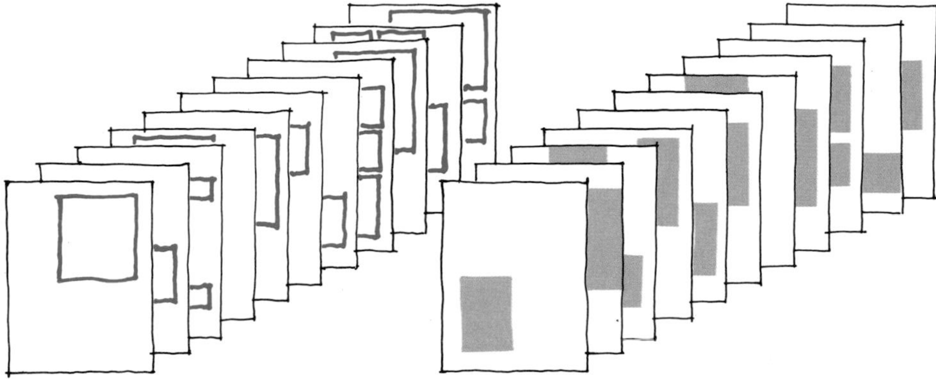

appropriate. It should also be special: avoid the obvious process colors: they are commonplace and not very handsome. Worse, because they are standard, everyone else has access to them and uses them because they are inexpensive. If you must use them, choose a blend of screens of the process colors with each other or with black. Or reserve a specially mixed ink. At the time of this writing, ramping the screen from light to dark is becoming fashionable, because the computer can produce the effect easily.

There are more recommendations about this in the section on diagrams (see page 46). What to do and how to do it can be rather complex. Yet the principle is simple: color should be deliberately restricted so that it becomes a valued, character-yielding attribute, instead of just colorful enrichment.

Color used as a locator signal

Here we discuss elements whose repetition makes them candidates for thinking about their color handling, as are folios or panel backgrounds. They differ from folios, headers, panel backgrounds, and other elements that are connected with the product as a whole in that they are a hybrid element—though they repeat, they refer more to the material itself. The same color-use theory holds.

Department headings and logos. Most multipage publications are assembled in sections. Often such a string of elements has to be explained to the user, and the most effective way to do this is by topic. Such labels are specific to the material in the section. They are also a chain of signals within the product as a whole. Controlling their color in the context of the chain is the reason for their inclusion here.

Their format needs to be unified, allowing necessary variation in each individual use. Clearly, the graphic variety of such formats is unlimited. Decisions about whether they should appear at the head or side of the page, whether they should bleed or not, whether they should be pale with dark type or dark with white type, and so on, are specific to each situation. It would be irresponsible to make generalized recommendations. Suffice it to say that this is an area where colorfulness pays off.

Numbers and locator tabs. Though they are a subset of department headings and logos, and demand similar handling, these deserve to be thought about separately. Their function is primarily that of a locator device. Not much thinking has to be done about what a numeral *5* may mean. It is just a *5*. We deduce that there are four units preceding it and probably several more following, if what we hold in our hands is heavy enough.

The prime attribute such numbers demand is visibility. They must be large enough and different enough from their background to be immediately noticeable. More important: they must be easy to find in the product as a whole. They must therefore be placed where they will be exposed most easily. This means that they should be on the outside of the page, as close to the top corner as possible, because this is where people tend to look first.

What color to use? A strong one. One that will jump off the page, because this is what you want it to do. Should the color bleed? And should the number therefore be in a panel? Yes, if at all possible technically, because the sliver of color visible on the edge of the pages as they are stacked makes the page easier to find. As the edges of the pages are shifted by the thumb, the tabs are revealed and make reference that much easier.

If the product's organization demands it, make each tab a different color to identify a separate section (and then use that hue within each section). This variation of the system does not change the basic principle. It enriches it.

Color used to define sections of the publication

An example of a successful merchandising application of color is the yellow pages. Wherever telephone directories are found, the yellow pages define—well, you know what they are. How much clearer can anything be? Its definition has been carefully controlled and nurtured until it has become a form of communication that requires no explanation.

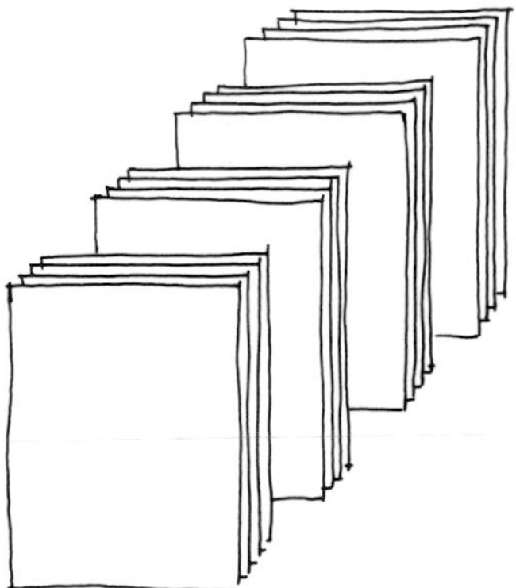

Any special section can be identified in a similar way. Not necessarily with yellow. The yellow pages are printed on a special colored stock, of course. Special-stock inserts require much careful planning. They tend to be expensive. Are there cheaper equivalents? A substitute will always remain a substitute, and it has to be your decision whether a substitute can meet the standard that you set. (A substitute may not necessarily be bad. Witness the market success of a spread sold as "substitute margarine.")

Color the outside of the page. How are the yellow pages first identified by the viewer as the publication is held in the hand? By the outside edge of the product.

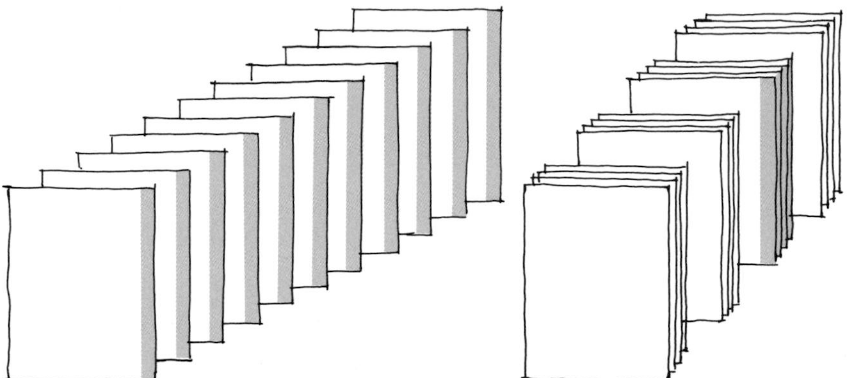

Why not print a strip of color up the edges so that the section you want to identify is highlighted? The rest of the pages can remain plain. How wide should the strip be? Wide enough to be able to accommodate imprecision of trimming (if the publication is bound and trimmed, like a magazine). The narrower it is, the more critical does precision become: ¼-inch is too narrow; ¾-inch is more than ample. However, if you want to print identifying wording in the color strip (sideways, please, never vertically!) it probably has to be ¾-inch.

If the publication is assembled of individual leaves printed simplex or duplex as individual 8½-×-11-inch sheets, such imprecision of trimming will probably not be a problem. Therefore, you can make the strip slightly narrower.

Color the section breaks. Breaking out a single section (as in the yellow pages, above) may be inappropriate, because no one single unit is more important than the others. Yet the sequence of chapters or units of which a publication is constructed needs to be explained as clearly as possible. The most obvious signal is that of identifying the starts of each section. Careful planning is necessary to make the most of every opportunity.

Ideally, all openers should be right-hand pages. That way they can be designed independently as dramatic "covers." Right-hand pages are also maximally noticeable in the package.

Left-hand pages are more difficult to handle as "covers" because they are hard to separate from the right-hand pages opposite. A full two-page spread, however, is an opportunity for major visual fireworks. Besides, we read from left to right and look up at the top-left corner first.

Whether you choose left- or right-hand openers, avoid mixing them. A random mixture weakens the impact of their accumulated rhythmic sequence. People miss either those on the left or those on the right, depending on the way they examine the product.

Your important signals are compromised. The product is not as clear as it would have been, had it been more rigidly structured.

4. CHARTS AND GRAPHS

Using color to explain and to persuade

The purpose of diagrams is to make complex relationships understandable by turning verbal concepts and mathematical data into visual form. The usual diagram is a stand-alone figure with a label that identifies the subject. Viewers are expected to study, analyze, absorb, and draw their own conclusions. Sometimes a caption or legend describes important factors or points out salient features.

Every time a new page is looked at, the first element to be noticed and studied is the visual, nontextual one—the diagram. Too often the information contained in the diagram is repeated in the text, much to the annoyance of the reader, who is forced to identify and then skip the duplication.

Making effective graphics is a complex process, no matter how helpful the software. It is not just a mechanical process that plots masses of data and then colorizes them to make the result pretty. It is, rather, the process of responsible interpretation. Its complexity is like that of an equation with three unknowns. An equation, however, usually has a correct answer. In using charts and graphs there is no such thing as a correct or incorrect answer. The only criterion is whether the idea, the substance, the reason for publishing, comes across to the viewer/reader clearly, vividly, and memorably.

Color contributes to the clarity, vividness, and memorableness of a diagram. Ideas sparkle when color is tied to the function, coupled with the type, the line weights, and the basic geometry of the piece. This is why it is folly to start with the goal of dressing up the chart to make it as pretty as possible. The goal should be to *illuminate the purpose of the chart*. If the avowed purpose is to show data without attempting to draw a conclusion, encouraging the viewer to deduce his or her own, then by all means make the chart as simple, forthright, and neutral as possible. Where the purpose is merely to *show* without explanation or persuasion, nothing should be allowed to come between the statistics and their interpreter. Such purity and elegant simplicity is praiseworthy.* It is not just appropriate but essential to the serious scholar, specialist, statistician—anyone whose avowed intention is to derive conclusions from published data.

*See Edward R. Tufte, *The Visual display of Quantitative Information* (Cheshire, Conn.: Graphics Press, 1983).

If, however, there is some intention at persuasion or a particular point of view in whose support the facts are being presented, then a new dimension is added to the problem of preparation. In this case, the data has to be presented in such a way that the viewer will indeed reach the intended interpretation.

Since there is a point of view, something has to be stressed. This means that some elements are brought into the foreground of noticeability, while others are pushed into the supporting background.** Thus the hidden agenda becomes noticeable.

Clearly, presentation that emphasizes some aspect of the information must be responsibly controlled by the editor. The degree of point making can be gentle or flagrant, subtle or exaggerated. Whatever the degree of stress may be, the color, type size, line weights, shapes, areas, and the basic geometry of the figure are used to make the point.

Charts must be assembled in a manner that fulfills the needs of the specific circumstances. Color can never be used successfully if it is merely an afterthought. To make maximum use of its potential, color must be thought of from the very inception of an idea, when the information is being planned for presentation. While the "what" and the "how" are being decided is the time to conceive of the way in which color will be exploited. Retrofitting it as a cosmetic detail will not allow it to make a significant contribution.

**See Jan V. White, *Using Charts and Graphs* (New York: R. R. Bowker, 1984).

Most business graphics share some characteristics that form a vocabulary of diagram making. They are the basics to which color can be added.

Most charts, graphs, and diagrams have some fundamental elements in common. If color is to be assigned logically, it is a good idea to define these elements and to see them as commonalities.

Past X-AXIS Future

NOW = 0

Increase (positive)

Neutral = 0

Y AXIS

Decrease (negative)

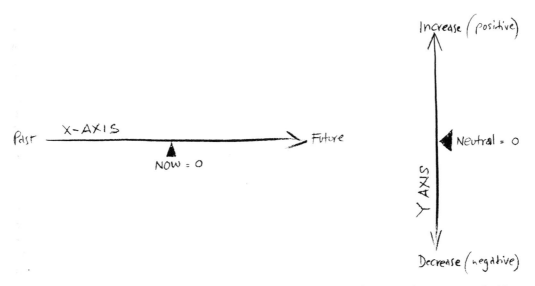

Most have the x- and y-coordinates. They are needed because most sets of information show some form of comparison, in terms of size, rate of changes, development over time, and so forth.

To make comparisons understandable, the elements that represent them need a common starting point as well as a common scale against which they can be measured. Whether that scale is actually shown or not is immaterial: without it, no chart would be credible. Visible or not, scale is implied.

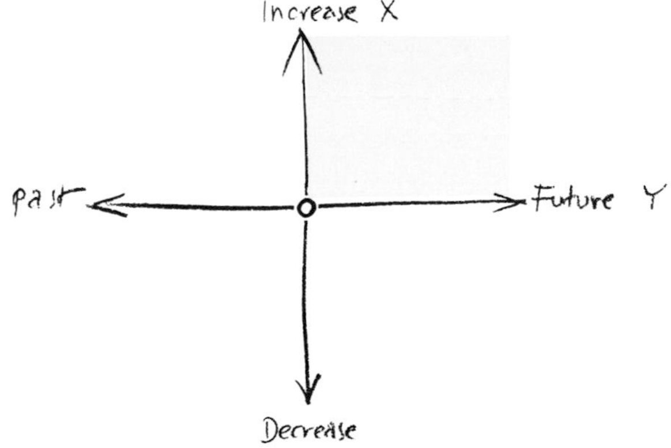

The horizontal x-axis crossing the vertical y-axis creates a field. This is the area on which the symbols representing the data are plotted and displayed, be they bars, lines, dots, or whatever. Each format (graph or fever chart, vertical columns, horizontal bars, or surface charts, histograms, and so forth) organizes a specific set of data for a specific purpose. The area is often turned into a color panel "to dress up the chart." Done with taste and care, it can be an aid to understanding, because the color defines the background clearly.

Color, however, must be used with care and restraint. Too often, colorization becomes an end in itself, and if one color is seen as being good, two are thought to be better. The resultant document looks like a coat of many colors.

The only format that does not require a coordinate field is the pie chart, which is a self-contained figure. Pies, however, can be placed on a tabletop covered with a blue tablecloth, even though blue is not intrinsic to the pie's message. A common background panel color can thus tie the pie to the other charts in a group.

Often an entire pie chart is placed in a box of some sort. Such a frame bears no relation to the specifics of the information displayed. It is only concerned with the chart as a graphic object and is used as an opportunity for adding some visual individuality to the statistics. Further, family resemblance in the frames can be used to tie disparate units throughout the publication. Color can be used to advantage here. Standard color schemes coupled with standard frames can be major aids in establishing corporate identity. (For twenty-four examples of patterns for boxes and frames, see page 96.) Frames can be used to cluster smaller units into bunches. (For twelve examples of patterns for clusters, see page 99.)

Frames or backgrounds can also be used to depict the subject of a pie chart, comment on the substance, or make a very graphic illustration of the material. Such use is growing in popularity because it is the ultimate step in humanizing dry statistics, making them palatable as well as understandable to the nonspecialist. The data must be accurately shown, of course. The imaginative presentation should affect only the attitude of the reader.

Graphics carry a title normally placed above the diagram. Just like a headline, which refers to the text that follows, the title over a chart or graph should stand out as strongly as possible so that the reader can immediately identify the information beneath. It communicates—and intrigues—best when it is more informative than the usual terse label. Writing it as short as possible restricts potential interest. (For twelve ideas on how to tie headings to boxes, see page 98.)

Lines must respond to meaning, as well as technical presentation and color. The editorial evaluation of each element determines its importance. The more important the element represented by a line or area, the more visible the line or area should be. Visibility is a function of size and contrast. Thus, you must take into account the need to compensate for reduced contrast whenever color is used. A red line does not look as important as the same line in black, because red is less visible on white paper than black. Therefore, it must be drawn more heavily. (See page 122, where this principle is discussed in relation to type.)

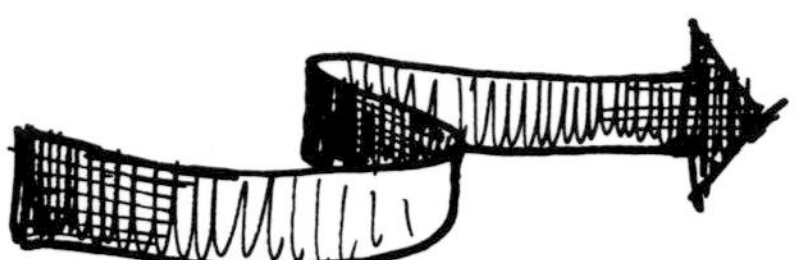

Arrows are a distinct element in chart making, Not only can they indicate direction, they can also point out highlighted elements. Further, they can guide the eye from one element to another facilitating the reading of charts and graphs. If this were not enough, they can also illustrate a concept. Color is the material that enables them to fulfill their potential. (For an analysis of arrows, see page 102.)

Repetitive sources of information, such as keys, sources, north points, scales, and so on, are all elements that should be thought of as integral parts of the chart and graphic presentation. Like color, they should not be afterthoughts. They should be brought into the planning process as early as possible in order to weave them into the fabric of the logic of the presentation.

A prototypical graph demonstrates the variety of which a single color is capable. The criterion for its use is whether the color makes significances vivid.

Charts, graphs, and diagrams are fertile opportunities for applying color to enriching effect. But the myriad combinations that color, its screens, and its applications are capable of must be used with discretion and—wherever possible—with purpose deeper than mere colorfulness.

The prototypical graph used as the following illustration is merely a compendium of the basics of charts and graphs: a title, a field, scales, grids, charted lines—all representing data to transmit. It is shown in twenty-two (obvious) variations on a theme.

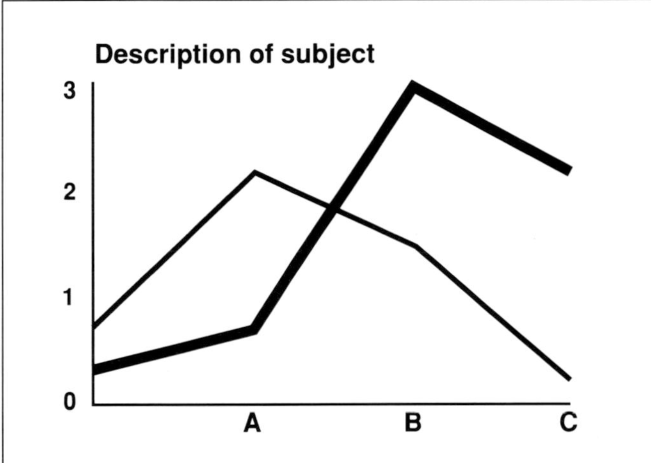

The raw original

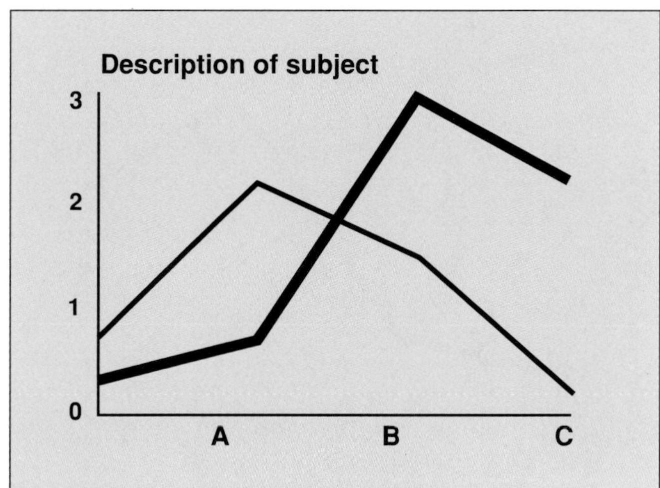

Tint background: a slightly embarrassed neutral

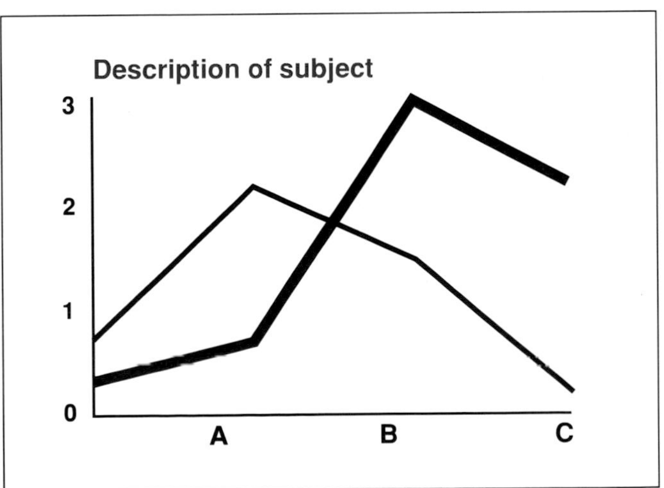

Title in color: not very thrilling

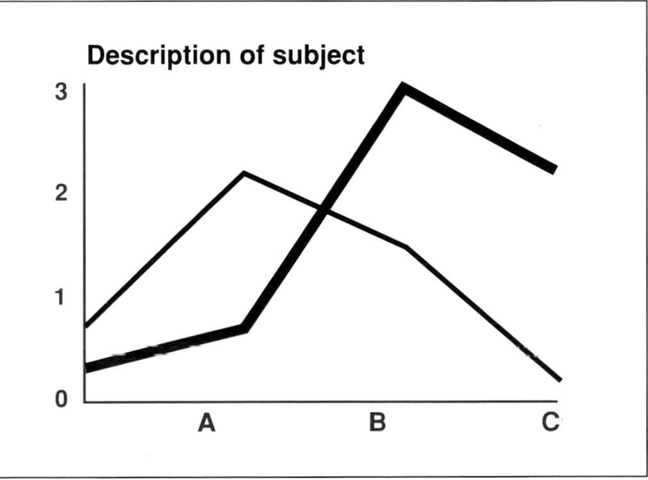

Indices and scales in color: underwhelming

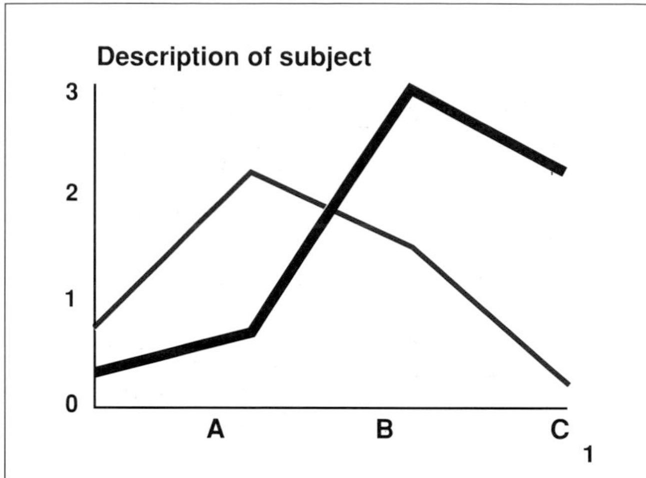

The wrong line in color: color implies emphasis

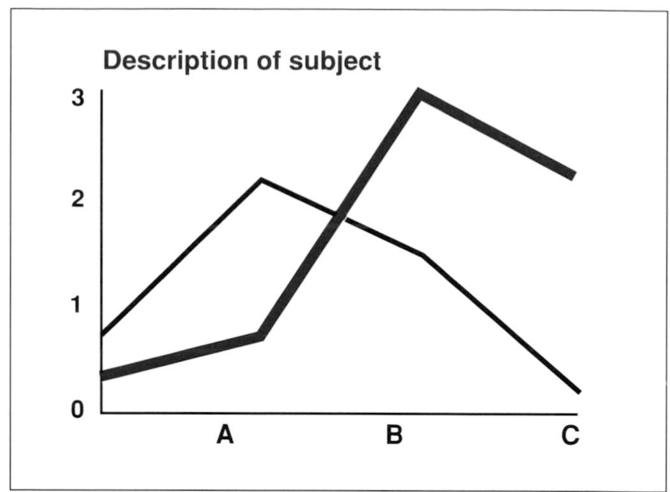

Color emphasizes the correct line and ties it to title

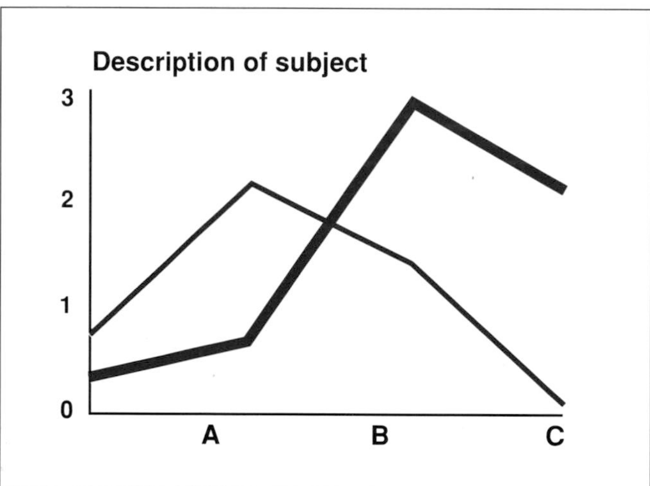

Both lines in color: bland and vague

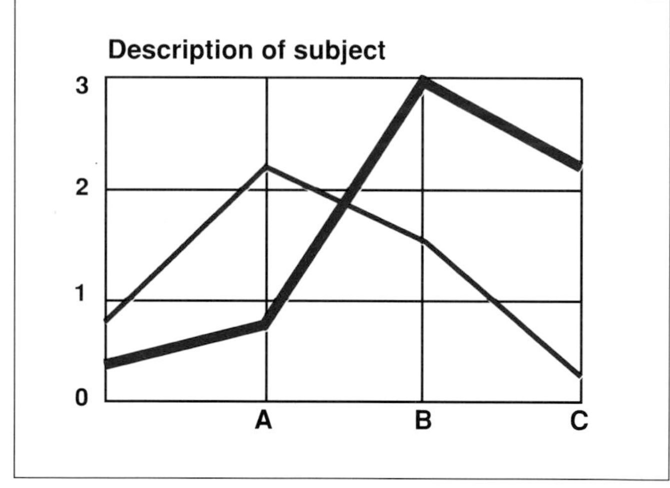

Black grid lines "behind" data lines in color

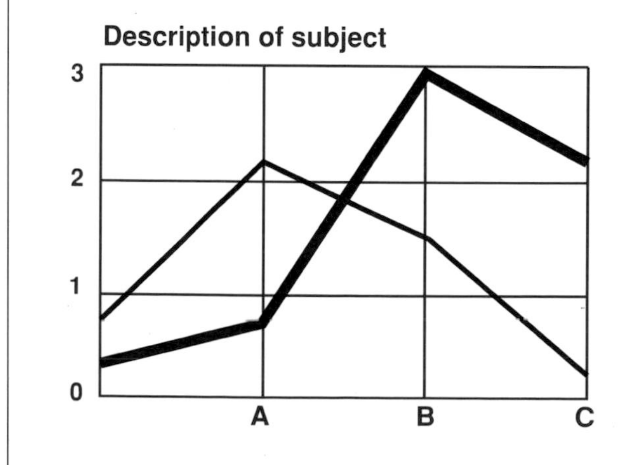

Black lines on red grids: reads well

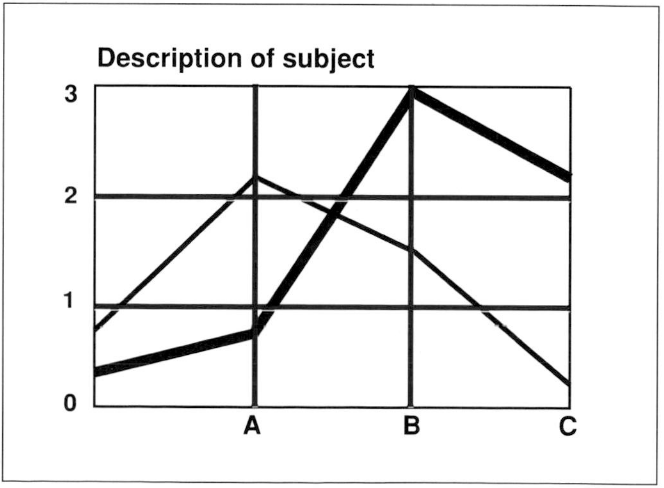

Grid lines in bold color: look like prison bars

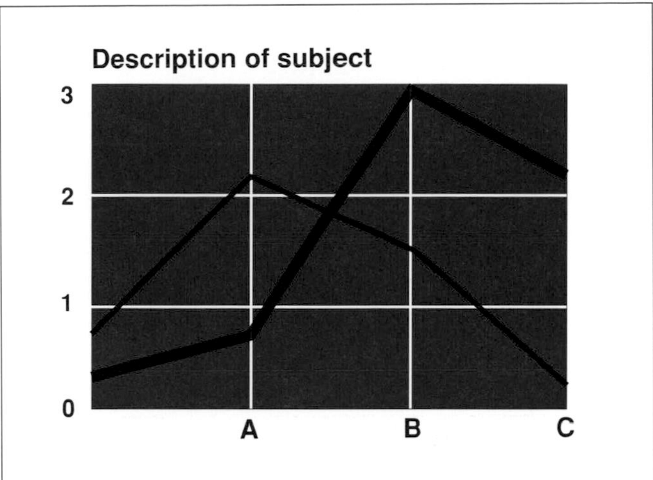

Grid lines dropped out from color field

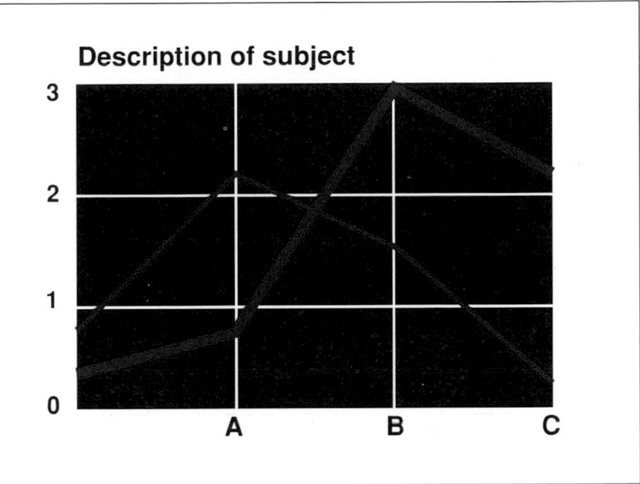

Black field, white grid, colored lines: dramatic

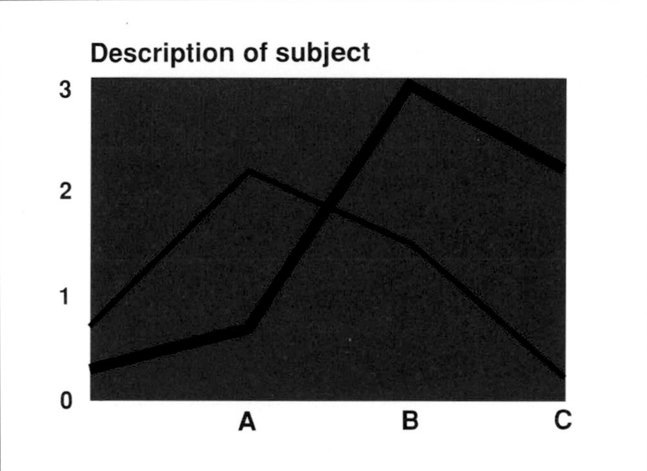

Field in solid color: perhaps too strong

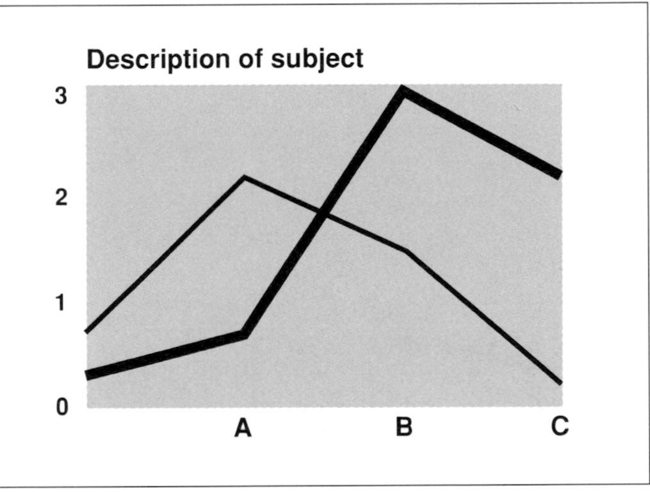

Field in tint of color: better when many charts are needed

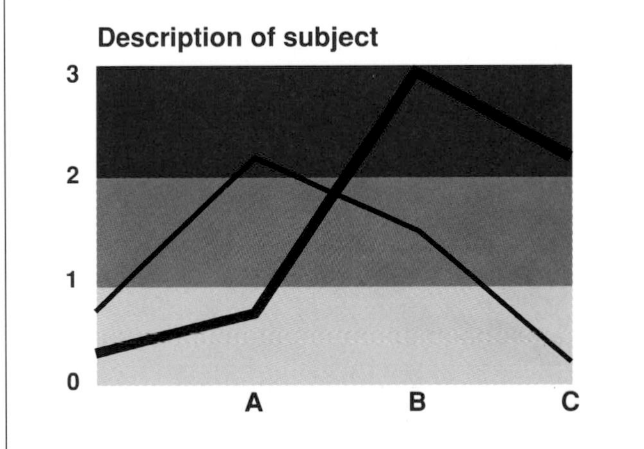

Field stepped in increments. (See page 84)

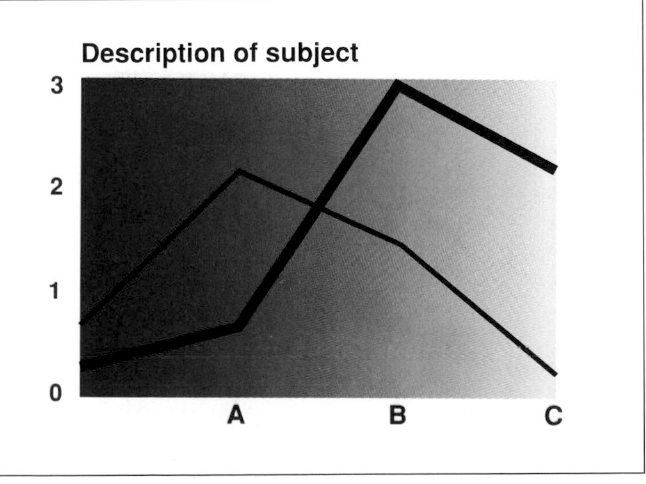

Field ramped left-to-right. (See page 87)

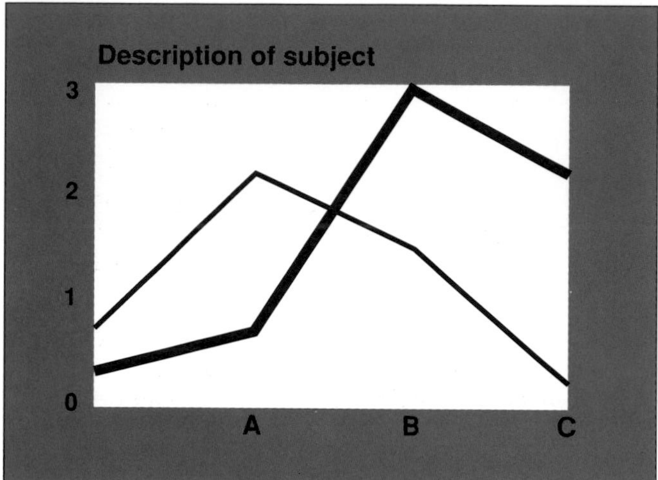

White window in tinted area concentrates attention

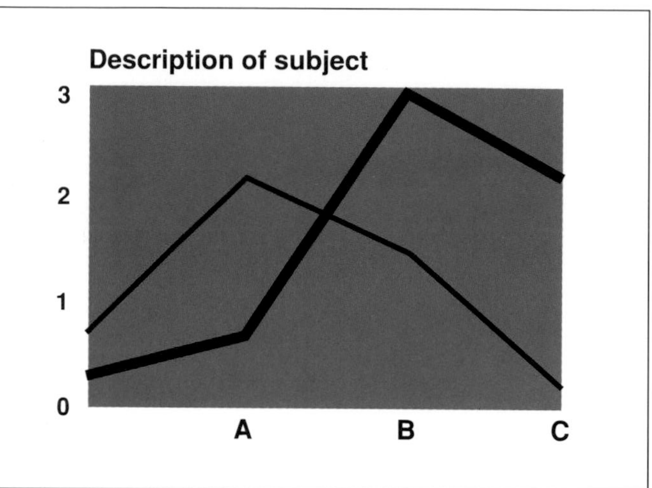

Colored field in white frame: looks smaller

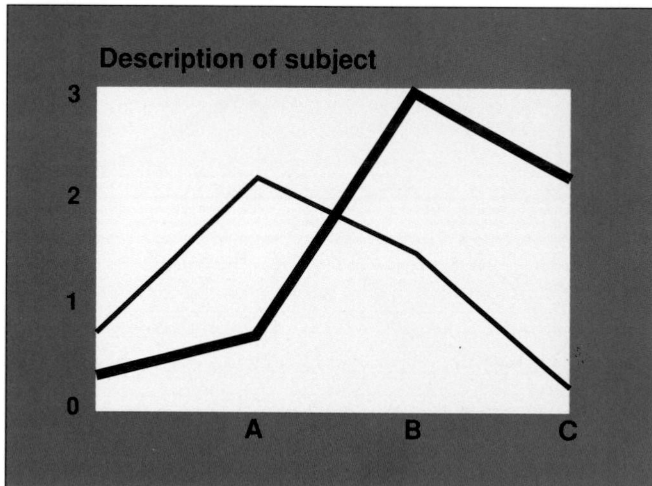

Pale color field in colored frame: colorful

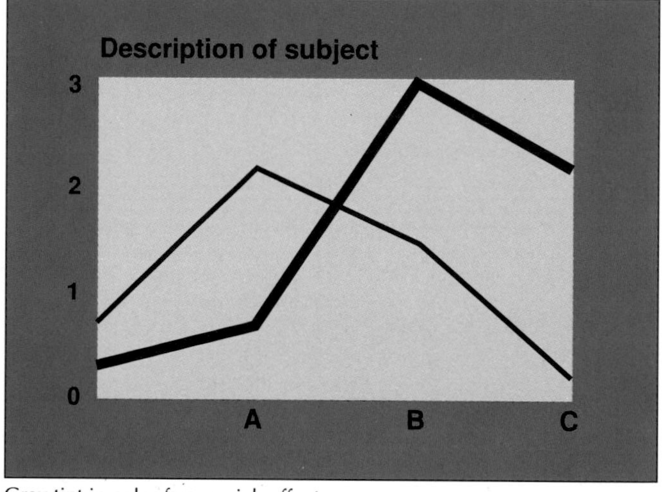

Gray tint in color frame: rich effect

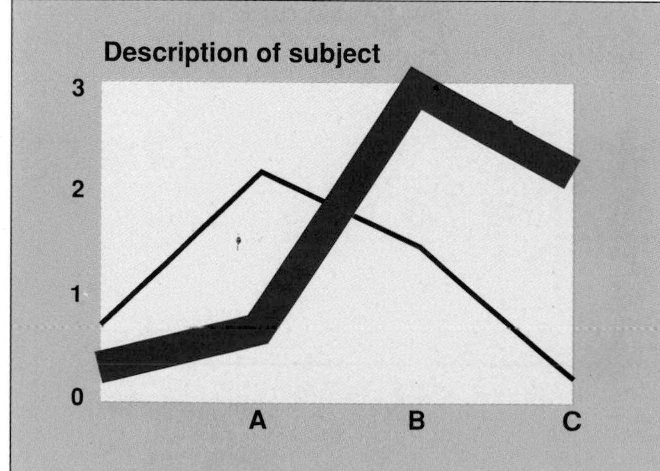

Bold line in color, frame in pale tint: functional

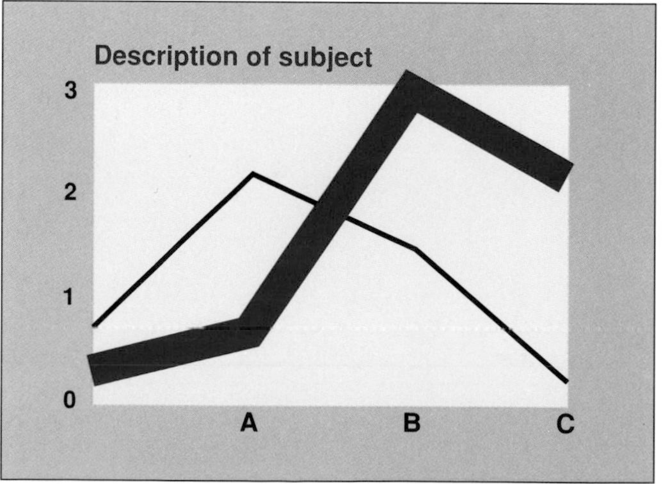

Bold color line, gray frame: powerful communication

The meaning of a chart or graph can be highlighted by color to help the viewer understand it faster. But the way in which color is used affects the diagram's interpretation.

Few statistical presentations in graphic form are mere statements of numbers, published as raw data. In those rare instances, the information is material intended for the recipient's use or personal deduction. Scientific research, for instance, is an area where such purity is expected.

More commonly, statistical data is published to make a specific point, to prove a theory, to back up an opinion. In other words, though statistics can appear neutral, they seldom are. Cynical as this may sound, it is a statement of fact for whose proof ample statistics can be found.

If you know what this purpose is, you can use graphics and color to catapult it into the viewer's mind. Deciding what the point is sounds easier than it is, but making it visible is easier than it sounds. Just make it bigger and fatter, then color it.

Three *fever curves* have been plotted as a simple graph. At first glance, the lines look alike, despite the fact that they have been drawn with different textures. None is deemed more important than the others. Therefore the viewer is not guided to any deduction. The color background adds nothing to the interpretation of the information. It only makes the figure a little more decorative. Were the subject of the graph the orange-produce business, it might make sense to tint the background a symbolic orange color. But even that would not be very rewarding or revealing.

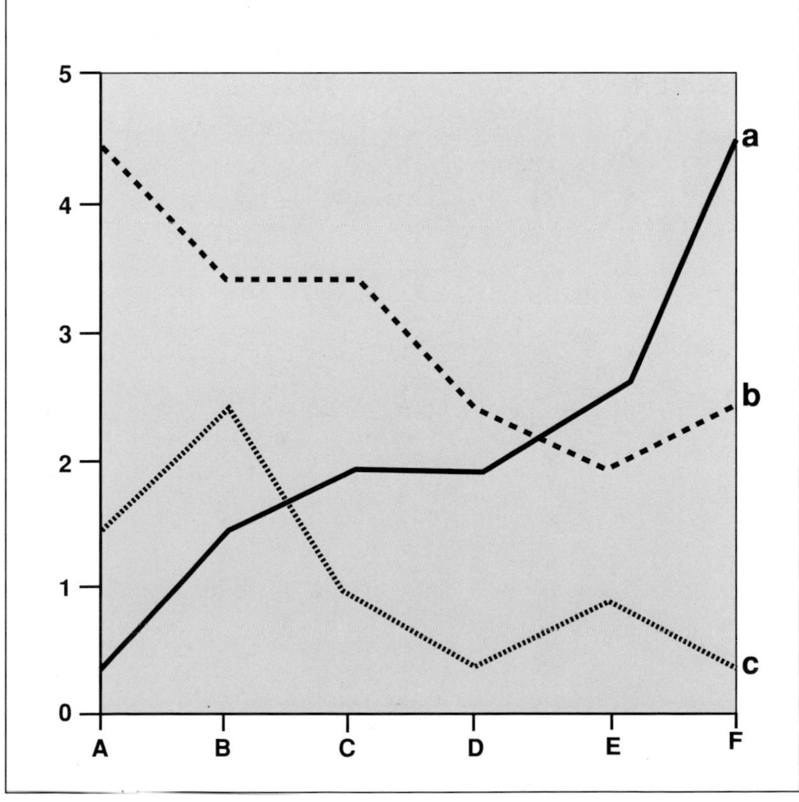

The same data presented with a point of view. Clearly, line A is going to be interpreted as carrying the important facts because it dominates the others through its thickness and color. If this was the intention, then the graphic format is successful.

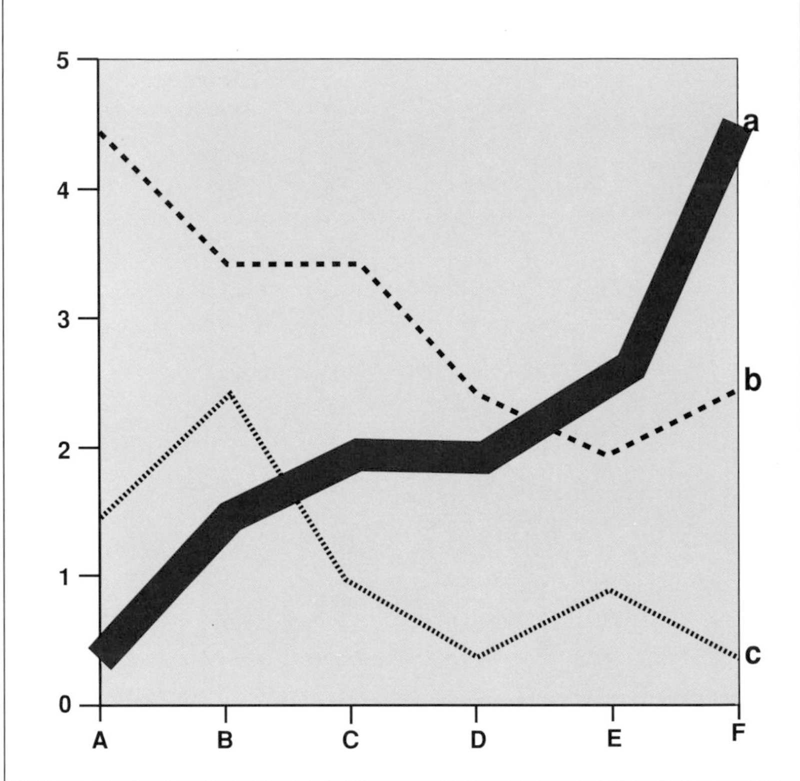

The viewer's attention is forced to line A. The two other sets of statistics are reduced to background status against which the dramatic rise of line A can be seen. They can be studied if the title and caption give the reader a reason to bother. Otherwise they are likely to be ignored. This is not a falsification of the factual data. Strict statistical accuracy is maintained. It is, however, an exaggeration of the way in which they are likely to be interpreted. Is it ethical to mislead? Never say never. This example is intended merely to illustrate what color can achieve.

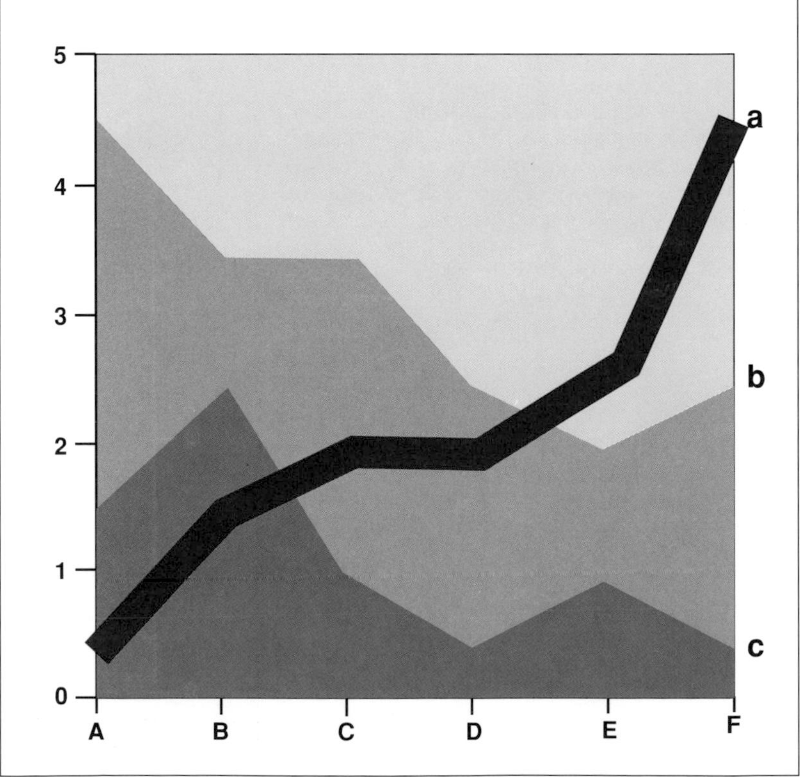

Complex relationships can be simplified by using color as a coding device. Similar colors relate similar elements to each other.

People instinctively assume that similar colors relate the elements that bear them. If there are three balls, two of them are red and one blue, the two red ones "belong" together, and the blue one is the outsider. Canny communicators can make use of this logic in presenting diagrammed information so that color is used to group and encode related elements.

A generic two-line graph illustrates how color relationships can be used to advantage. The statistics are shown here charted in plain black.

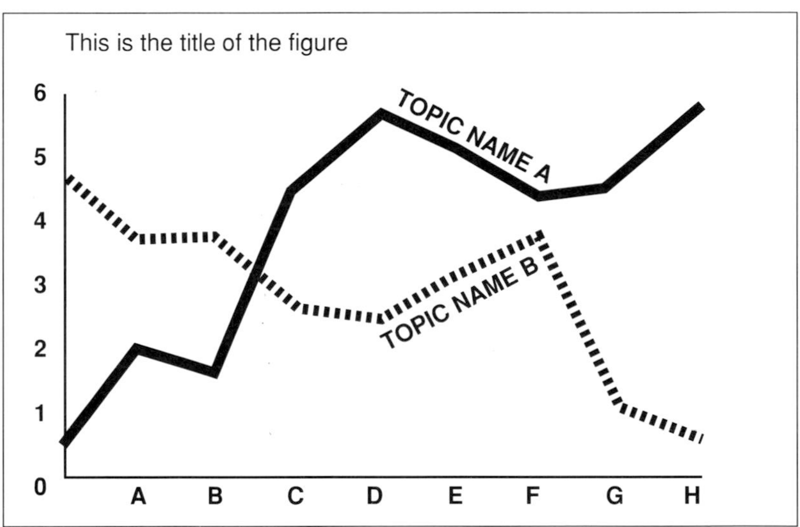

The red line carries the red label, the blue line carries the blue label. (The title is in black, because it is a neutral color.)

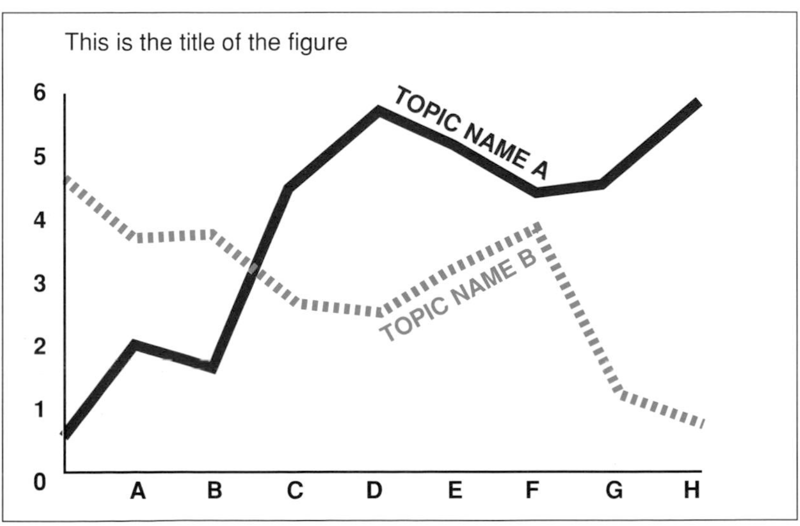

Reversing the colors creates confusion.

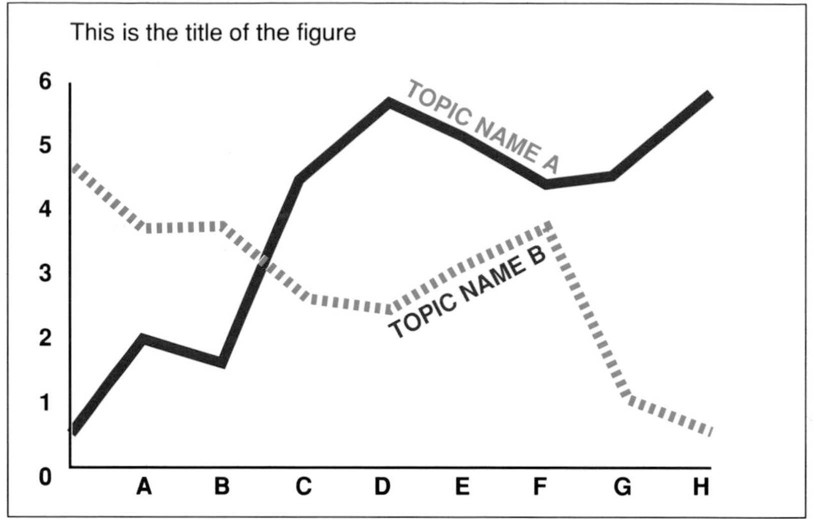

A more complex situation, where the colors define more than merely a line and its label. Here the field is in two colors: the red indices refer to the red material at left, the blue ones to the blue material at right. Such information would be much harder to understand without color.

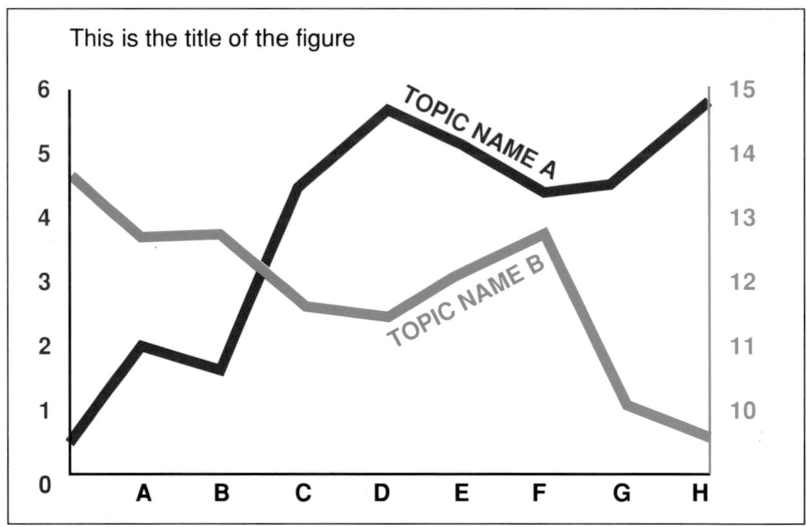

The identical information presented in black with just one additional color. The interpretation is subtler here. Because color is usually used to highlight the important material, the black part is assumed to be the background against which the red (the important part) is compared.

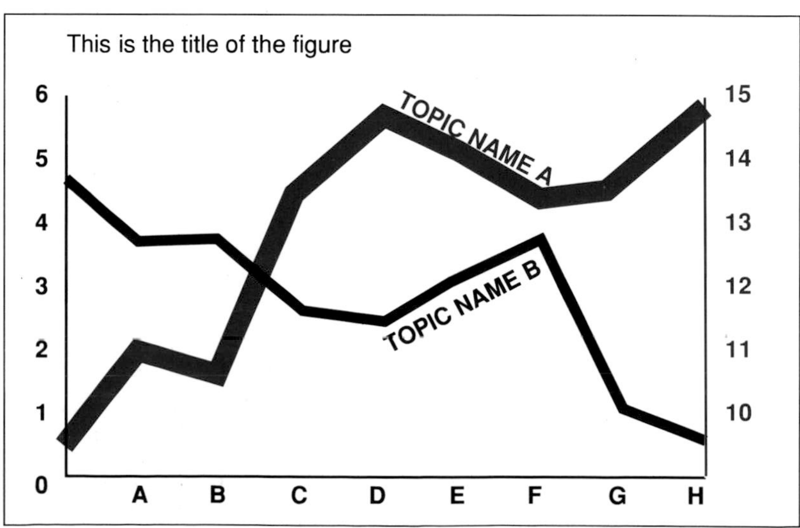

Plain statistical tabulations are difficult to access because they require study and analysis. Color can accelerate the search for the bottom line.

Plain statistics are seldom thrilling to look at. Eye-appeal is never their purpose. Their purpose is to arrange facts in clear, logical, and easy-to-understand fashion. Color can help with the easy-to-understand aspect.

As in any charting (and what is a spreadsheet tabulation but an alphanumeric chart?) there are always elements that deserve to be stressed. Culminations, high points, bottom lines, projections—all can be brought out in such a way that they stand out from their background. Ranking information by such emphasis helps the viewer to distinguish the important from the less important at first glance. The onerous process of studying raw data can thus be shortened.

CIRCUM VENTILATOR CORPORATION
First Quarter 1989
Sales Department Statistics
(Dollars in Thousands)

Rank	Salesperson	Jan. Sales	Feb. Sales	Mar. Sales	Tot. Quarter Sales	Avg. Monthly Sales	Pct. of Tot. Sales
1	C. Zachary	$450	$1,100	$950	$2,500	$833	17.6%
2	E. Daniels	$650	$670	$690	$2,010	$670	14.1%
3	L. Gregory	$360	$900	$410	$1,670	$557	11.7%
4	A. Gregory	$410	$560	$700	$1,670	$557	11.7%
5	R. Alexis	$830	$170	$400	$1,400	$467	9.8%
6	O. McCourtney	$250	$290	$840	$1,380	$460	9.7%
7	D. Morgan	$190	$270	$570	$1,030	$343	7.2%
8	I. Stopher	$350	$320	$330	$1,000	$333	7.0%
9	N. Tobin	$170	$280	$400	$850	$283	6.0%
10	A. Nichols	$340	$280	$100	$720	$240	5.1%
	Total	$4,000	$4,840	$5,390	$14,230	$4,743	100.0%
	Percent	28.1%	34.0%	37.9%	100.0%		

06-Apr-89

Raw spreadsheet data spewed out by the computer can make the heart sink. The information is there, but what a job it is to find the conclusions. If certain information is highlighted by color, the type to be run in color needs to be bolder, otherwise the emphasized elements disappear. (Watch out for red ink: if the numbers represent dollars, use red only for losses.)

CIRCUM VENTILATOR CORPORATION
First Quarter 1989
Sales Department Statistics
(Dollars in Thousands)

Rank	Salesperson	Jan. Sales	Feb. Sales	Mar. Sales	Tot. Quarter Sales	Avg. Monthly Sales	Pct. of Tot. Sales
1	C. Zachary	$450	$1,100	$950	$2,500	$833	17.6%
2	E. Daniels	$650	$670	$690	$2,010	$670	14.1%
3	L. Gregory	$360	$900	$410	$1,670	$557	11.7%
4	A. Gregory	$410	$560	$700	$1,670	$557	11.7%
5	R. Alexis	$830	$170	$400	$1,400	$467	9.8%
6	O. McCourtney	$250	$290	$840	$1,380	$460	9.7%
7	D. Morgan	$190	$270	$570	$1,030	$343	7.2%
8	I. Stopher	$350	$320	$330	$1,000	$333	7.0%
9	N. Tobin	$170	$280	$400	$850	$283	6.0%
10	A. Nichols	$340	$280	$100	$720	$240	5.1%
	Total	$4,000	$4,840	$5,390	$14,230	$4,743	100.0%
	Percent	28.1%	34.0%	37.9%	100.0%		

06-Apr-89

Here the salient points have been separated from the rest of the spreadsheet by color. The information is classified, but there is one problem: the color tint decreases the contrast of black ink on white paper, so the very elements that should pop out are instead harder to read.

CIRCUM VENTILATOR CORPORATION
First Quarter 1989
Sales Department Statistics
(Dollars in Thousands)

Rank	Salesperson	Jan. Sales	Feb. Sales	Mar. Sales	Tot. Quarter Sales	Avg. Monthly Sales	Pct. of Tot. Sales
1	C. Zachary	$450	$1,100	$950	$2,500	$833	17.6%
2	E. Daniels	$650	$670	$690	$2,010	$670	14.1%
3	L. Gregory	$360	$900	$410	$1,670	$557	11.7%
4	A. Gregory	$410	$560	$700	$1,670	$557	11.7%
5	R. Alexis	$830	$170	$400	$1,400	$467	9.8%
6	O. McCourtney	$250	$290	$840	$1,380	$460	9.7%
7	D. Morgan	$190	$270	$570	$1,030	$343	7.2%
8	I. Stopher	$350	$320	$330	$1,000	$333	7.0%
9	N. Tobin	$170	$280	$400	$850	$283	6.0%
10	A. Nichols	$340	$280	$100	$720	$240	5.1%
	Total	$4,000	$4,840	$5,390	$14,230	$4,743	100.0%
	Percent	28.1%	34.0%	37.9%	100.0%		

06-Apr-89

Since black on white is more highly visible, this version of coloring the background in panels is much more functional. The salient points are brighter, the body of information is duller.

Tables usually carry information of varying importance. The viewer can be led to understand ranking by varying the brightness of colors.

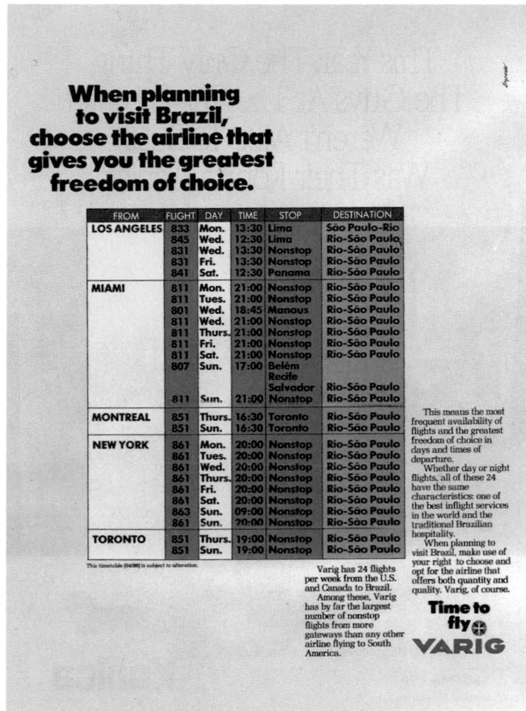

Used with permission of Espressão Brasileira de Propaganda

The receding and advancing characteristics of color should be taken advantage of. As in all communication, the editor must establish which point of view or element needs emphasizing over another. Then color can be used to fulfill the task of making the intended point stand out.

Bright yellow, such as process yellow (used below) advances most obviously. Dull blues and greens recede. How much they advance or recede depends entirely on the specific hues and the relationships of the areas they cover. The example taken from the advertisement (see original at left) shows the effect clearly.

FROM	FLIGHT	DAY	TIME	STOP	DESTINATION
LOS ANGELES	833	Mon.	13:30	Lima	São Paulo-Rio
	845	Wed.	12:30	Lima	Rio-São Paulo
	831	Wed.	13:30	Nonstop	Rio-São Paulo
	831	Fri.	13:30	Nonstop	Rio-São Paulo
	841	Sat.	12:30	Panama	Rio-São Paulo
MIAMI	811	Mon.	21:00	Nonstop	Rio-São Paulo
	811	Tue.	21:00	Nonstop	Rio-São Paulo
	801	Wed.	18:45	Manaus	Rio-São Paulo
	811	Wed.	21:00	Nonstop	Rio-São Paulo
	811	Thurs.	21:00	Nonstop	Rio-São Paulo
	811	Fri.	21:00	Nonstop	Rio-São Paulo
	811	Sat.	21:00	Nonstop	Rio-São Paulo
	807	Sun.	17:00	Belem	
				Recife	
				Salvador	Rio-São Paulo
	811	Sun.	21:00	Nonstop	Rio-São Paulo
MONTREAL	851	Thurs.	16:30	Toronto	Rio-São Paulo
	851	Sun.	16:30	Toronto	Rio-São Paulo
NEW YORK	861	Mon.	20:00	Nonstop	Rio-São Paulo
	861	Tue.	20:00	Nonstop	Rio-São Paulo
	861	Wed.	20:00	Nonstop	Rio-São Paulo
	861	Thurs.	20:00	Nonstop	Rio-São Paulo
	861	Fri.	20:00	Nonstop	Rio-São Paulo
	861	Sat.	20:00	Nonstop	Rio-São Paulo
	863	Sun.	09:00	Nonstop	Rio-São Paulo
	861	Sun.	20:00	Nonstop	Rio-São Paulo
TORONTO	851	Thurs.	19:00	Nonstop	Rio-São Paulo
	851	Sun.	19:00	Nonstop	Rio-São Paulo

Yellow areas are the vital ones. They exemplify the "freedom of choice" described in the headline. The green area also advances, though not nearly as dramatically. It should advance because it lists the destinations, which are important, though less than the destinations and dates in the yellow areas. The blue areas in the background list the background information: flight numbers, times, stops.

Would it have made better sense to list them FROM/DAY/DESTINATION and then the housekeeping facts? Probably. But this would not follow the normal way in which airline flight information is listed, and so it might cause confusion to the user. Worse, the color contrasts would be reduced, so DAY would not stand out as dramatically—and so the point of the message would be obscured.

FROM	DAY	DESTINATION	FLIGHT	TIME	STOP
LOS ANGELES	Mon.	São Paulo-Rio	833	13:30	Lima
	Wed.	Rio-São Paulo	845	12:30	Lima
	Wed.	Rio-São Paulo	831	13:30	Nonstop
	Fri.	Rio-São Paulo	831	13:30	Nonstop
	Sat.	Rio-São Paulo	841	12:30	Panama
MIAMI	Mon.	Rio-São Paulo	811	21:00	Nonstop
	Tue.	Rio-São Paulo	811	21:00	Nonstop
	Wed.	Rio-São Paulo	801	18:45	Manaus
	Wed.	Rio-São Paulo	811	21:00	Nonstop
	Thurs.	Rio-São Paulo	811	21:00	Nonstop
	Fri.	Rio-São Paulo	811	21:00	Nonstop
	Sat.	Rio-São Paulo	811	21:00	Nonstop
	Sun.		807	17:00	Belem
					Recife
		Rio-São Paulo			Salvador
	Sun.	Rio-São Paulo	811	21:00	Nonstop
MONTREAL	Thurs.	Rio-São Paulo	851	16:30	Toronto
	Sun.	Rio-São Paulo	851	16:30	Toronto
NEW YORK	Mon.	Rio-São Paulo	861	20:00	Nonstop
	Tue.	Rio-São Paulo	861	20:00	Nonstop
	Wed.	Rio-São Paulo	861	20:00	Nonstop
	Thurs.	Rio-São Paulo	861	20:00	Nonstop
	Fri.	Rio-São Paulo	861	20:00	Nonstop
	Sat.	Rio-São Paulo	861	20:00	Nonstop
	Sun.	Rio-São Paulo	863	09:00	Nonstop
	Sun.	Rio-São Paulo	861	20:00	Nonstop
TORONTO	Thurs.	Rio-São Paulo	851	19:00	Nonstop
	Sun.	Rio-São Paulo	851	19:00	Nonstop

What is the viewer conscious of first in this version? TIME and STOP. Neither is very important. FROM is so dark that it would probably be ignored. DESTINATION and FLIGHT seem related to each other because the green links them visually. But emphasizing such a close relationship is not helpful.

FROM	FLIGHT	DAY	TIME	STOP	DESTINATION
LOS ANGELES	833	Mon.	13:30	Lima	São Paulo-Rio
	845	Wed.	12:30	Lima	Rio-São Paulo
	831	Wed.	13:30	Nonstop	Rio-São Paulo
	831	Fri.	13:30	Nonstop	Rio-São Paulo
	841	Sat.	12:30	Panama	Rio-São Paulo
MIAMI	811	Mon.	21:00	Nonstop	Rio-São Paulo
	811	Tue.	21:00	Nonstop	Rio-São Paulo
	801	Wed.	18:45	Manaus	Rio-São Paulo
	811	Wed.	21:00	Nonstop	Rio-São Paulo
	811	Thurs.	21:00	Nonstop	Rio-São Paulo
	811	Fri.	21:00	Nonstop	Rio-São Paulo
	811	Sat.	21:00	Nonstop	Rio-São Paulo
	807	Sun.	17:00	Belem	
				Recife	
				Salvador	Rio-São Paulo
	811	Sun.	21:00	Nonstop	Rio-São Paulo
MONTREAL	851	Thurs.	16:30	Toronto	Rio-São Paulo
	851	Sun.	16:30	Toronto	Rio-São Paulo
NEW YORK	861	Mon.	20:00	Nonstop	Rio-São Paulo
	861	Tue.	20:00	Nonstop	Rio-São Paulo
	861	Wed.	20:00	Nonstop	Rio-São Paulo
	861	Thurs.	20:00	Nonstop	Rio-São Paulo
	861	Fri.	20:00	Nonstop	Rio-São Paulo
	861	Sat.	20:00	Nonstop	Rio-São Paulo
	863	Sun.	09:00	Nonstop	Rio-São Paulo
	861	Sun.	20:00	Nonstop	Rio-São Paulo
TORONTO	851	Thurs.	19:00	Nonstop	Rio-São Paulo
	851	Sun.	19:00	Nonstop	Rio-São Paulo

A prototypical table illustrates the variety that the addition of a single color can create, despite the fact that tables are seldom as dramatic as charts and graphs.

There is an infinity of ways to combine the elements in a table with color. Just think of the colors themselves and the changes that can be made by screening; then add black; then add reverses (white type on black or color); then use clever ways to handle rules and lines. And then put the whole thing in a box that makes the title stand out. The variety of ways to mix these materials is indeed infinite. What is definitely not infinite is what you are trying to accomplish with the presentation. Apart from making the object look prettier, color can expose or it can hide. It can reveal or camouflage. It can also remain neutral.

The generic table that follows is shown in fifteen variations to illustrate the very simplest of ways that color can be applied. The captions explain how the color would probably affect the viewer. Process blue has been used because it is used so often for precisely this purpose.

Topic title

Stub head	Column head	Column head
Stub topic	mmmmmm	mmmmm
Stub topic	mmmmm	mmmm
Stub topic	mmmmmm	mmmmmm
Stub topic	mmmm	mmmmm
	mmmmm	mmmmm

Topic title

Stub head	Column head	Column head
Stub topic	mmmmmm	mmmmm
Stub topic	mmmmm	mmmm
Stub topic	mmmmmm	mmmmmm
Stub topic	mmmm	mmmmm
	mmmmm	mmmmm

The simple color panel that covers the black type is not very helpful; too dark.

Topic title

Stub head	Column head	Column head
Stub topic	mmmmmm	mmmmm
Stub topic	mmmmm	mmmm
Stub topic	mmmmmm	mmmmmm
Stub topic	mmmm	mmmmm
	mmmmm	mmmmm

Additional colorfulness, but little improvement in communication value. No elements are emphasized.

Topic title

Stub head	Column head	Column head
Stub topic	mmmmmmm	mmmmmm
Stub topic	mmmmmm	mmmmm
Stub topic	mmmmmmm	mmmmmmm
Stub topic	mmmmm	mmmmmm
	mmmmmm	mmmmmm

The color makes totals pop out. They would be more dramatically visible were they set in bold type as well as in color.

Topic title

Stub head	Column head	Column head
Stub topic	mmmmmmm	mmmmmm
Stub topic	mmmmmm	mmmmm
Stub topic	mmmmmmm	mmmmmmm
Stub topic	mmmmm	mmmmmm
	mmmmmm	mmmmmm

The title and the bottom line it refers to are tied together and make the rest of the information skippable.

Topic title

Stub head	Column head	Column head
Stub topic	mmmmmmm	mmmmmm
Stub topic	mmmmmm	mmmmm
Stub topic	mmmmmmm	mmmmmmm
Stub topic	mmmmm	mmmmmm
	mmmmmm	mmmmmm

A single topic line is highlighted with a band of color.

Topic title

Stub head	Column head	Column head
Stub topic	mmmmmmm	mmmmmm
Stub topic	mmmmmmm	mmmmmmm
Stub topic	mmmmmm	mmmmm
Stub topic	mmmmm	mmmmmm

The highlighting of a topic line is even more noticeable here than in the example at left.

Topic title

Stub head	Column head	Column head
Stub topic	mmmmmmm	mmmmmm
Stub topic	mmmmmm	mmmmm
Stub topic	mmmmmmm	mmmmmmm
Stub topic	mmmmm	mmmmmm
	mmmmmm	mmmmmm

A screened color panel separates a column from its neighbors, presumably signaling its specialness.

Topic title

Stub head	Column head	Column head
Stub topic	mmmmm	mmmmmm
Stub topic	mmmmmmm	mmmmmm
Stub topic	mmmmmm	mmmmm
Stub topic	mmmmmmm	mmmmmmm
	mmmmmm	mmmmmm

Screened color areas separate layers from each other.

Topic title

Stub head	Column head	Column head
Stub topic	mmmmmmm	mmmmmm
Stub topic	mmmmmm	mmmmm
Stub topic	mmmmmmm	mmmmmmm
Stub topic	mmmmm	mmmmmm
	mmmmmm	mmmmmm

Tinting the field encourages the headings to stand out. The grid of lines adds another element to manipulate in color.

Topic title

Stub head	Column head	Column head
Stub topic	mmmmmmm	mmmmmm
Stub topic	mmmmmm	mmmmm
Stub topic	mmmmmmm	mmmmmmm
Stub topic	mmmmm	mmmmmm
	mmmmmm	mmmmmm

Tinting the surroundings encourages the field to stand out. Compare the effect with the example at left.

Topic title

Stub head	Column head	Column head
Stub topic	mmmmmmm	mmmmmm
Stub topic	mmmmmm	mmmmm
Stub topic	mmmmmmm	mmmmmmm
Stub topic	mmmmm	mmmmmm
	mmmmmm	mmmmmm

Rules in color separate columns and rows. The rule above the totals is in black.

Topic title

Stub head	Column head	Column head
Stub topic	mmmmmmm	mmmmmm
Stub topic	mmmmmm	mmmmm
Stub topic	mmmmmmm	mmmmmmm
Stub topic	mmmmm	mmmmmm
	mmmmmm	mmmmmm

Type in color separated by vertical rules in black. Since type in color is more unusual, it will gain attention.

Topic title

Stub head	Column head	Column head
Stub topic	mmmmmmm	mmmmmm
Stub topic	mmmmmm	mmmmm
Stub topic	mmmmmmm	mmmmmmm
Stub topic	mmmmm	mmmmmm
	mmmmmm	mmmmmm

An arrangement that is perhaps a little more complex than the subject warrants.

Topic title

Stub head	Column head	Column head
Stub topic	mmmmmmm	mmmmmm
Stub topic	mmmmmm	mmmmm
Stub topic	mmmmmmm	mmmmmmm
Stub topic	mmmmm	mmmmmm
	mmmmmm	mmmmmm

The bold black rules add horizontal emphasis as well as visibility to heads and totals.

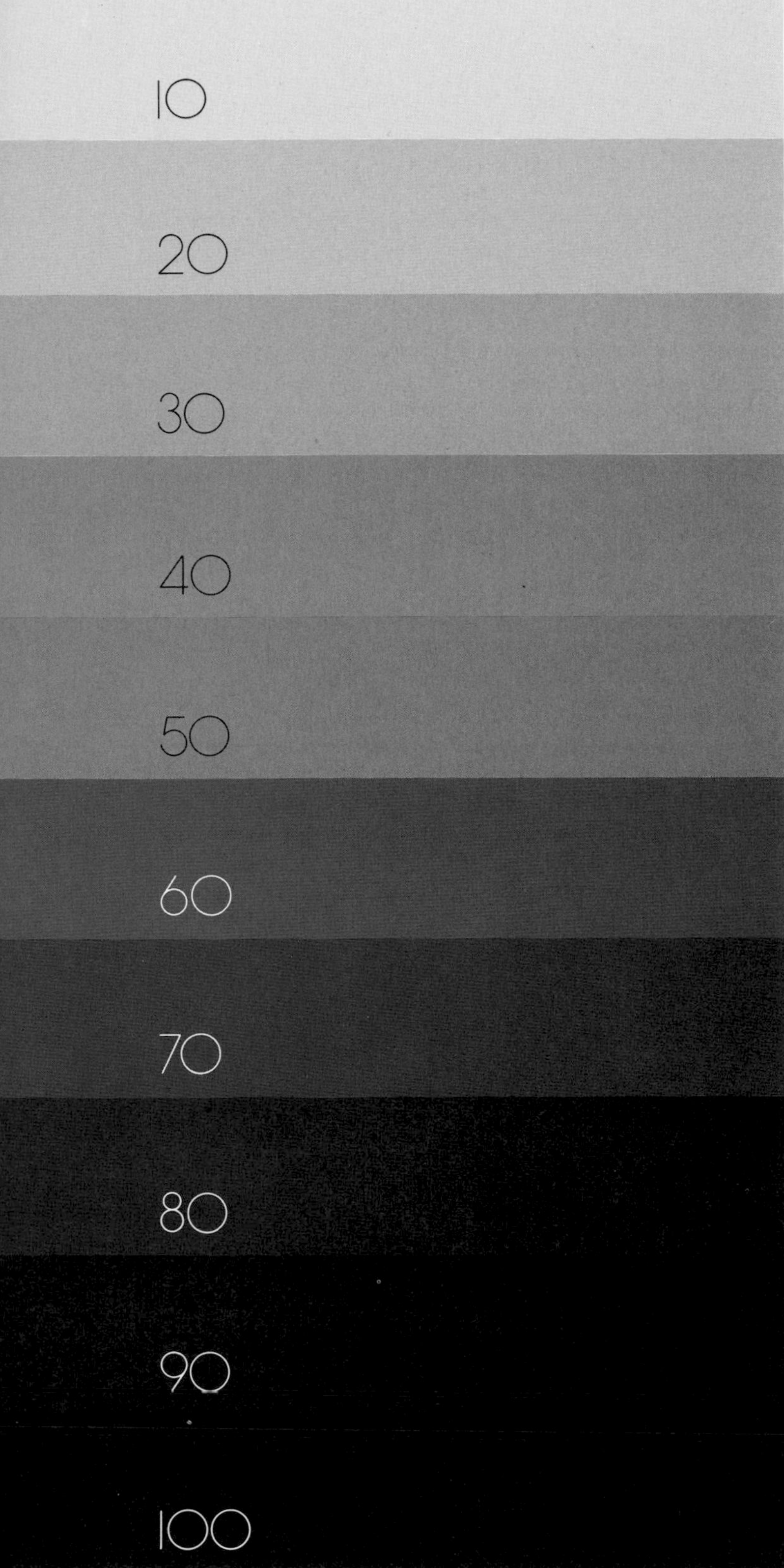
10
20
30
40
50
60
70
80
90
100

The value (lightness and darkness) of background colors used in charts and graphs has a strong effect on how they will be interpreted.

The greatest contrast in print is that of black ink on white paper. (In slide presentations, the reverse is true: the strongest effect is that of white type on black background.)

Black type on a white background sparkles more vividly than the same black type on any other color. It is therefore very dangerous to run tables with layers of black on white between layers of black on yellow (or black on whatever). The black on white springs forward and catches the eye first. The implication is that this is the important material, and that the other is of secondary importance. It may not be so in fact, but the viewer will jump to that conclusion simply because of the physical visual reaction to the printed image.

Black on yellow does stand out more strikingly, but this is a function of the combination of hue more than of contrast. It is startling, but not conducive to long-term study. Why is text seldom run on yellow? Because it hurts to read it.

First-class citizenship is held by material in the layers whose contrast is greatest.

This type, which is printed on a dark background, is harder to discern than . . .

this type, which is printed on a white background, and stands out more vividly than . . .

this type, which is printed on a dark background, and is harder to discern than . . .

this type, which is printed on a white background, and stands out more vividly than . . .

this type, which is printed on a dark background, and is harder to discern than . . .

this type, which is printed on a white background, and stands out more vividly than . . .

this type, which is printed on a dark background, and is therefore harder to discern.

Balanced color backgrounds equalize the interpretation of the data.

This type, which is printed on a colored background, is no harder to discern than . . .

this type, which is on a colored background whose tone is similar, therefore . . .

this type, which is printed on a colored background, is no harder to discern than . . .

this type, which is on a colored background whose tone is similar, therefore . . .

this type, which is printed on a colored background, is no harder to discern than . . .

this type, which is on a colored background whose tone is similar, therefore . . .

this type, which is printed on a colored background, is no harder to discern.

The whole question of color contrast in backgrounds for type is tricky. White type on color, black type on color: both are problematic. You have to handle them with care.

Plan color with contrast of tone in mind. To ensure legibility, the background must be dark enough to drop out the type in white, or it must be light enough to allow the type to be surprinted on it in black. The table is shown in black (below), and cyan (opposite). Problems are clearly evident at both ends of the scale. The tables are shown in increments of 10% screens. The type used is Times Roman, Helvetica Light, and Helvetica Medium, all in ten point. Notice how much better the bold type reads in the problem areas. If you intend to run type in color on color backgrounds, be extremely careful about the contrast that is likely to occur. Get samples. Run tests. Talk to the printer. Never experiment on the real thing.

10%	This type is surprinted in black..	this type is dropped out in white	10%
	This type is surprinted in black..	this type is dropped out in white	
	This type is surprinted in black..	**this type is dropped out in white**	
20%	This type is surprinted in black...	this type is dropped out in white	20%
	This type is surprinted in black...	this type is dropped out in white	
	This type is surprinted in black...	**this type is dropped out in white**	
30%	This type is surprinted in black...	this type is dropped out in white	30%
	This type is surprinted in black...	this type is dropped out in white	
	This type is surprinted in black...	**this type is dropped out in white**	
40%	This type is surprinted in black...	this type is dropped out in white	40%
	This type is surprinted in black...	this type is dropped out in white	
	This type is surprinted in black...	**this type is dropped out in white**	
50%	This type is surprinted in black...	this type is dropped out in white	50%
	This type is surprinted in black...	this type is dropped out in white	
	This type is surprinted in black...	**this type is dropped out in white**	
60%	This type is surprinted in black...	this type is dropped out in white	60%
	This type is surprinted in black...	this type is dropped out in white	
	This type is surprinted in black...	**this type is dropped out in white**	
70%	This type is surprinted in black...	this type is dropped out in white	70%
	This type is surprinted in black...	this type is dropped out in white	
	This type is surprinted in black...	**this type is dropped out in white**	
80%	This type is surprinted in black...	this type is dropped out in white	80%
	This type is surprinted in black...	this type is dropped out in white	
	This type is surprinted in black...	**this type is dropped out in white**	
	.	this type is dropped out in white	90%
	.	this type is dropped out in white	
	.	**this type is dropped out in white**	
	.	this type is dropped out in white	100%
	.	this type is dropped out in white	
	.	**this type is dropped out in white**	

10%

This type is surprinted in black..
This type is surprinted in black..
This type is surprinted in black..

20%

This type is surprinted in black.. this type is dropped out in white
This type is surprinted in black.. this type is dropped out in white
This type is surprinted in black.. this type is dropped out in white

20%

30%

This type is surprinted in black... this type is dropped out in white
This type is surprinted in black... this type is dropped out in white
This type is surprinted in black... this type is dropped out in white

30%

40%

This type is surprinted in black... this type is dropped out in white
This type is surprinted in black... this type is dropped out in white
This type is surprinted in black... this type is dropped out in white

40%

50%

This type is surprinted in black... this type is dropped out in white
This type is surprinted in black... this type is dropped out in white
This type is surprinted in black... this type is dropped out in white

50%

60%

This type is surprinted in black... this type is dropped out in white
This type is surprinted in black... this type is dropped out in white
This type is surprinted in black... this type is dropped out in white

60%

70%

This type is surprinted in black... this type is dropped out in white
This type is surprinted in black... this type is dropped out in white
This type is surprinted in black... this type is dropped out in white

70%

80%

This type is surprinted in black... this type is dropped out in white
This type is surprinted in black... this type is dropped out in white
This type is surprinted in black... this type is dropped out in white

80%

90%

This type is surprinted in black... this type is dropped out in white
This type is surprinted in black... this type is dropped out in white
This type is surprinted in black... this type is dropped out in white

90%

100%

This type is surprinted in black... this type is dropped out in white
This type is surprinted in black... this type is dropped out in white
This type is surprinted in black... this type is dropped out in white

100%

Most people choose hue, forgetting that the relationship of its value is probably more critical than its actual "color." Always be aware of the comparative gray scale.

Using color is always a bit risky, and you never know exactly what it will look like until it is finally printed, no matter how carefully you plot and plan. To avoid mistakes ahead of time, it is always a good idea to mock up the final as carefully as possible. Markers that correspond to PMS colors, for instance, are widely available. It would be wise to invest in a full set, if you use a lot of color.

Print out a copy of the black-on-white base drawing (there are few charts and graphs that lack such a thing), and cover it with a tracing-paper overlay. Use specially made tissue, which does not allow the color to bleed through. Sketch in the color with the marker. Then, having decided which you intend to use, identify each with a swatch from the color-sample book. If you are using process colors, any color you choose can be simulated by a combination of the four process inks.

Then pull your swatches together and compare them for balance (or contrast) to the gray scale, like the one on the opposite page.

You want them to be in close range, 20% is probably safest, so that none screams or overwhelms the others. Place the swatch atop the gray. Half-close the eyes so that you become conscious only of the tones. When they match, this is the gray value that you are seeking.

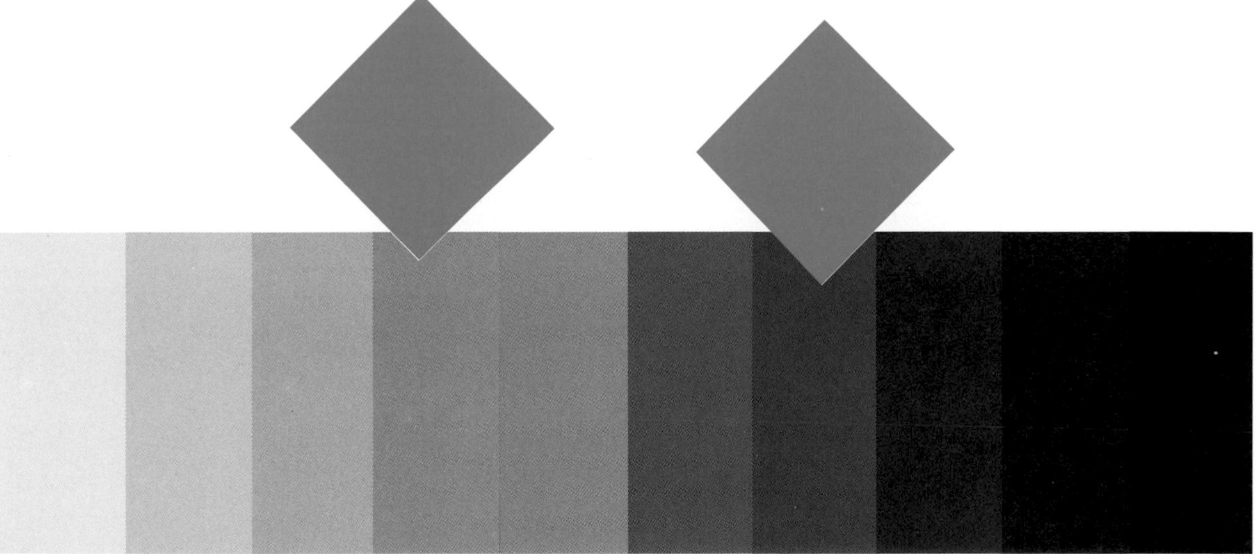

Beware, because colors darker than an equivalent of 60% on the gray scale will probably hide the drawing beneath, but this is about the darkness you need for dropping out type in white most effectively. So be aware of the area that such a dark color is being used on.

Colors paler than 15%, however, tend to look a bit washed out, though they are an ideal background for black text. The actual hue may affect the effect.

To create color contrast (for instance, to ensure that type stands out from its colored background) make the difference in gray-scale value at least 30%.

This message is easy to read because white type contrasts clearly against the 70% screen of black

This message is much harder to read despite the brightness of its color, because there is hardly any contrast in tone

This is much better: the color of the type is the same green as in the example above, but the black is paler: 30%

The headline at the top is perfectly legible. It is white on 70% black. The headline in the middle is invisible. The background is the same 70% screen of black, but the lettering is made up of 100% cyan, 100% yellow, and 20% magenta—a nice bright color that happens to have a tonal value very similar to the 70% black. The headline in the bottom panel uses the same green, but the background has been lightened to 30% black. It reads well. Not as well as the white on gray, perhaps, but considerably better than the one in the middle. The problem, therefore, is not that green does not read well on gray, but what sort of green and what sort of gray do you attempt to contrast with each other?

Gentle, light colors are kinder and friendlier when type is to be read on them. Bright, dark ones are more decorative, perhaps. But they can hinder reading.

Any screen over 40% tends to be too strong and dark, and therefore dangerous, if type is to be surprinted. You can surprint black on yellow even if it is 100% solid. Its brashness and vulgarity, however, increase in proportion to its intensity.

Process blue (cyan) is safest in screens. It is perceived as calm and cool, and it is preferred by people over fifty-five.

Process red (magenta) turns into a crude and unattractive pink when used alone in screen form.

Both cyan and magenta, used as single screens, denote ordinariness. They are the cheapest way of getting color onto the page, and they look it.

More subtle colorization, using muted tones, is preferred by upscale, sophisticated audiences. Adding 5% black screen is usually the easiest way to take the curse off plain magenta or cyan.

Light tones in the brighter, primary hues are popular with younger audiences as well as with the less affluent.

The examples on the next two pages are made of various combinations of process-color screens. They are shown in 5% and 10% combinations. Some are gentler and more appealing than others. Remember that they seldom exist by themselves but are seen in combination with their surroundings. As a result, the initially cheerful, sunny combination of 5% yellow and 5% magenta will look aggressively hot when seen in a context of blues or greens.

On a more technical level: when you print screens in layers on top of each other, as in all color printing, you have to "angle the screens." If the tiny dots were all printed directly above each other, you would get mud. If they were not placed at just the right distances and angles to each other, however, the dots would form moiré patterns or stars in the final printed picture. Do not worry, though. Your suppliers (and your computers) know that black goes down at forty-five degrees, magenta (red) at seventy-five degrees, yellow at ninety degrees, and cyan (blue) at 105 degrees from the vertical. You just need to be aware of this technicality.

5% yellow + 5% magenta

10% yellow + 5% magenta

10% yellow + 10% magenta

5% yellow + 5% cyan

10% yellow + 5% cyan

10% yellow + 10% cyan

5% yellow + 5% black

10% yellow + 5% black

10% yellow + 10% black

5% magenta + 5% cyan
10% magenta + 5% cyan
10% magenta + 10% cyan
5% magenta + 5% black
5% magenta + 10% black
10% magenta + 10% black
5% cyan + 5% black
10% cyan + 5% black
10% cyan + 10% black

Color's capacity to indicate change can be shown as a progression of staged hues or tones. It creates arresting and expressive backgrounds.

The representation of a sequence of change is a commonly needed device. The usual way to represent this is to number items, 1, 2, 3, and then to ask the reader to follow the numbers. Primitive as the method may be, it works well enough to describe a series of discrete events. Such a flow, however, can be made to sparkle more vividly with color. The technique is founded on two simple facts: we read from left to right (which should be no news to anyone), and some colors appear to advance while others recede (which is somewhat trickier). To use the factors effectively requires understanding of three additional factors: color progression, geometrical progression, and how color progression and geometrical progression can be combined to strengthen the clarity of the flow.

Color progression

Variegation of hue and value effectively splits a series into separate components. Instead of creating unifying relationships, it disintegrates. It is indeed very colorful. Its variety, however, can disturb the feeling of flow, making it harder for the viewer to understand the sequence.

Progression can be exhibited most clearly by simplicity. Here, a single color is shown in a sequence of gradations. The screens used are: 15%, 25%, 40%, 60%, 80%, 100%. The darkest one (100%) seems to be closest, whereas the lightest one (15%) appears to be farthest away.

For an effect that uses the capacity of the new technology to best advantage and produces a colorful result that retains the deliberately organized effect, use the illusion of one color turning into another by stages. This can best be accomplished by starting with one pure color at left, ending with the other at right, and superimposing tints in the intervening units that change the balance. Shown here is 100% magenta, 0% cyan at left; 80% magenta, 20% cyan; 60% magenta, 40% cyan; 40% magenta, 60% cyan; 20% magenta, 80% cyan; 0% magenta, 100% cyan at right. The result is fairly balanced from left to right. If you want to build up to a crescendo, change the proportions of the screens. Check in a color book or experiment.

Geometrical progression

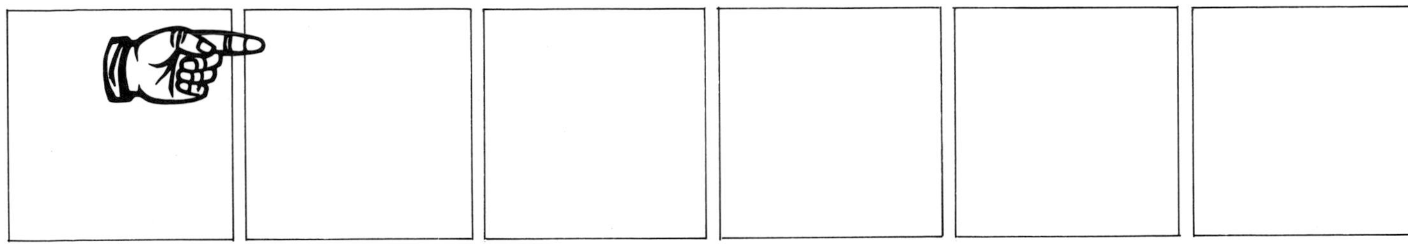

Six units on parade. Even without numbers showing, we assume numbering to begin at the far left, as convention dictates. The result is a static presentation without climax.

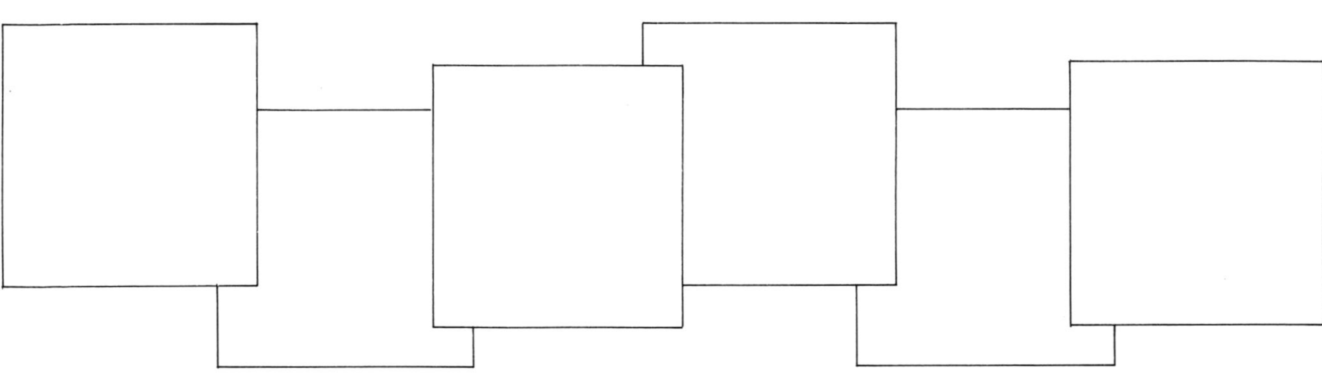

Six units shown overlapping in random fashion. Some appear to be in front, others behind.

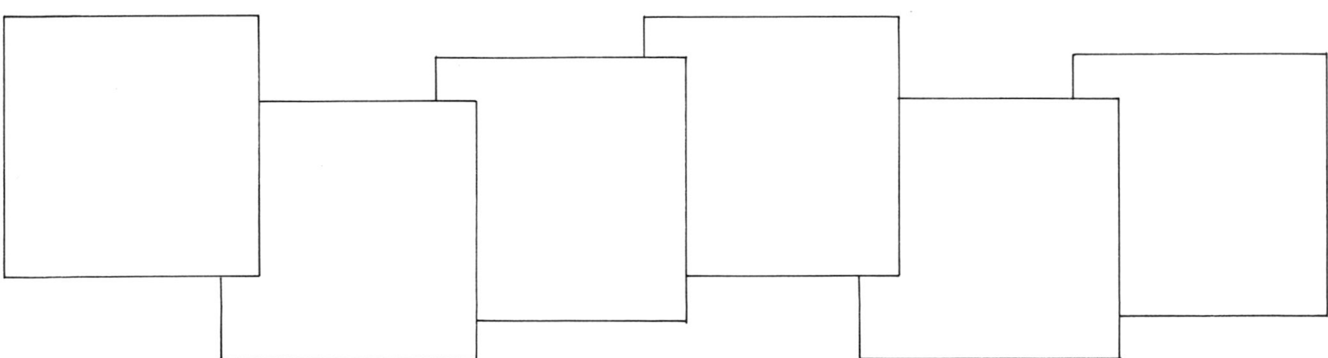

The six units all overlapping in the same direction. Since we read left to right, we interpret the ones above to be receding into the distance, whereas the ones below appear to be advancing.

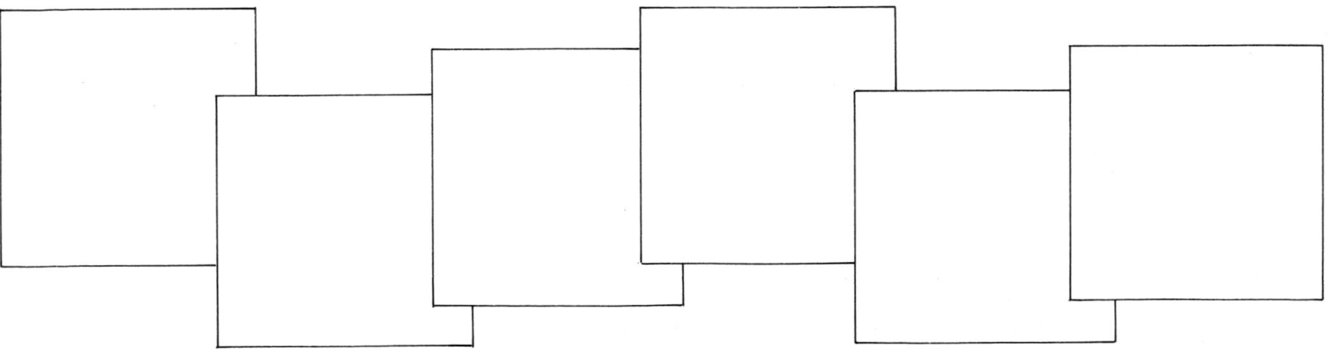

Combining the progressions

Adding colors at random to a random arrangement exacerbates the sense of disorganization. It is undoubtedly colorful, but it is confusing.

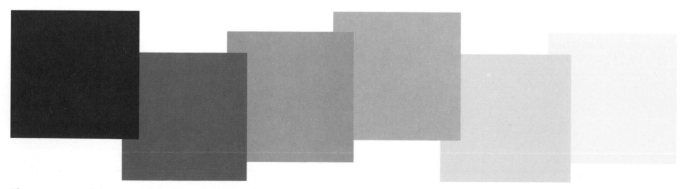

Organized color helps a little, but it cannot overcome the problem of the disorganization of the boxes.

The geometry of these overlaps appears to recede into the distance at far right. Stronger color at far left is also up front because of its own strength. The sequence proceeds from there into the distance.

The colors work at cross-purposes with the geometry here. The weakest, palest color is in the "front" at left, whereas the strongest one is in the box that is supposed to look the farthest away.

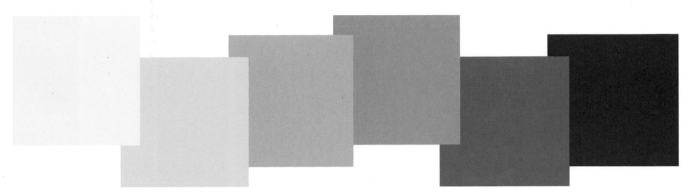

Overlaps that appear to advance toward the viewer at far right seem to culminate in a climax. This is why the strongest color at far right is more successful than if it were the palest.

Color progression in use: here is an example of a simple bar chart. It illustrates how interpretation can be made to vary by the way the color is applied.

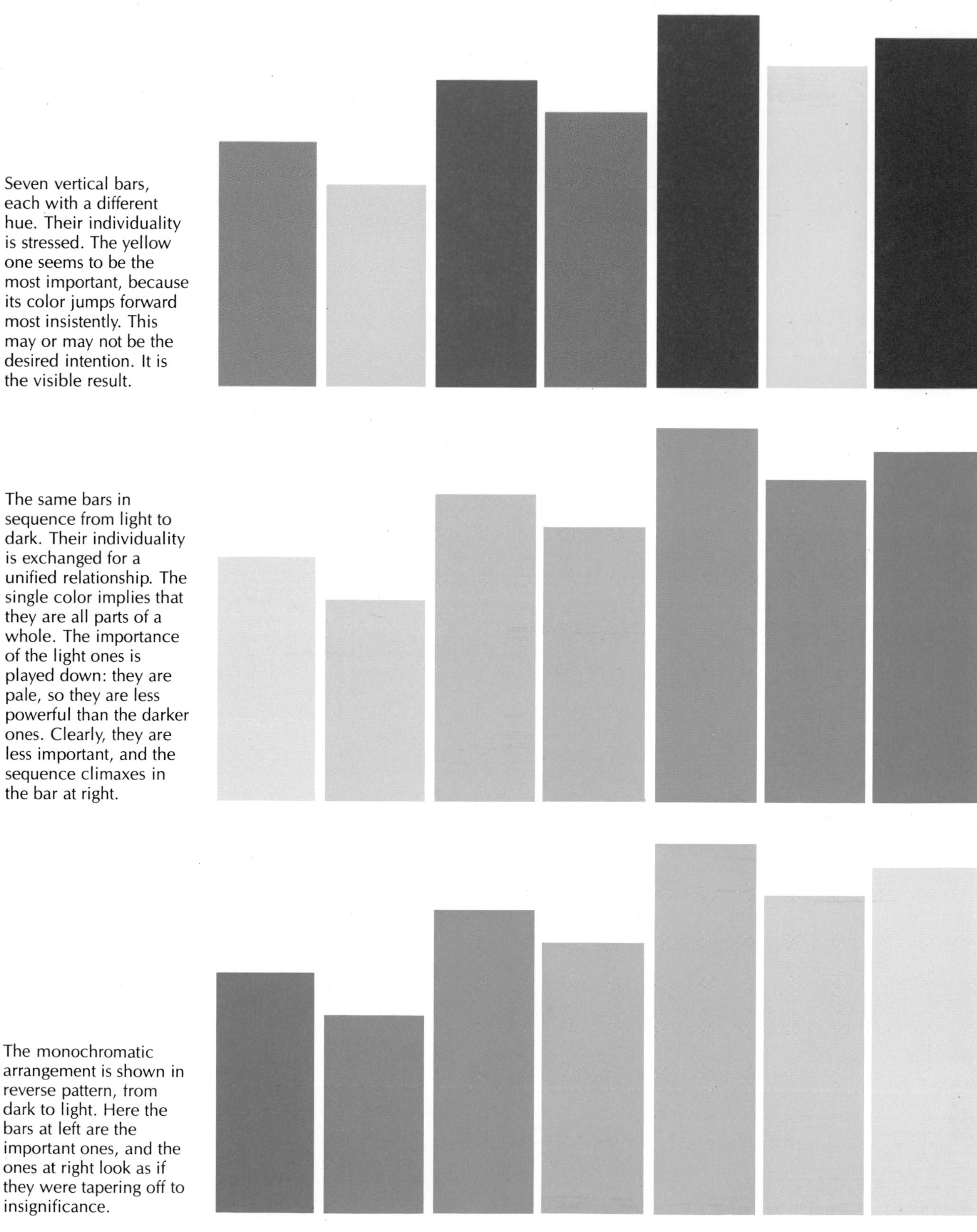

Seven vertical bars, each with a different hue. Their individuality is stressed. The yellow one seems to be the most important, because its color jumps forward most insistently. This may or may not be the desired intention. It is the visible result.

The same bars in sequence from light to dark. Their individuality is exchanged for a unified relationship. The single color implies that they are all parts of a whole. The importance of the light ones is played down: they are pale, so they are less powerful than the darker ones. Clearly, they are less important, and the sequence climaxes in the bar at right.

The monochromatic arrangement is shown in reverse pattern, from dark to light. Here the bars at left are the important ones, and the ones at right look as if they were tapering off to insignificance.

Two or more colors add variety but complicate the interpretation. The brightness, vividness, and the advancing and recessive qualities of each hue must be taken into account. The quiet green is outscreamed by the brilliant orange. Though the orange is indeed "lighter" than the green, its intensity advances it in front of the green, and we interpret that as emphasis.

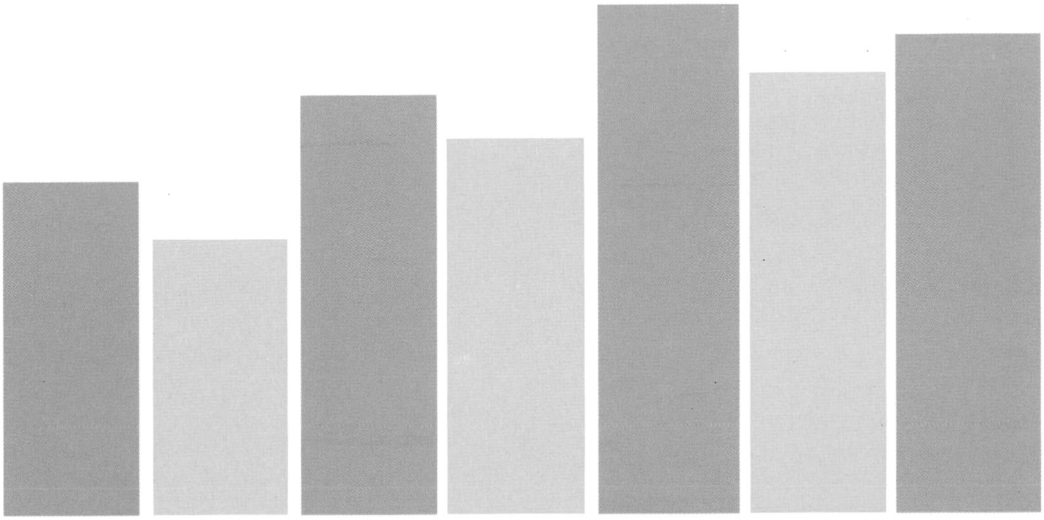

Reaching a climax at far right, using a sequence of colors . . .

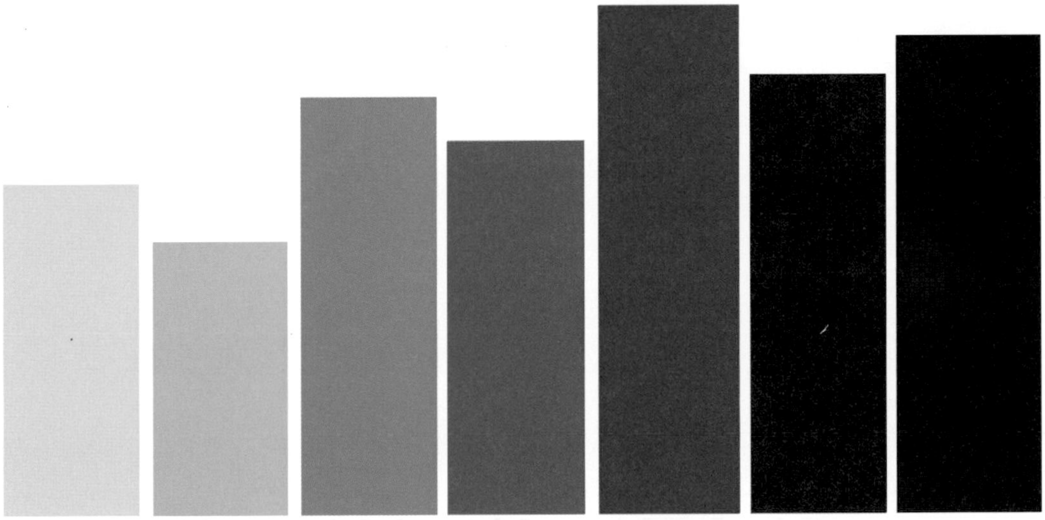

. . . and descending from a climax at left, using the same colors.

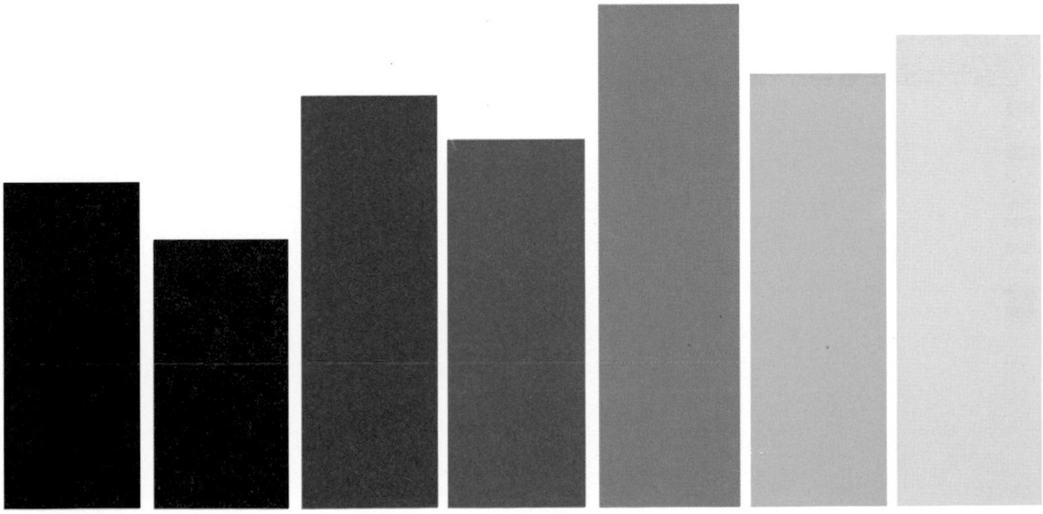

Stepped color progression can be used to advantage as a more expressive background in the panel behind the chart, graph, or table.

This is a background area rendered in a single color. It is simple and cheap to create. It also adds a touch of color to the page or the slide. Its advantage is neutrality. Its disadvantage is dullness. It is shown here without a frame or title block, both of which are opportunities for more color use.

The vertical subdivisions of the chart or graph that are to be displayed on the background can be indicated by color. This technique may well be more captivating and effective than the usual horizontal lines. Here the background is shown in six steps, from light at the top to dark at the bottom.

Here the sequence is reversed from dark at the top to light at the bottom. Which is better? It depends on what is to be made to stand out most strikingly.

Maximal contrast between the background and the superimposed lines will occur where the background is darkest and the lines are white . . .

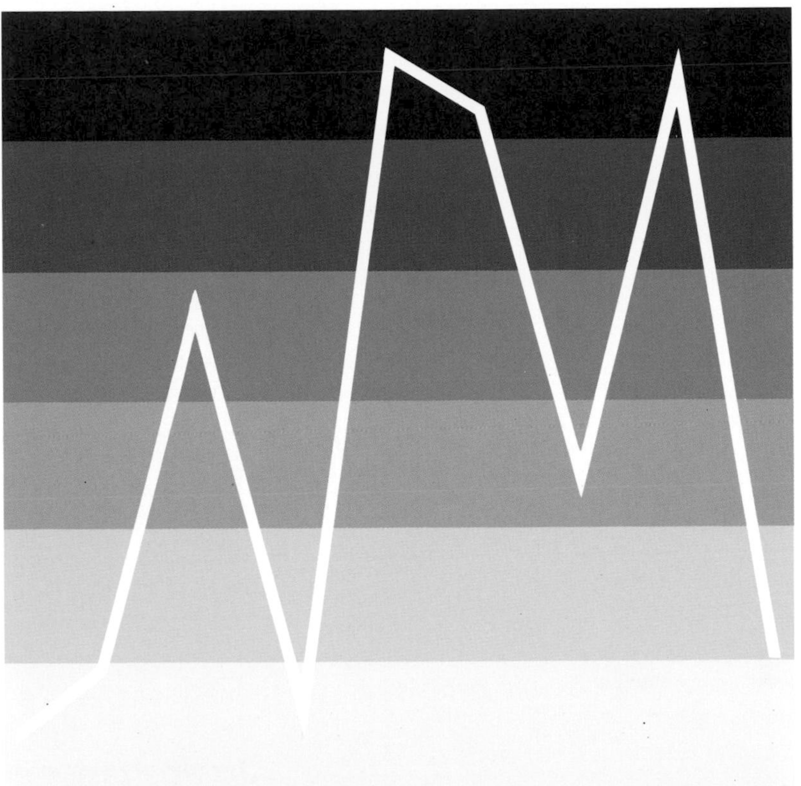

. . . or, in reverse, where the background is lightest and the lines are dark.

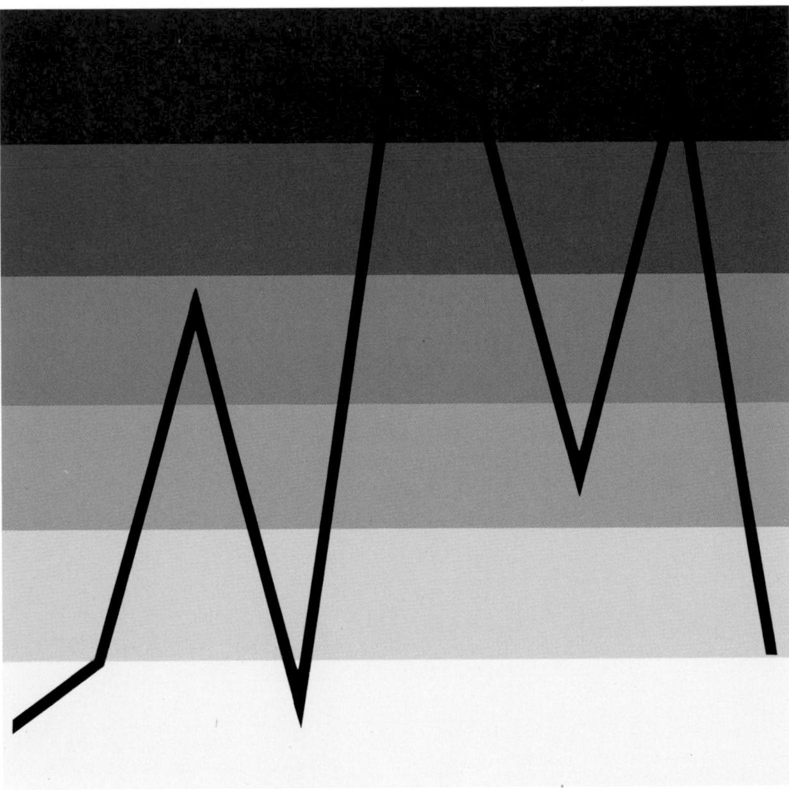

Color progression can be a far better medium of subtle communication when the colors are ramped rather than stepped.

A background color panel need no longer be a flat tint. What could only be accomplished at great trouble and expense by airbrushing has been made easy by electronics. Now you can have a background that goes from dark to light or light to dark at any rate of darkening you specify. Further, *dithering* intersperses pixels of various hues so that you can create the illusion of going from one color to another.

Ramped backgrounds are visually the most interesting, most decorative, richest, and certainly the most enjoyable. There is no doubt that a color tint going from pale blue at the top of the page to dark purple at the bottom adds startling originality. Nonetheless, if it is merely a background that is beautiful for its own sake, then it remains just that—a background—no matter how beautiful or unique.

People start scanning at the top and follow downward.

From dark sky down to light horizon.

From light sky down to dark horizon.

If there is something guiding them along, they also start at the left and follow toward the right.

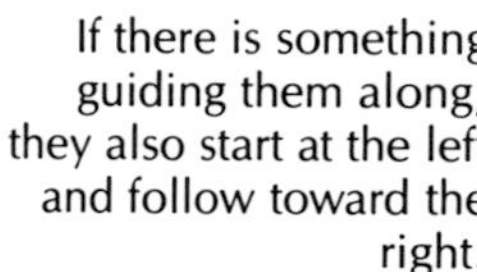

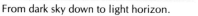

From warm to cold.

From cheerful to somber.

The technique can go beyond the ordinary, and it can be exploited to help clarify ideas, especially in diagrams, charts, and graphs. The trick lies in realizing that ramping creates the illusion of "from . . . to." Ramping appears to move from dark to paler, or pale to darker; it flows from warm red to cool blue, from cheerful yellow to somber brown.

If this capacity of direction is superimposed on the motion of a graph, then the "from . . . to" effect is reinforced. This becomes especially significant if the message of the graph lies at either end of the time line. The contrast of line against background must be used: the greater the contrast, the greater its noticeability. Thus the area most worth noticing should be placed where the contrast will be the most dramatic: dark line atop palest background, or light line dropped out from darkest background.

A line going up, no matter how dramatic the statistics, is just a line on a colored background. It does not appear particularly exciting, despite the implication of good news. It just lies motionless on the page.

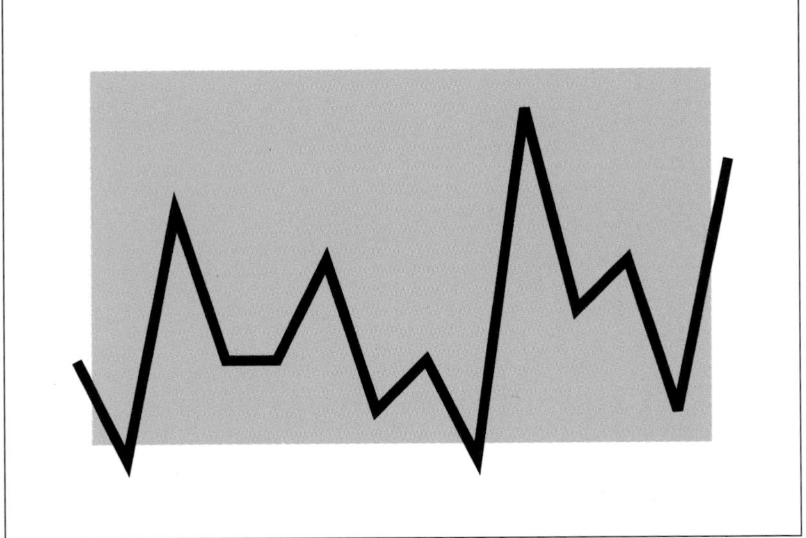

By ramping the background color, the idea of good news is brought out.

The past is shown in the murky darkness. The good news at the far right shines out from the contrast of the black line against pale color. The effect builds from left to right, following the way people normally study.

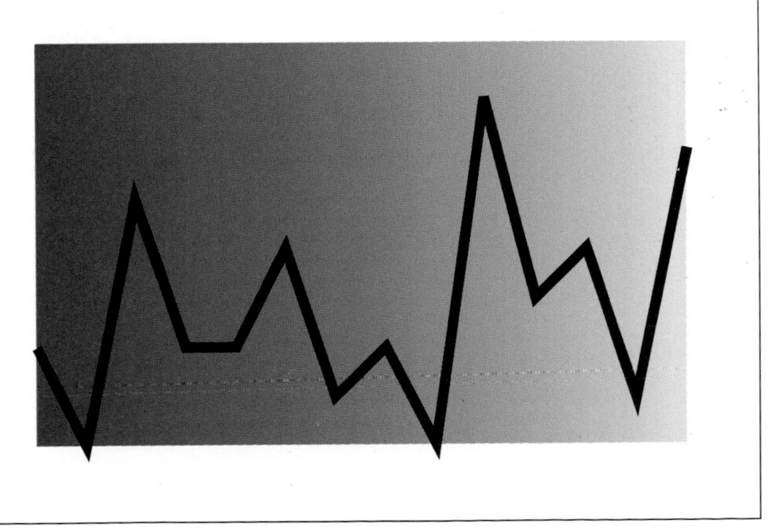

Color can be used to show progression from front to back. The illusion of depth can be created by controlling tonalities and by judicious use of shadows.

We judge distance by paleness. The farther away a mountain is, the paler it appears. The mountain also turns bluer as distance from the viewer increases, regardless of its makeup: green trees, brown rocks, or white glaciers.

The dust particles and water vapor floating in the intervening air are the physical causes of the illusion. When they are missing, as in the crystal air of the desert, distances are much harder to determine. The intervening air is seldom neutral gray, however. Its color is bluish, purplish. At dawn it is pinkish. At sunset it can be multicolored.

Shadows create the appearance of three-dimensional modeling and can be added to the tonal procession that disappears into the distance. The human reaction and interpretation of these illusions is universal: we see and perceive similarly. Capturing them and applying them adds not merely visual dimension but also an intellectual one. It makes the material feel more realistic, more comfortable, and thus more credible.

Here is a diagram of planes overlapped in space. To make the principle more accessible, think of them as representing the facades of four doghouses standing in front of each other.

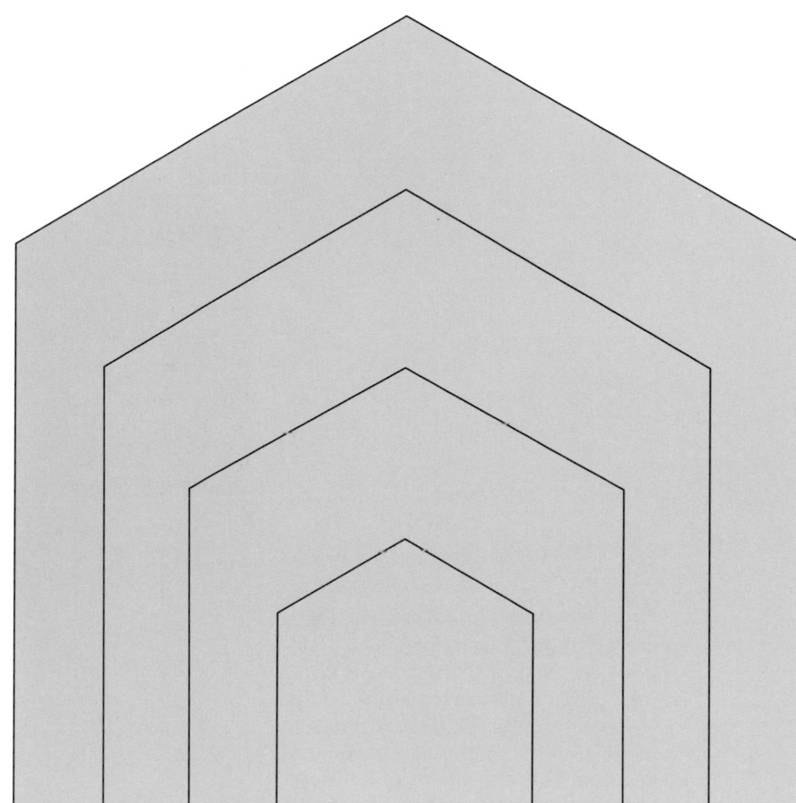

The four planes have been painted the same shade of blue. The color gives no clue as to which of the doghouses is closest, which the farthest away.

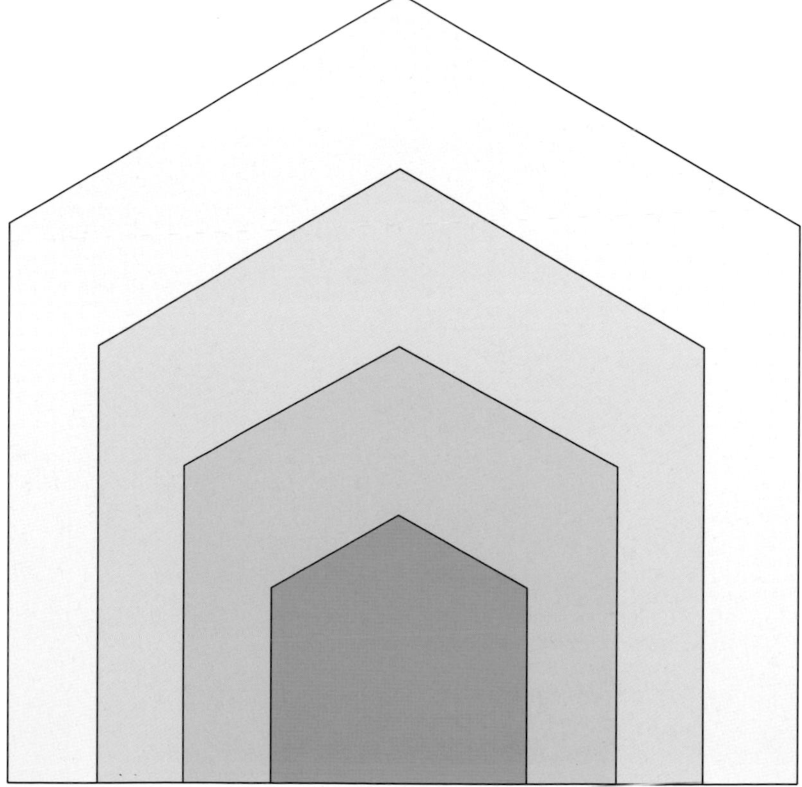

The small one looks closest, the largest one farthest away. This is because the closest one is dark, and the distant one pale. The intervening planes step back in logical sequence.

Here the color confuses depth perception, because the smallest is the palest, whereas the large one is dark. The stepping continues logically. So the confusion is not serious. We just conclude that the doghouses have been painted different shades of the same color, or are we looking down a tunnel?

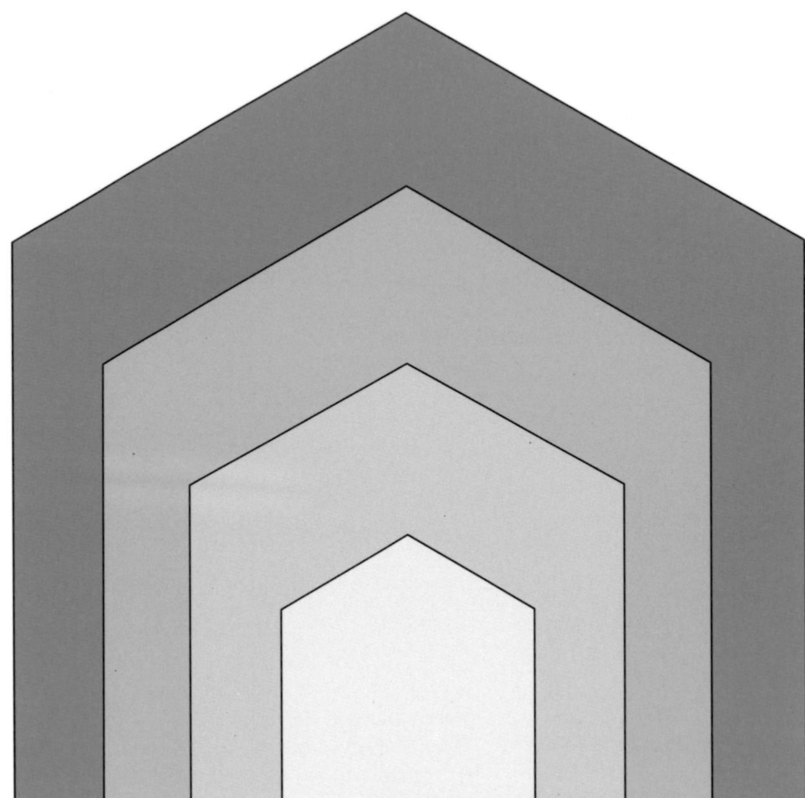

Lightness and darkness are arbitrarily rendered. This causes consternation. It is illogical. The illusion of progression in depth has been shattered, and the colors appear random and unrelated. Normal, expected relationships are broken.

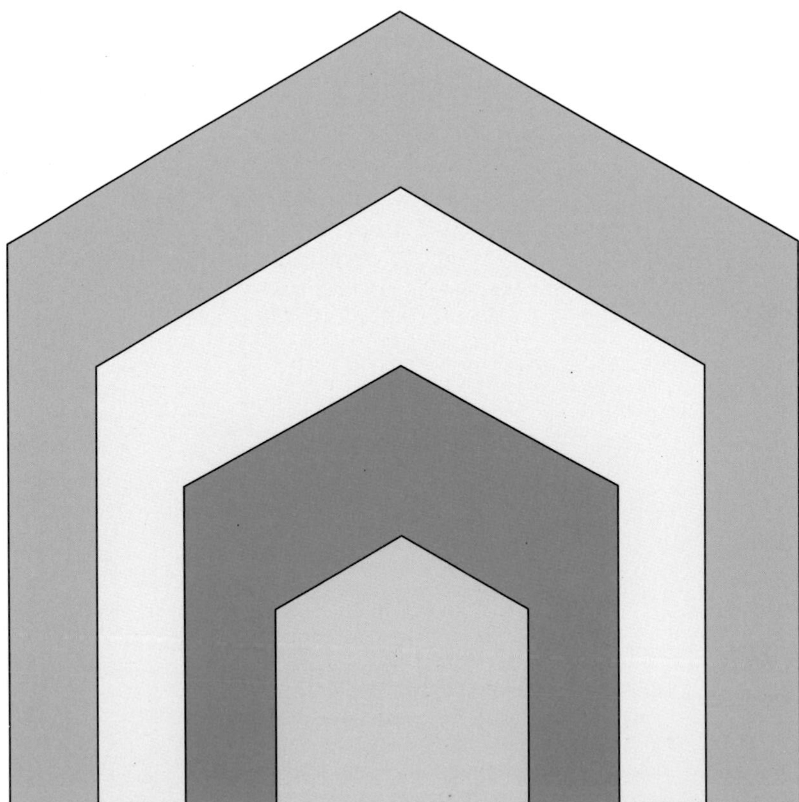

The illusion of depth by means of receding color tones can be reinforced by the addition of shadows apparently cast by the panel.

The illusion of three-dimensional reality can be created on the two-dimensional surface of the paper or slide. The technique's steps are shown here in black and white for simplicity's sake. But we live in a colorful world, so color increases the realism and thus the credibility and effectiveness of the illusion.

Here are two sheets of paper. The smaller one is lying on the larger one at a slight angle.

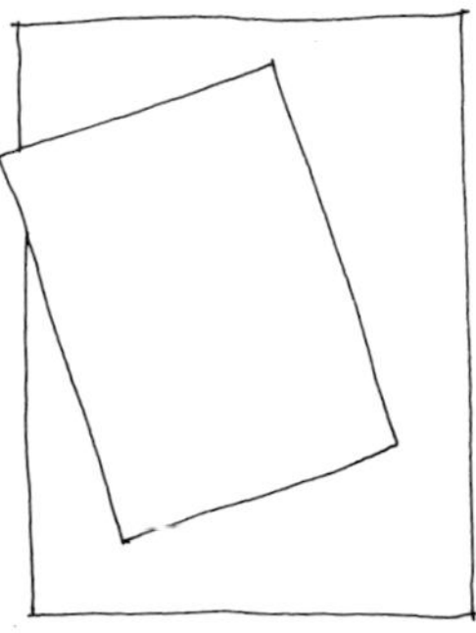

The smaller one appears to be floating above the surface because it appears to be casting a shadow.

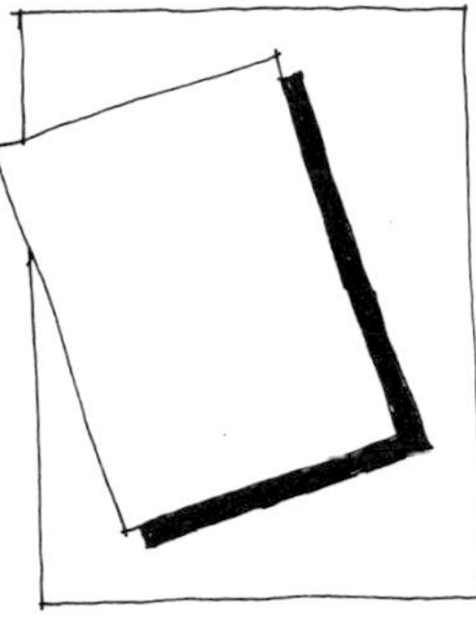

The width of the shadow determines how we interpret the distance between the background and the foreground. The wider the shadow, the greater the distance.

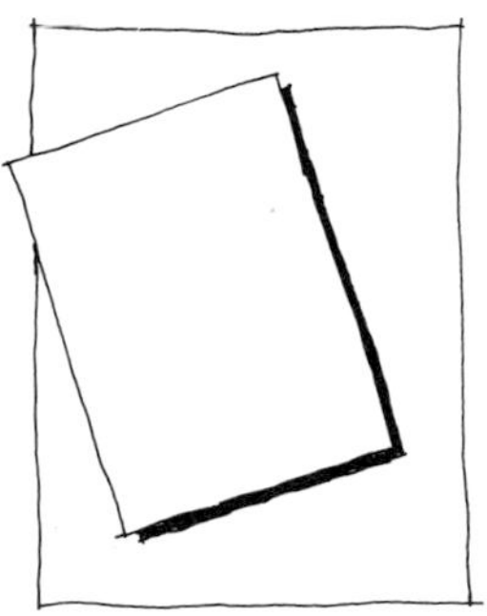

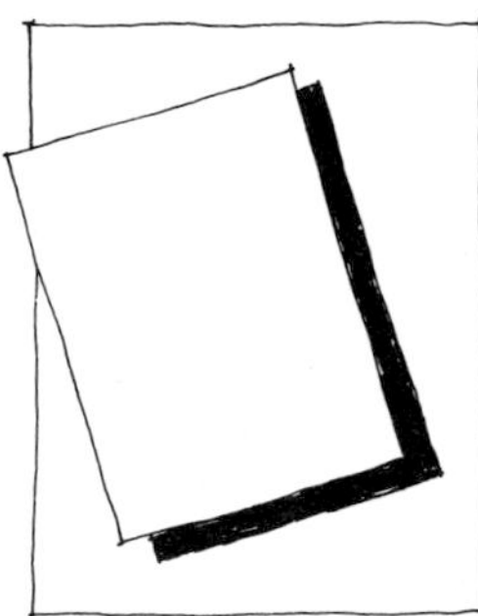

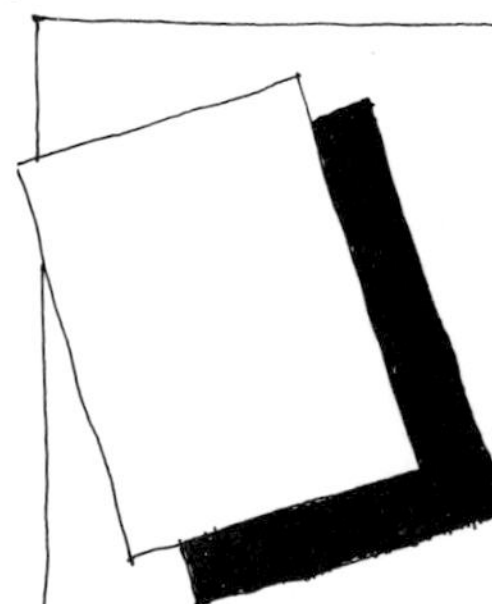

As in the illusion created by distance, where the most distant object appears to be the palest, the intensity of shadow color adds to the illusion of distance. The closer the two elements are, the darker the shadow should be. The farther apart they are, the paler the shadow should be.

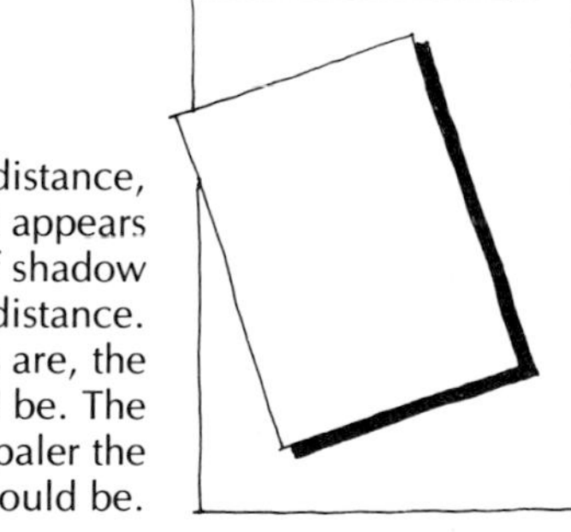

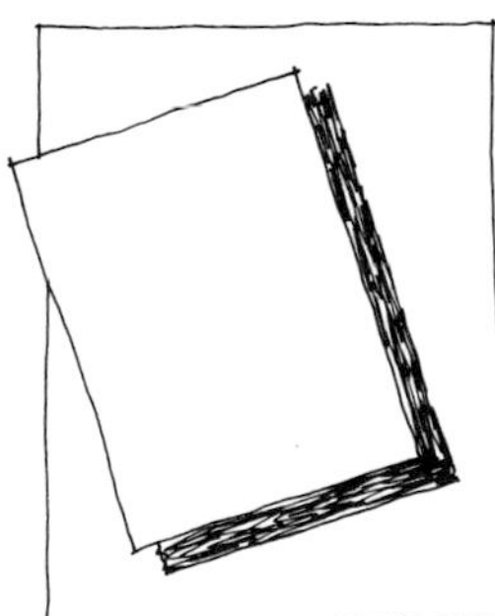

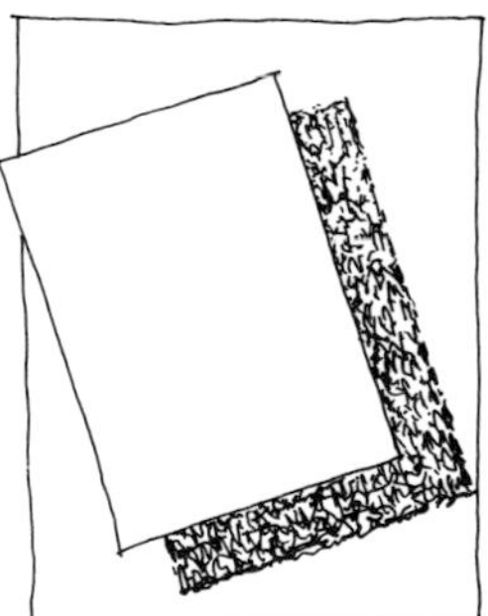

For trompe-l'oeuil (fool-the-eye) realism, the outer edges of the shadow should be darker than the inside area. We simply assume that light is reflected from the hidden underside of the smaller piece of paper.

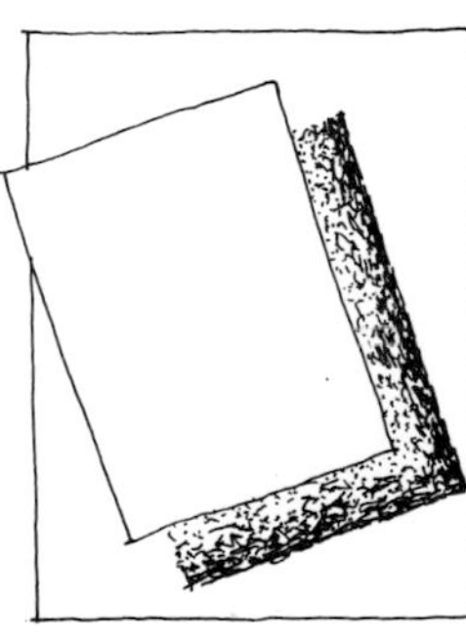

Where there are multiple overlapping planes, it is vitally important to imagine the planes and their interrelationships and to depict the shadow widths to conform to the logic of distance. The geometry apparently becomes increasingly complex, but it just looks complicated. It is, in fact, very simple. Once the principle of the illusion of distance created by shadow width is understood, it becomes a simple matter of addition and subtraction.

Neither of the two planes appears to be in front of the other. Why? Because the shadows are arbitrary, unrealistic, and of equal width. They don't overlap. They are lying next to each other.

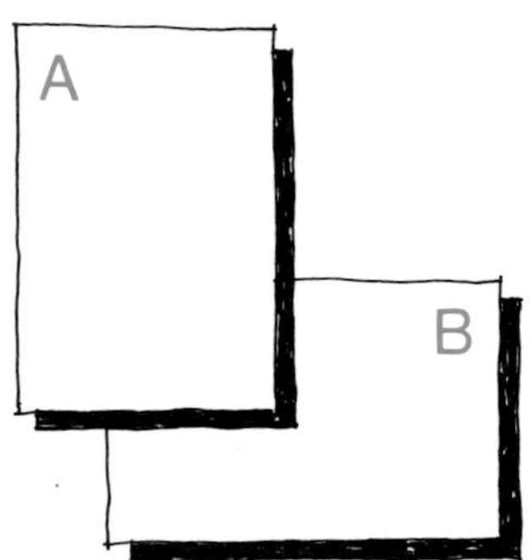

The determination of distance must be made first. To make the point dramatically, assume that plane A is five millimeters from the background (and therefore the shadow it casts is five millimeters wide) and that plane B is one millimeter away (which is why its shadow is one millimeter wide).

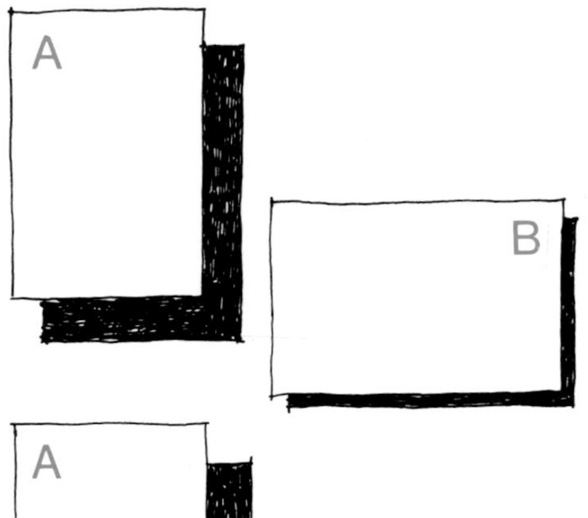

The illusion that B overlaps A is not believable. The shadows deny what the rest of the drawing depicts. The logic of shadow widths must be taken into account to make A overlap B. Why does A appear to float in front of B? It casts its 5-millimeter shadow on the back plane, but the shadow it casts over B is only 4 millimeters wide. (Subtract the 1 millimeter that B itself casts from the total 5 and you are left with 4. Not too difficult a calculation, once you visualize the need for it.)

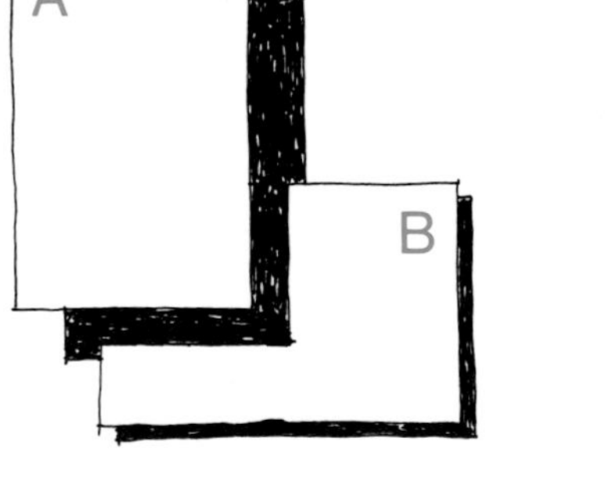

Now add the principle of lightening the color of the shadow in accordance to its width (or distance) and you are creating credible illusions.

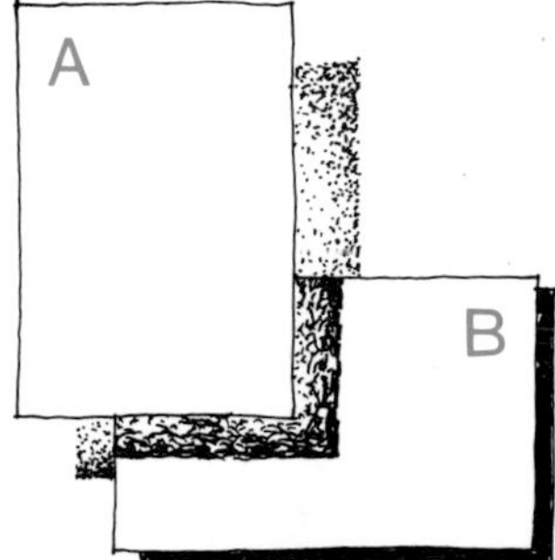

All illusions are fragile. They must be carried out with consistency and care. This is why it is vital to understand about the placement of the light source. It establishes the direction in which the shadows fall. The light source should logically be the same when it is shining on a coordinated group of elements. This helps to ensure the success of the illusion.

Convention places the shadows at the lower right. This implies that the Sun is above your left shoulder. Further, making the width of both sides of the shadow the same implies that the Sun is exactly halfway between the horizon and the top of your head (at forty-five degrees).

Here is the illusion of the Sun traveling from left to right.

The conventional placement of the light source can be changed at will. Its implications can affect the way in which the image is perceived and interpreted. (Bela Lugosi's Dracula-face is spooky simply because it is lit from below.) Here are four diagonals. The top left is the usual version of casting a shadow.

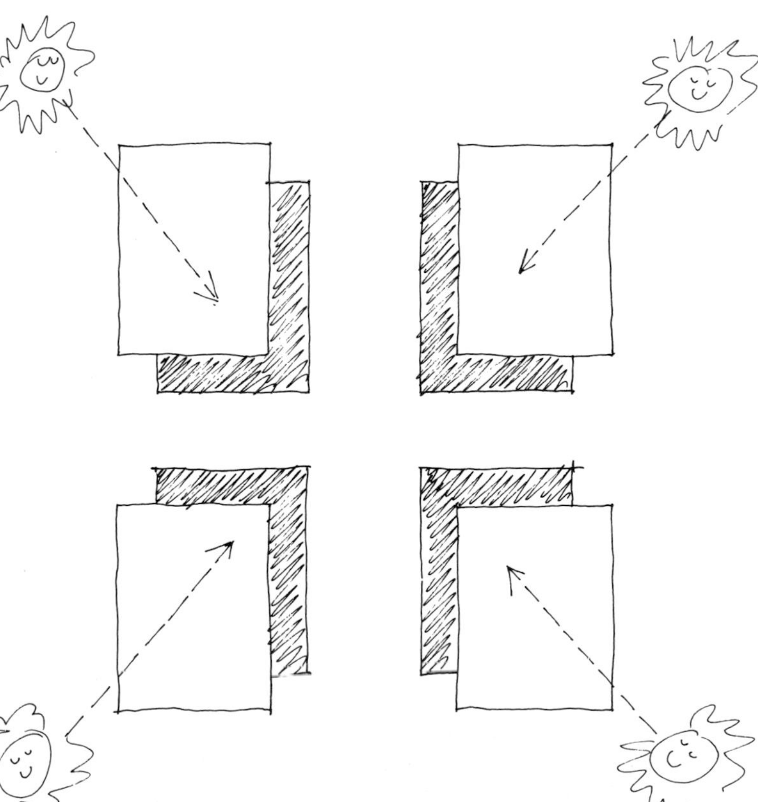

The shape of the shadow describes the position and shape of the object that is casting it. These examples are "standing up," but the backgrounds on which the shadow is cast are ambiguous: they could all be flat (with the light source moving), or they could all be at different angles (with the light source steady).

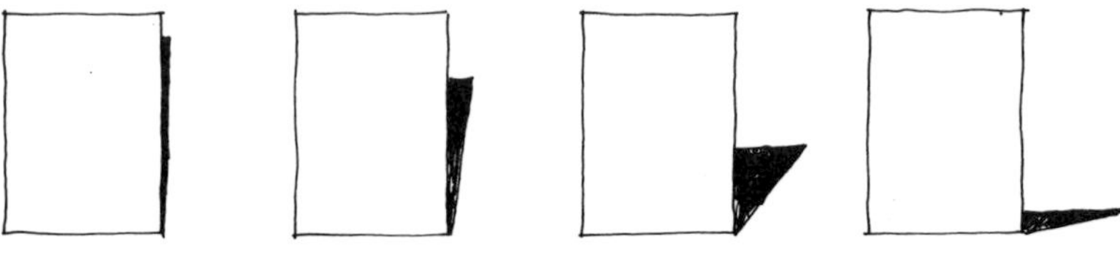

The object in the foreground is curved, the background is flat.

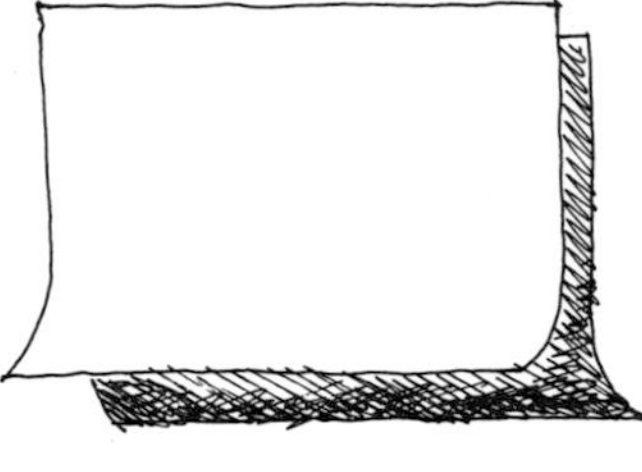

The shape of the shadow describes the shape of the object onto which the shadow is cast. Here a flat plane is floating in front of the curved background.

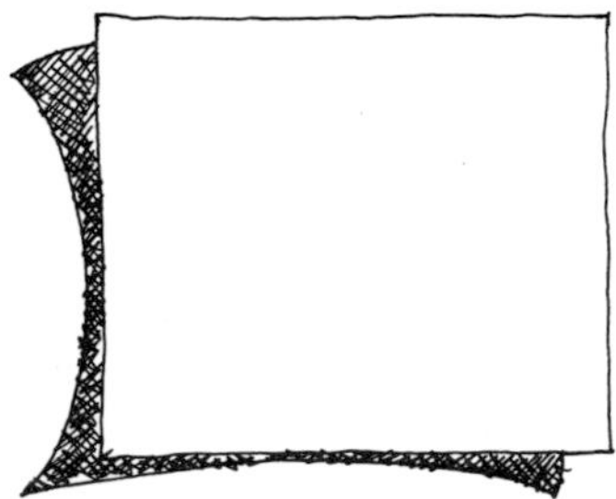

Shadows are thought of as gray. This is why they have been depicted in black or gray in the preceding examples. This, however, is merely an accepted convention. It is not how they occur in nature.

Gray is the right color when the background has "no" color. Most commonly this occurs when the background happens to be a piece of paper. Since gray can easily be produced from black ink or toner by using a screen, grayness is the commonest, easiest, and cheapest method of creating the illusion of shadow in printed matter. This, however, is an oversimplified cliché.

A shaded area looks darkened because some of the light falling on it has been blocked by the object casting a shadow. If the original area was red, it continues being red. The shaded area is darker red—not gray. An apple continues being a Golden Delicious, it doesn't suddenly get gangrene, which makes a part of it turn gray. Its gold color becomes a darker gold.

If you visit any area where the sun shines brightly, such as Spain, and become conscious of the colors of the shadows cast on the whitewashed buildings, you'll discover that gray is seldom among them. Shadows reflect the light, the sky, the trees, the flowerbeds; they are purple, blue, brown, greenish. Further, the colors vary from one side of the shadow to the other. And they change as the sun moves. They are not static clichés. They are alive, vibrant, exciting, dramatic. Most of all, they are unexpected.

Is there a rule or guideline for doing shadows in color? Is it always right to change from gray to blue? Or purple? One wishes there were. Given the variety of contexts, uses, and resultant meanings, no formulas that make sense can be devised. The only one that makes sense: open your eyes and observe, then experiment. Play with the infinite possibilities that the technology now allows. Then have the courage to try something beyond the safely expected norm.

Charts, graphs, and diagrams can be inserted in frames, which presents yet another opportunity for using color as individual enrichment or identifying continuity.

Boxes and panels are not just boxes and panels. Use your ingenuity and imagination to make more of them. They are shown here in plain black on white. Start thinking color: change the lines into color, fill the spaces with color, surround the spaces with contrasting or matching color, combine elements. Each is an opportunity to use color for its own decorative sake. The color can be in the background, without disturbing the statistics or whatever the content of the frames may be. Is this decoration? It is. But it, too, has its legitimate place, so long as it is used responsibly and with restraint.

Twenty-four frames and boxes

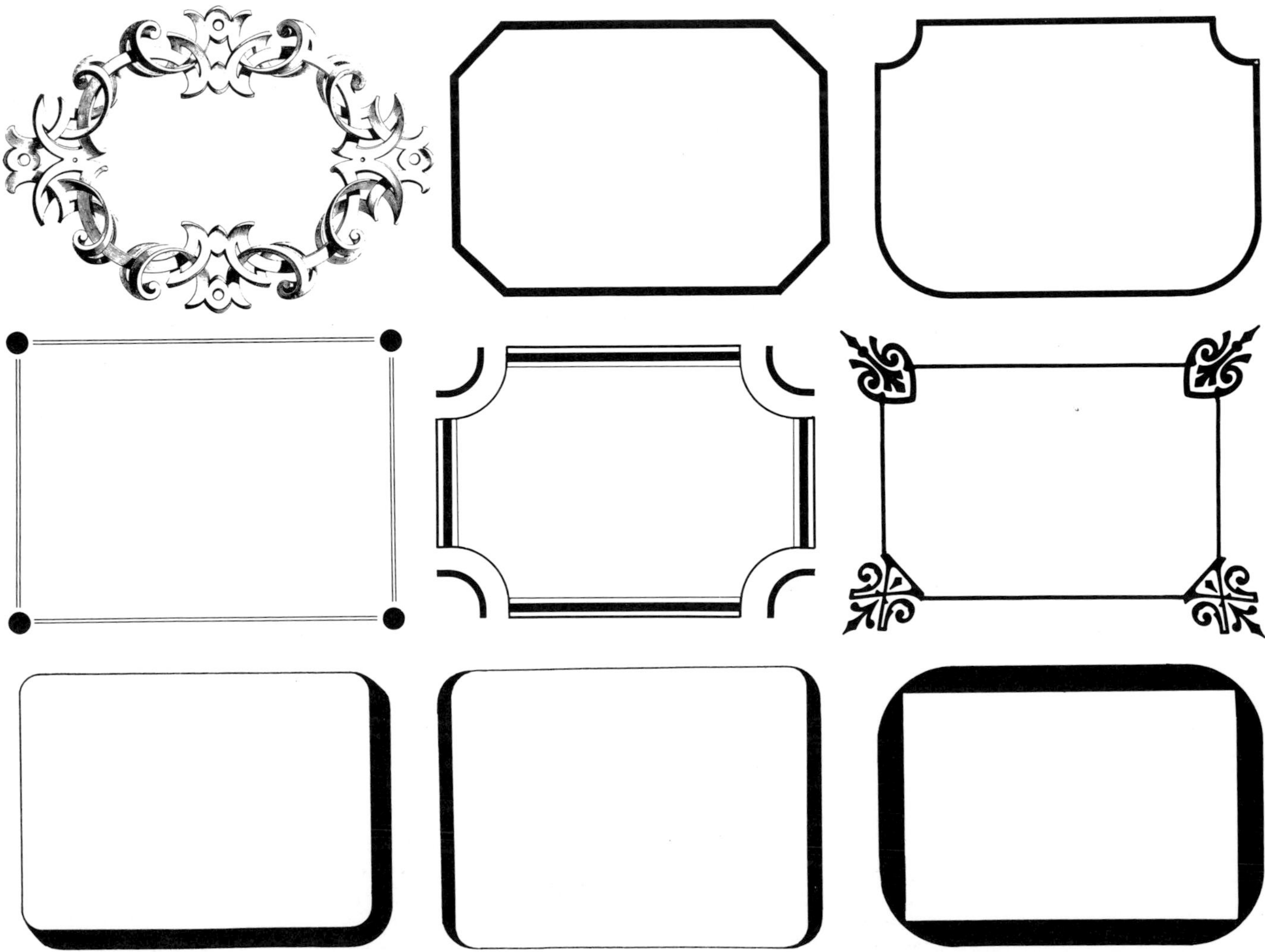

From Jan V. White, *Using Charts and Graphs* (New York: R. R. Bowker, 1984).

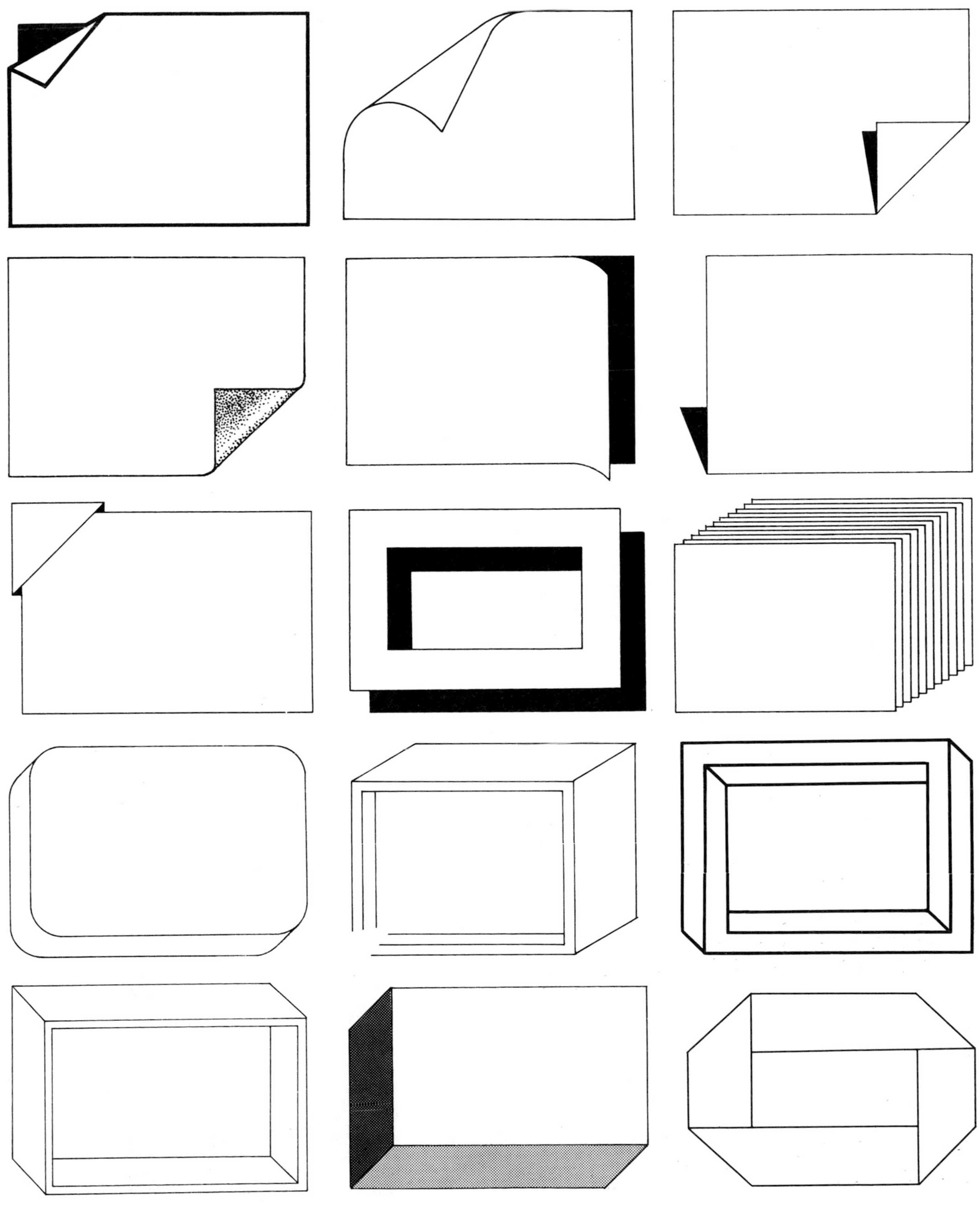

Twelve panels with headings

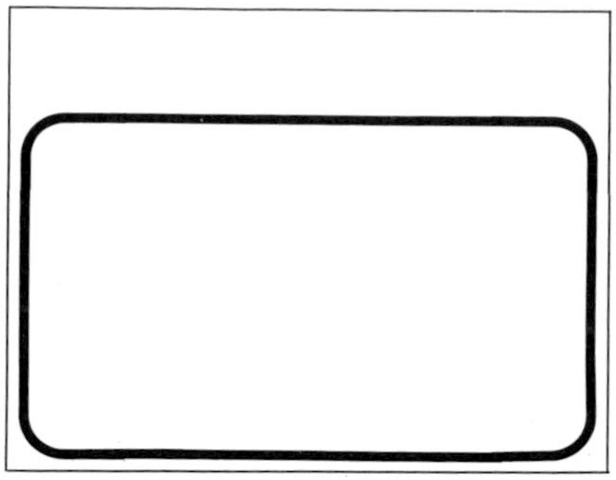

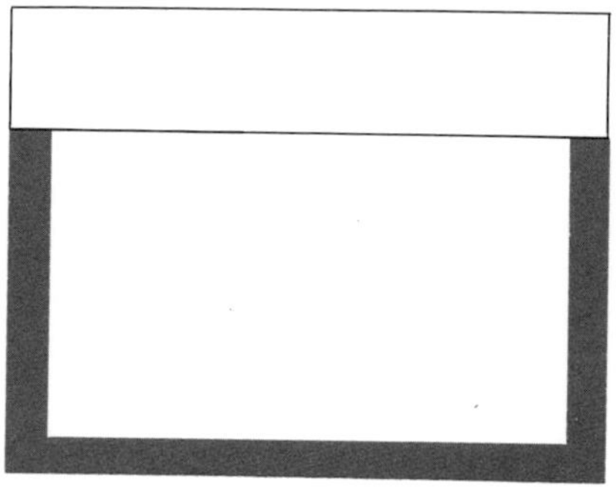

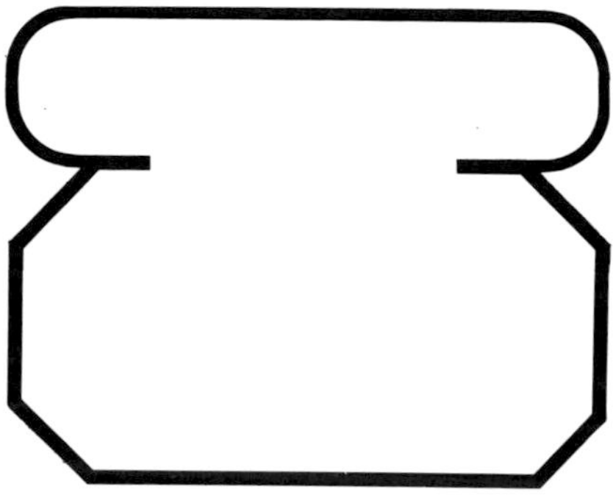

Bold rules could be in color or in black. Title drops out or surprints in black, depending on the background.

Background needs to be darker to create the illusion of a plane floating in front of it. Title in white.

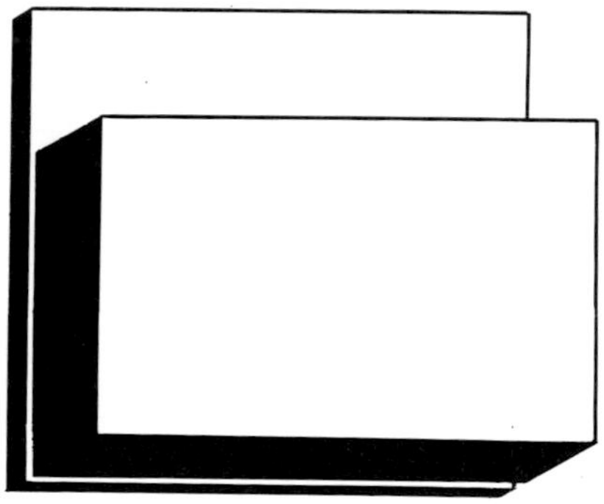

One three-dimensionalized box atop another. Shaded edges of the boxes must be in two tones.

Title floats near but separate from the field of the illustration.

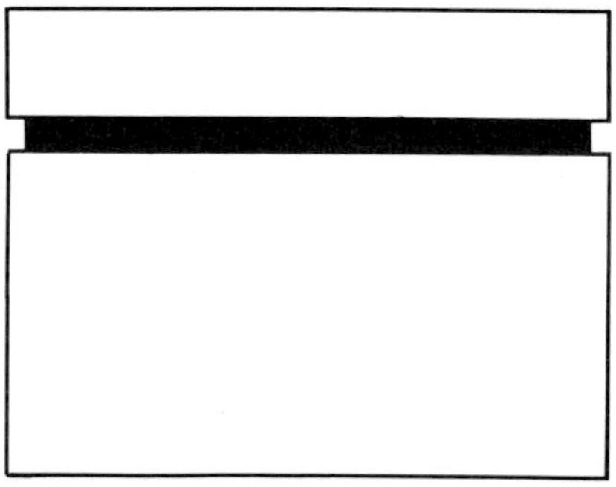

Tints separate the functions of the two boxes.

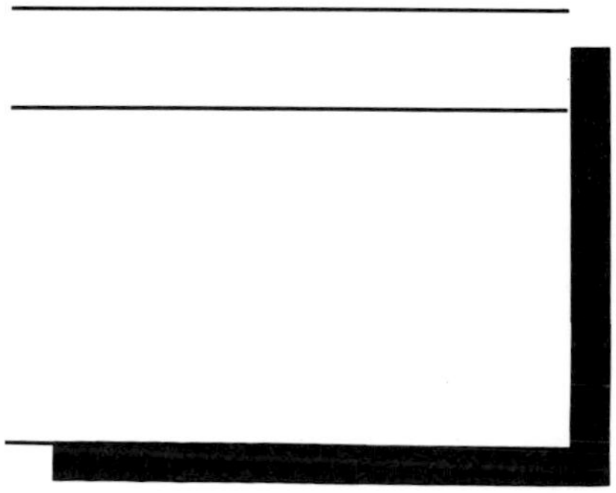

The shadow creates the illusion of a sheet of paper floating over the surface.

Twelve panel clusters

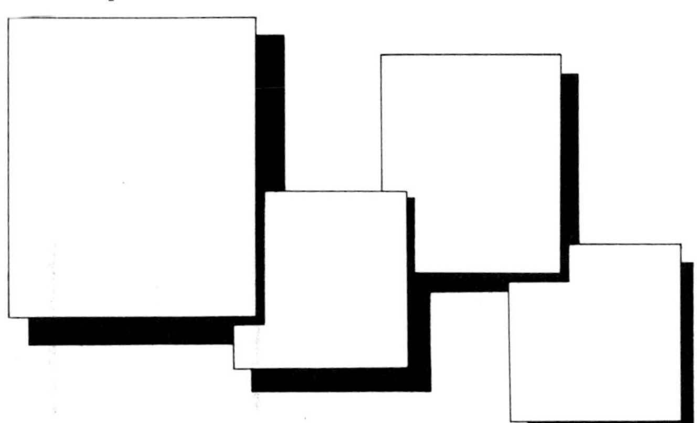

Overlapping units stepped back are shown by means of shades and shadows (see page 92).

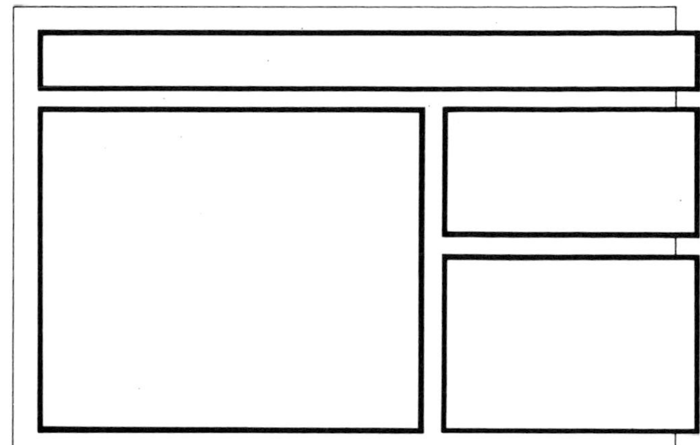

Three-dimensionalized boxes with color on the faces, black edges.

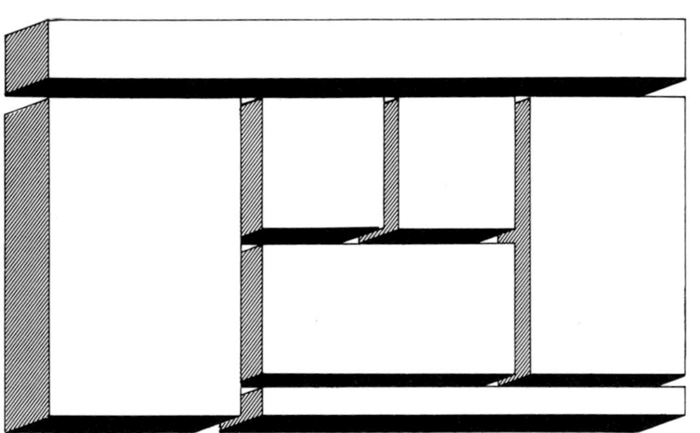

White panels outlined in bold black, with background a gentle, light color.

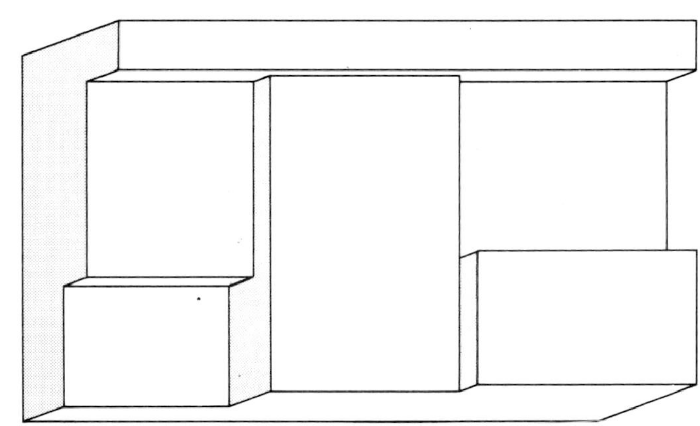

Panels carved out from a solid, with the faces shown at different levels.

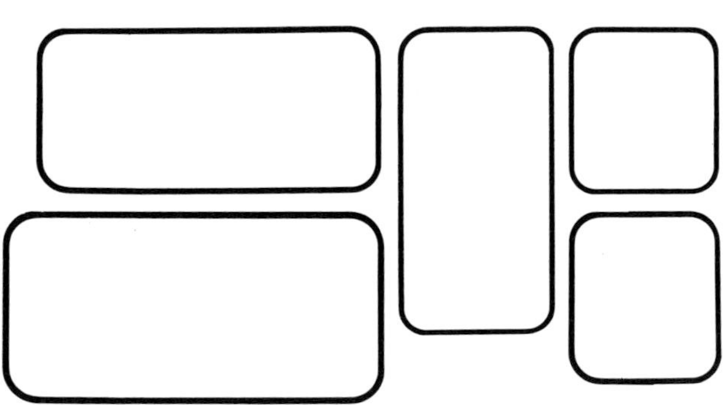

Varied proportions of individual panels are accommodated by assembling the panels in a group and making the spaces between them constant. Rounded corners add personality.

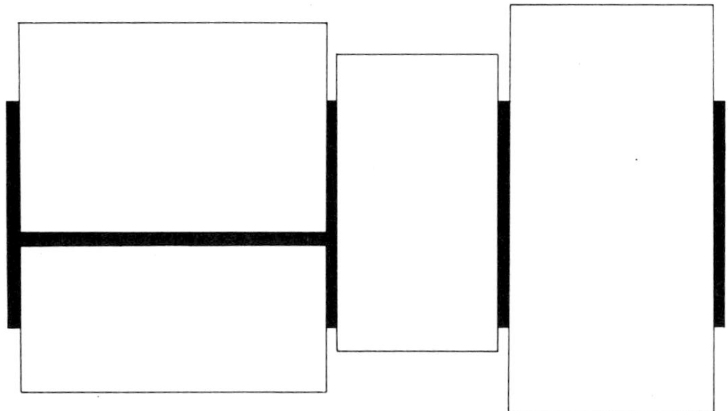

Series of rectangles held together by a unifying ribbon in the background. Shown in black here, it could, of course, be in another—strong—color.

White panels on a colored background.

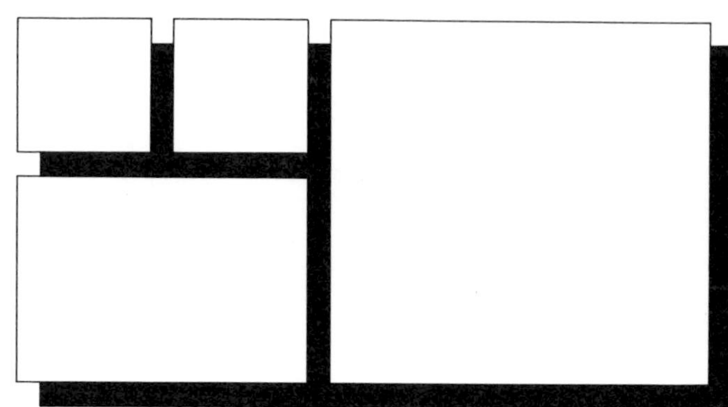

Colored areas on a black background.

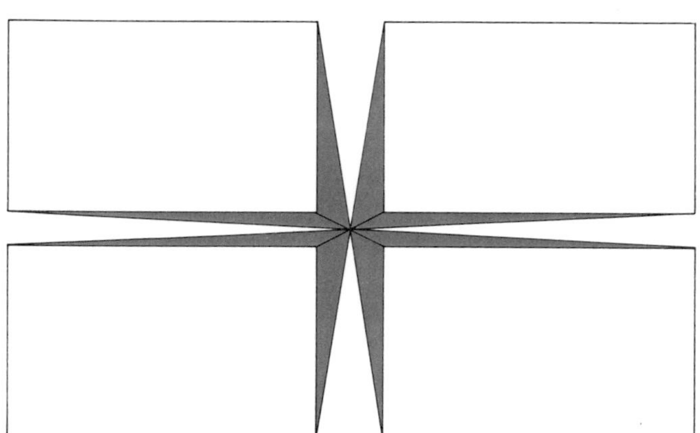

Panels are carved out from a block, but they are shown disappearing in perspective.

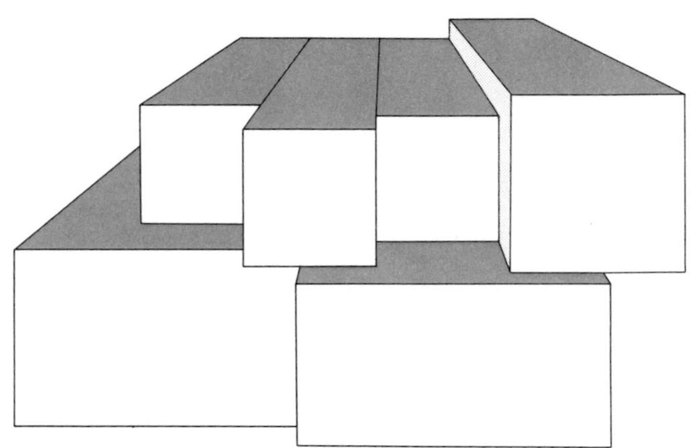

Panels are the ends of long, rectangular blocks all vanishing at a common point. The rectangular two-by-fours are an opportunity for color variation.

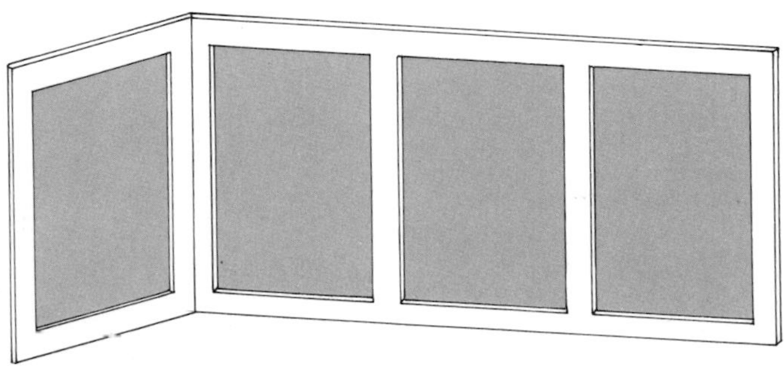

Pictorialization: think of the panels as something other than what they are: just a panel or two. Imagine them as being billboards on a green hillside; or anything else that makes sense and where color can be fruitfully employed.

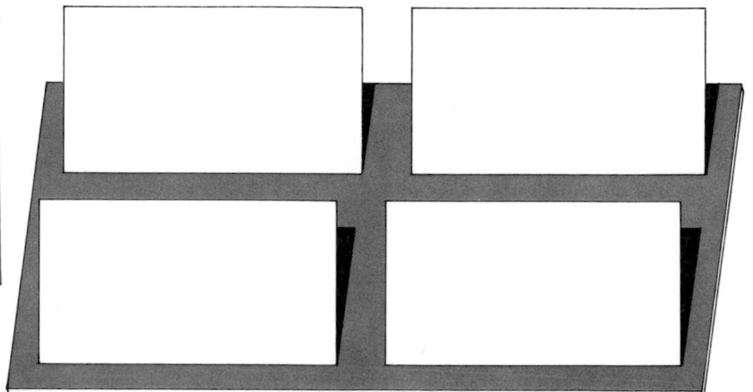

Color and rules, bars, arrowheads, pointers, bullets, icons, circles, triangles, ballot boxes, and other symbols used to identify, rank, organize, or emphasize.

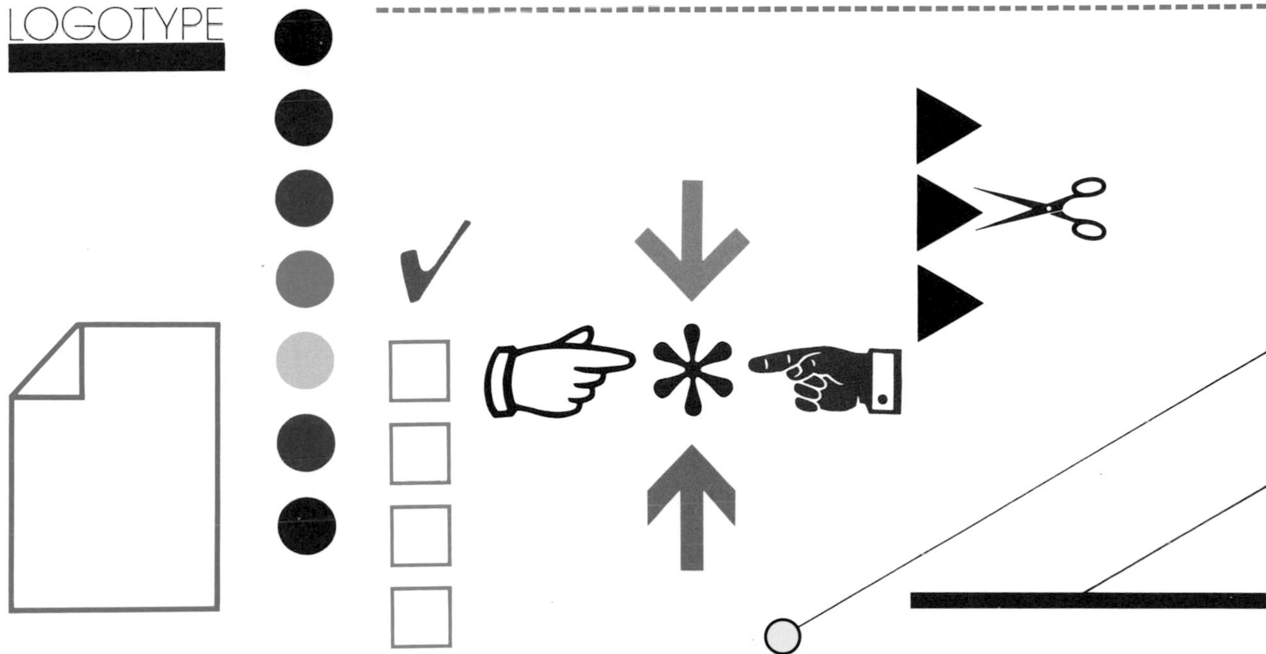

Since color helps to identify, rank, organize, emphasize, and all those other good things, then it should be used. Unfortunately, color is too often applied to these visual elements for no other reason than that they are *not words*. Words mean something, so coloring them requires a justification that emphasizes the meaning in some way. But rules, bars, stars, and all those other marks are just visual symbols. They have no meaning other than that given them by the way they are applied. They can apparently be made colorful with impunity. The rationale is simple. The rationalizing monologue runs something like this: "We've got lists of bulleted items to accommodate on the page. They look so boring, like most lists. Let's dress'em up somehow. Hey! We've got color available—but there's no real reason to "coke" up any of the text with color. The list is too big to put a tint behind it, but we've got to do *something*. So let's colorize the neutral stuff. Okay, let's make the bullets a green. *I like green*."

Then the supervisor, client, spouse—whoever—objects, "Let's don't make 'em green, that's boring. Let's make them like the rainbow—hey, that's fun! Red, orange, yellow, green, blue, violet, wow!" (Fortunately this turns out to be too expensive, so they wind up with a pea-green instead.)

Color is a marvelous material with which to embellish the page or the presentation. Simple embellishment may well be exactly the right touch in some circumstances. All this book argues for is that color not be misused merely in order to make flamboyant use of its embellishing qualities. It has to be used with purpose. If color fulfills a clearly defined need, and its presence makes communication clearer or more vivid, then go for it. (Yes, even if it means making bullets look like confetti on the page.)

Arrows and pointers are parts of business graphics that deserve more care and attention. Coupled with color they can do more for you than point or identify.

Arrows

and pointers

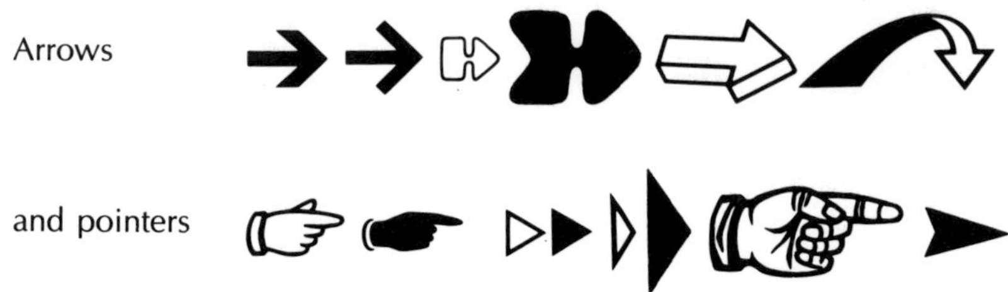

can be used to fulfill four distinct purposes.

Indicating the way The most obvious use for an arrow is to show the direction of flow, course, orientation, compass bearing, or even responsibility. The point is so clear to start with that color can add little to its interpretation. It can, however, help to make the sign stand out from its surroundings, to ensure the visibility of the message.

Pointing out The act of pointing toward something identifies it, singles it out from its surroundings, and makes it noticeable.

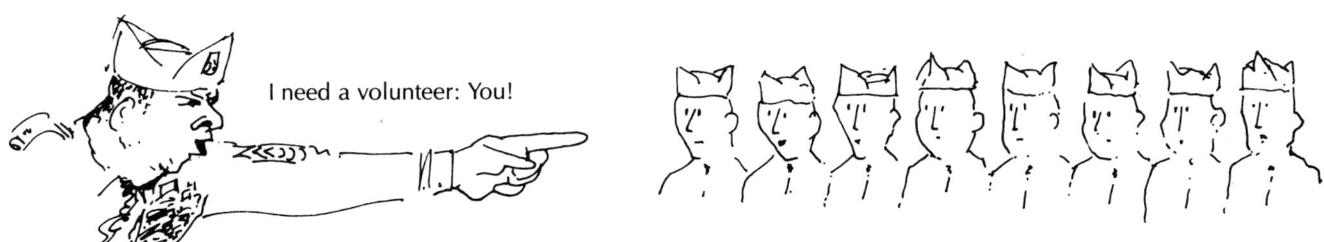

I need a volunteer: You!

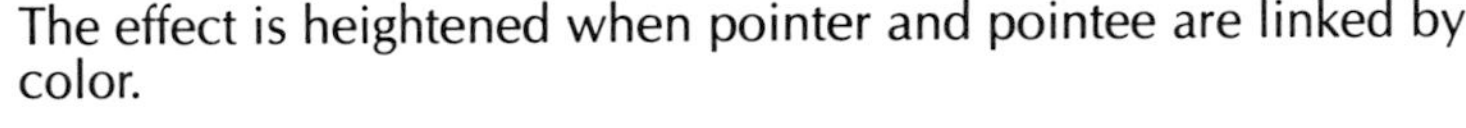

The effect is heightened when pointer and pointee are linked by color.

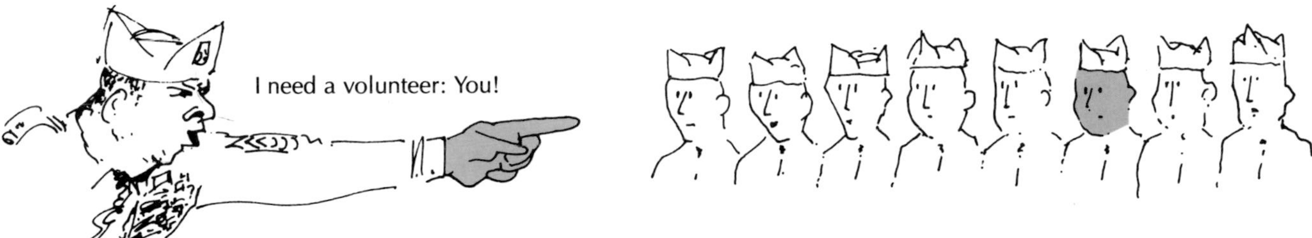

I need a volunteer: You!

Illustrating a concept The arrow pointing upward is symbol for good news, downward is bad news—as the standard graph cliché implies. The arrow becoming narrow shows weakening, while its fattening out symbolizes strengthening. The arrow curving past an obstacle is understood as overcoming a difficult situation, and so on. The context in which it is seen affects the way in which the symbol will be interpreted.* The following figure, for instance, could be interpreted to mean:

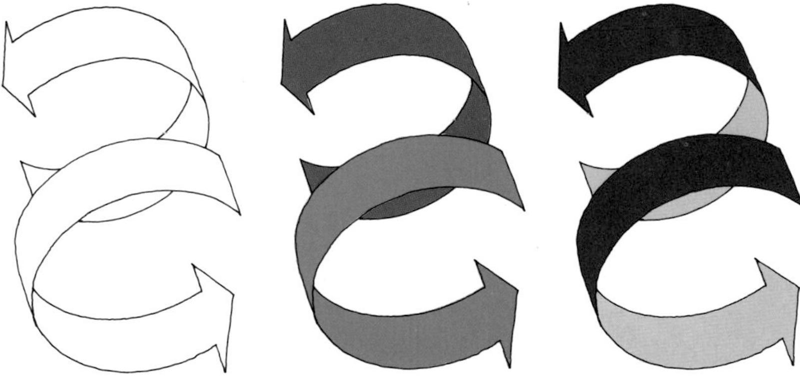

Torsion . . . working at cross purposes . . . tanning all over

*For 132 variations on arrows and their interpretation see Jan V. White, *Using Charts and Graphs* (New York: R. R. Bowker, 1984).

Leading from here to there Linkage shows the relationship of the original to the resultant. It depicts development by leading from cause to effect:

The strongest "from . . . to" effect is created by forcing the arrow to overlap the figures at both ends:

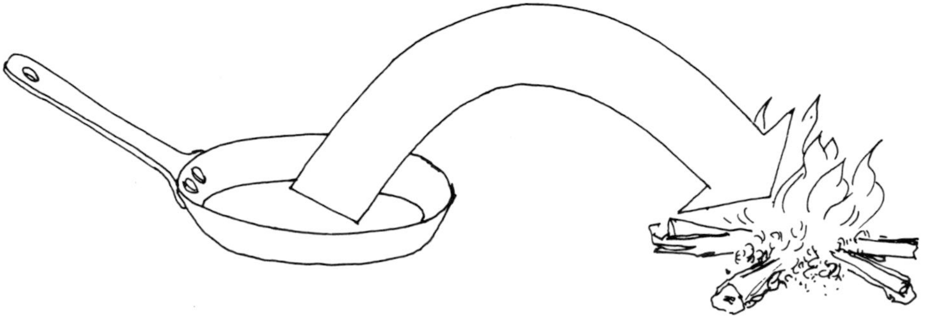

Color must be used to split the arrow from its background so that it is recognized as floating on a plane apart from the elements it overlaps:

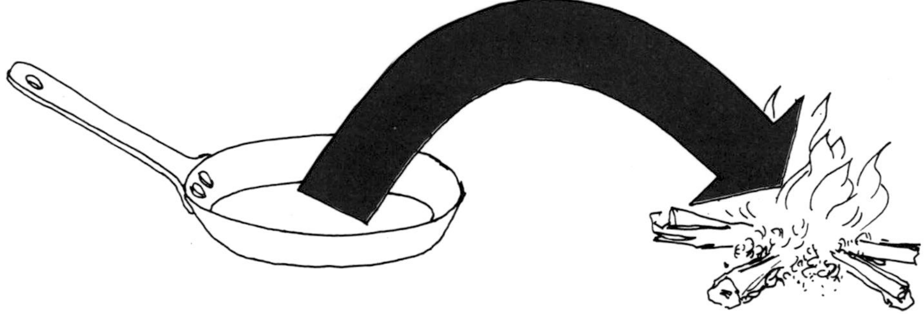

Changing the color from one end of the arrow to the other reinforces the idea of change:

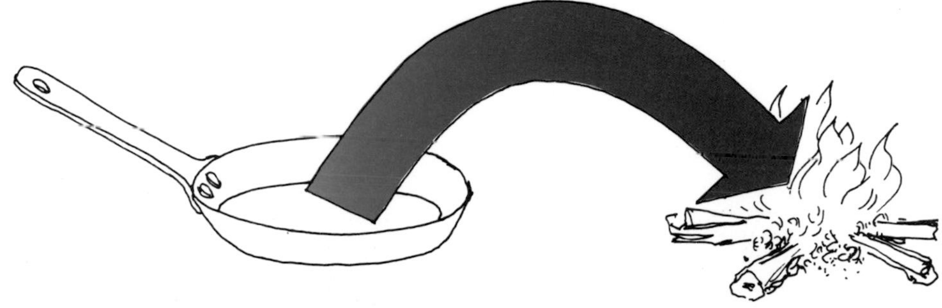

The degree of intensity of change can be expressed by color ramping. The varying color saturation can lead from strong and dissipate into weak, or start weak and build to strong:

The illusion of realistic dimension, receding into space or coming closer to the viewer, can be created by the way the arrow is drawn:

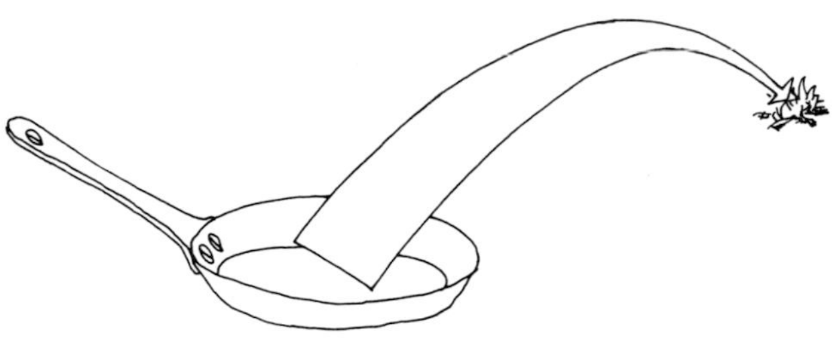

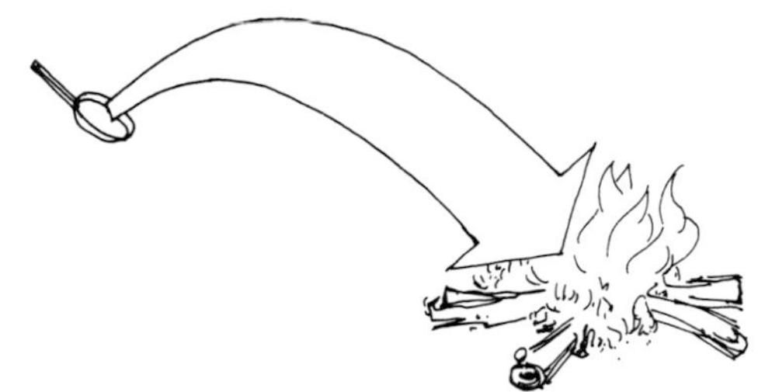

The feeling of depth is emphasized by simultaneous color ramping:

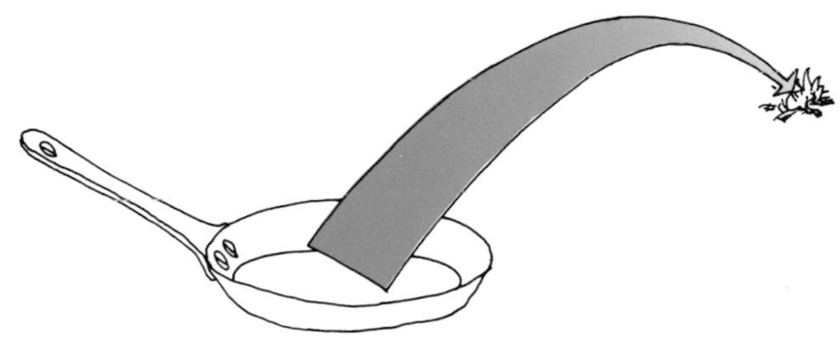

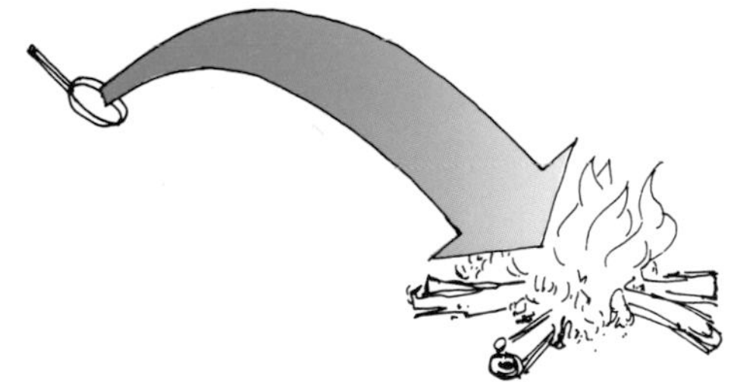

Note that motion is most successfully followed by the viewer/reader when the "from" is at left and the "to" is at right. We are used to reading left to right and find flow that follows that direction as most natural and least puzzling. It is therefore sensible to use it, because a diagram is often just a sentence shown in pictures.

5. TYPE

Using color to highlight meaning

People are used to reading black ink on white paper. We may call them "black" and "white" for convenience, but they are hardly ever that. Black ink and black toner are seldom truly black. They may be brownish, bluish, purplish, grayish. Let's describe black more accurately: *very dark*.

Paper that is pure white is nigh well impossible to fabricate, no matter how little expense is spared. It is grayish, yellowish, creamish, or any other kind of *-ish* you wish. It also changes color with age. Let's just call it *very light*.

People are used to the contrast of very dark ink on very light paper. It is the traditional way of printing, and it may also be the easiest to read. The contrast of color against white is inevitably lower than that of "black." Each hue has a different effect. The darker the color, the stronger the contrast. The paler the color, the weaker the contrast, Being aware of this will guide you in compensating by size and boldness.

To complicate matters, the effects differ markedly when you print type in color on a white background, or whether you print the background in color and "drop out" the type in white. (Please do not forget that dropping out type is technically more difficult, because the lines tend to fill up with ink except under the most strictly quality-controlled conditions.) In presentations, where light type is seen on dark screen, you have to handle type and color with even greater care than in any printed medium.

To prove the claim that the effects vary markedly, the next eight pages show the same text, Hamlet's "To be or not to be" soliloquy, set several different ways for easy comparison. It is set in four typographic variations: Galliard, Helvetica light, Helvetica medium, Helvetica bold; in three sizes: 8/8, 10/10, 12/12; using color in four methods: type in color on white, type in color on black, type in white on color, type in black on color.

To examine a segment at a time, take some sheets of plain paper and cover the surroundings. Compare the effect of one unit against another. Here are some pointers you may agree with:

☐ You can get away with the smaller sizes of the type on white background if you use the bolder versions.
☐ All the larger sizes read better.
☐ Small sizes of type that are run on dark backgrounds (whether black or color) do not read nearly as well as the larger ones.
☐ A serif type, with its thick-and-thin lines, is more fragile and harder to decipher when used with color than any of the sans-serif versions.

Remember, this example illustrates a single, though typical, set of relationships. What is true of one face in one color may not be true of another. Here we used cyan because it is a color commonly used.

One other consideration to take into account is the muchness, or the total volume, of text to be handled in color. The fewer the lines, the more freedom you have to take risks. You can get away with unexpected tricks, especially when the material is worthy of the implied emphasis. It will get read no matter how badly you may mess it up, simply because it is so important. The more lines there are, the surer you must be that the color handling will not hinder legibility.

To be, or not to be: that is the question:
Whether 'tis nobler in the mind to suffer
The slings and arrows of outrageous fortune,
Or to take arms against a sea of troubles,
And by opposing, end them? To die: to sleep;
No more; and by a sleep to say we end
the heart-ache and the thousand natural shocks
That flesh is heir to, 'tis a consummation
Devoutly to be wish'd. To die, to sleep;
To sleep: perchance to dream: ay, there's the rub;
For in that sleep of death what dreams may come
When we have shuffled off this mortal coil,
Must give us pause: there's the respect
that makes calamity of so long life;
For who would bear the whips and scorns of time,
The oppressor's wrong, the proud man's contumely,
The pangs of despised love, the law's delays,
The insolence of office, and the spurns
That patient merit of the unworthy takes,
When he himself might his quietus make
With a bare bodkin? Who would fardels bear,
To grunt and sweat under a weary life,
But that the dread of something after death,
The undiscover'd country from whose bourn
No traveller returns, puzzles the will,
And makes us rather bear those ills we have
Than fly to others that we know not of?
Thus conscience does make cowards of us all;
And thus the native hue of resolution
Is sicklied o'er with the pale cast of thought,
And enterprises of great pitch and moment
With this regard their currents turn awry,
And lose the name of action.

To be, or not to be: that is the question:
Whether 'tis nobler in the mind to suffer
The slings and arrows of outrageous fortune,
Or to take arms against a sea of troubles,
And by opposing, end them? To die: to sleep;
No more; and by a sleep to say we end
the heart-ache and the thousand natural shocks
That flesh is heir to, 'tis a consummation
Devoutly to be wish'd. To die, to sleep;
To sleep: perchance to dream: ay, there's the rub;
For in that sleep of death what dreams may come
When we have shuffled off this mortal coil,
Must give us pause: there's the respect
that makes calamity of so long life;
For who would bear the whips and scorns of time,
The oppressor's wrong, the proud man's contumely,
The pangs of despised love, the law's delays,
The insolence of office, and the spurns
That patient merit of the unworthy takes,
When he himself might his quietus make
With a bare bodkin? Who would fardels bear,
To grunt and sweat under a weary life,
But that the dread of something after death,
The undiscover'd country from whose bourn
No traveller returns, puzzles the will,
And makes us rather bear those ills we have
Than fly to others that we know not of?
Thus conscience does make cowards of us all;
And thus the native hue of resolution
Is sicklied o'er with the pale cast of thought,
And enterprises of great pitch and moment
With this regard their currents turn awry,
And lose the name of action.

To be, or not to be: that is the question:
Whether 'tis nobler in the mind to suffer
The slings and arrows of outrageous fortune,
Or to take arms against a sea of troubles,
And by opposing, end them? To die: to sleep;
No more; and by a sleep to say we end
the heart-ache and the thousand natural shocks
That flesh is heir to, 'tis a consummation
Devoutly to be wish'd. To die, to sleep;
To sleep: perchance to dream: ay, there's the rub;
For in that sleep of death what dreams may come
When we have shuffled off this mortal coil,
Must give us pause: there's the respect
that makes calamity of so long life;
For who would bear the whips and scorns of time,
The oppressor's wrong, the proud man's contumely,
The pangs of despised love, the law's delays,
The insolence of office, and the spurns
That patient merit of the unworthy takes,
When he himself might his quietus make
With a bare bodkin? Who would fardels bear,
To grunt and sweat under a weary life,
But that the dread of something after death,
The undiscover'd country from whose bourn
No traveller returns, puzzles the will,
And makes us rather bear those ills we have
Than fly to others that we know not of?
Thus conscience does make cowards of us all;
And thus the native hue of resolution
Is sicklied o'er with the pale cast of thought,
And enterprises of great pitch and moment
With this regard their currents turn awry,
And lose the name of action.

**To be, or not to be: that is the question:
Whether 'tis nobler in the mind to suffer
The slings and arrows of outrageous fortune,
Or to take arms against a sea of troubles,
And by opposing, end them? To die: to sleep;
No more; and by a sleep to say we end
the heart-ache and the thousand natural shocks
That flesh is heir to, 'tis a consummation
Devoutly to be wish'd. To die, to sleep;
To sleep: perchance to dream: ay, there's the rub;
For in that sleep of death what dreams may come
When we have shuffled off this mortal coil,
Must give us pause: there's the respect
that makes calamity of so long life;
For who would bear the whips and scorns of time,
The oppressor's wrong, the proud man's contumely,
The pangs of despised love, the law's delays,
The insolence of office, and the spurns
That patient merit of the unworthy takes,
When he himself might his quietus make
With a bare bodkin? Who would fardels bear,
To grunt and sweat under a weary life,
But that the dread of something after death,
The undiscover'd country from whose bourn
No traveller returns, puzzles the will,
And makes us rather bear those ills we have
Than fly to others that we know not of?
Thus conscience does make cowards of us all;
And thus the native hue of resolution
Is sicklied o'er with the pale cast of thought,
And enterprises of great pitch and moment
With this regard their currents turn awry,
And lose the name of action.**

To be, or not to be: that is the question:
Whether 'tis nobler in the mind to suffer
The slings and arrows of outrageous fortune,
Or to take arms against a sea of troubles,
And by opposing, end them? To die: to sleep;
No more; and by a sleep to say we end
the heart-ache and the thousand natural shocks
That flesh is heir to, 'tis a consummation
Devoutly to be wish'd. To die, to sleep;
To sleep: perchance to dream: ay, there's the rub;
For in that sleep of death what dreams may come
When we have shuffled off this mortal coil,
Must give us pause: there's the respect
that makes calamity of so long life;
For who would bear the whips and scorns of time,
The oppressor's wrong, the proud man's contumely,
The pangs of despised love, the law's delays,
The insolence of office, and the spurns
That patient merit of the unworthy takes,
When he himself might his quietus make
With a bare bodkin? Who would fardels bear,
To grunt and sweat under a weary life,
But that the dread of something after death,
The undiscover'd country from whose bourn
No traveller returns, puzzles the will,
And makes us rather bear those ills we have
Than fly to others that we know not of?
Thus conscience does make cowards of us all;
And thus the native hue of resolution
Is sicklied o'er with the pale cast of thought,
And enterprises of great pitch and moment
With this regard their currents turn awry,
And lose the name of action.

To be, or not to be: that is the question:
Whether 'tis nobler in the mind to suffer
The slings and arrows of outrageous fortune,
Or to take arms against a sea of troubles,
And by opposing, end them? To die: to sleep;
No more; and by a sleep to say we end
the heart-ache and the thousand natural shocks
That flesh is heir to, 'tis a consummation
Devoutly to be wish'd. To die, to sleep;
To sleep: perchance to dream: ay, there's the rub;
For in that sleep of death what dreams may come
When we have shuffled off this mortal coil,
Must give us pause: there's the respect
that makes calamity of so long life;
For who would bear the whips and scorns of time,
The oppressor's wrong, the proud man's contumely,
The pangs of despised love, the law's delays,
The insolence of office, and the spurns
That patient merit of the unworthy takes,
When he himself might his quietus make
With a bare bodkin? Who would fardels bear,
To grunt and sweat under a weary life,
But that the dread of something after death,
The undiscover'd country from whose bourn
No traveller returns, puzzles the will,
And makes us rather bear those ills we have
Than fly to others that we know not of?
Thus conscience does make cowards of us all;
And thus the native hue of resolution
Is sicklied o'er with the pale cast of thought,
And enterprises of great pitch and moment
With this regard their currents turn awry,
And lose the name of action.

To be, or not to be: that is the question:
Whether 'tis nobler in the mind to suffer
The slings and arrows of outrageous fortune,
Or to take arms against a sea of troubles,
And by opposing, end them? To die: to sleep;
No more; and by a sleep to say we end
The heart-ache and the thousand natural shocks
That flesh is heir to, 'tis a consummation
Devoutly to be wish'd. To die, to sleep;
To sleep: perchance to dream: ay, there's the rub;
For in that sleep of death what dreams may come
When we have shuffled off this mortal coil,
Must give us pause: there's the respect
That makes calamity of so long life;
For who would bear the whips and scorns of time,
The oppressor's wrong, the proud man's contumely,
The pangs of despised love, the law's delays,
The insolence of office, and the spurns
That patient merit of the unworthy takes,
When he himself might his quietus make
With a bare bodkin? Who would fardels bear,
To grunt and sweat under a weary life,
But that the dread of something after death,
The undiscover'd country from whose bourn
No traveller returns, puzzles the will,
And makes us rather bear those ills we have
Than fly to others that we know not of?
Thus conscience does make cowards of us all;
And thus the native hue of resolution
Is sicklied o'er with the pale cast of thought,
And enterprises of great pitch and moment
With this regard their currents turn awry,
And lose the name of action.

To be, or not to be: that is the question:
Whether 'tis nobler in the mind to suffer
The slings and arrows of outrageous fortune,
Or to take arms against a sea of troubles,
And by opposing, end them? To die: to sleep;
No more; and by a sleep to say we end
The heart-ache and the thousand natural shocks
That flesh is heir to, 'tis a consummation
Devoutly to be wish'd. To die, to sleep;
To sleep: perchance to dream: ay, there's the rub;
For in that sleep of death what dreams may come
When we have shuffled off this mortal coil,
Must give us pause: there's the respect
That makes calamity of so long life;
For who would bear the whips and scorns of time,
The oppressor's wrong, the proud man's contumely,
The pangs of despised love, the law's delays,
The insolence of office, and the spurns
That patient merit of the unworthy takes,
When he himself might his quietus make
With a bare bodkin? Who would fardels bear,
To grunt and sweat under a weary life,
But that the dread of something after death,
The undiscover'd country from whose bourn
No traveller returns, puzzles the will,
And makes us rather bear those ills we have
Than fly to others that we know not of?
Thus conscience does make cowards of us all;
And thus the native hue of resolution
Is sicklied o'er with the pale cast of thought,
And enterprises of great pitch and moment
With this regard their currents turn awry,
And lose the name of action.

To be, or not to be: that is the question:
Whether 'tis nobler in the mind to suffer
The slings and arrows of outrageous fortune,
Or to take arms against a sea of troubles,
And by opposing, end them? To die: to sleep;
No more; and by a sleep to say we end
the heart-ache and the thousand natural shocks
That flesh is heir to, 'tis a consummation
Devoutly to be wish'd. To die, to sleep;
To sleep: perchance to dream: ay, there's the rub;
For in that sleep of death what dreams may come
When we have shuffled off this mortal coil,
Must give us pause: there's the respect
that makes calamity of so long life;
For who would bear the whips and scorns of time,
The oppressor's wrong, the proud man's contumely,
The pangs of despised love, the law's delays,
The insolence of office, and the spurns
That patient merit of the unworthy takes,
When he himself might his quietus make
With a bare bodkin? Who would fardels bear,
To grunt and sweat under a weary life,
But that the dread of something after death,
The undiscover'd country from whose bourn
No traveller returns, puzzles the will,
And makes us rather bear those ills we have
Than fly to others that we know not of?
Thus conscience does make cowards of us all;
And thus the native hue of resolution
Is sicklied o'er with the pale cast of thought,
And enterprises of great pitch and moment
With this regard their currents turn awry,
And lose the name of action.

To be, or not to be: that is the question:
Whether 'tis nobler in the mind to suffer
The slings and arrows of outrageous fortune,
Or to take arms against a sea of troubles,
And by opposing, end them? To die: to sleep;
No more; and by a sleep to say we end
the heart-ache and the thousand natural shocks
That flesh is heir to, 'tis a consummation
Devoutly to be wish'd. To die, to sleep;
To sleep: perchance to dream: ay, there's the rub;
For in that sleep of death what dreams may come
When we have shuffled off this mortal coil,
Must give us pause: there's the respect
that makes calamity of so long life;
For who would bear the whips and scorns of time,
The oppressor's wrong, the proud man's contumely,
The pangs of despised love, the law's delays,
The insolence of office, and the spurns
That patient merit of the unworthy takes,
When he himself might his quietus make
With a bare bodkin? Who would fardels bear,
To grunt and sweat under a weary life,
But that the dread of something after death,
The undiscover'd country from whose bourn
No traveller returns, puzzles the will,
And makes us rather bear those ills we have
Than fly to others that we know not of?
Thus conscience does make cowards of us all;
And thus the native hue of resolution
Is sicklied o'er with the pale cast of thought,
And enterprises of great pitch and moment
With this regard their currents turn awry,
And lose the name of action.

To be, or not to be: that is the question:
Whether 'tis nobler in the mind to suffer
The slings and arrows of outrageous fortune,
Or to take arms against a sea of troubles,
And by opposing, end them? To die: to sleep;
No more; and by a sleep to say we end
the heart-ache and the thousand natural shocks
That flesh is heir to, 'tis a consummation
Devoutly to be wish'd. To die, to sleep;
To sleep: perchance to dream: ay, there's the rub;
For in that sleep of death what dreams may come
When we have shuffled off this mortal coil,
Must give us pause: there's the respect
that makes calamity of so long life;
For who would bear the whips and scorns of time,
The oppressor's wrong, the proud man's contumely,
The pangs of despised love, the law's delays,
The insolence of office, and the spurns
That patient merit of the unworthy takes,
When he himself might his quietus make
With a bare bodkin? Who would fardels bear,
To grunt and sweat under a weary life,
But that the dread of something after death,
The undiscover'd country from whose bourn
No traveller returns, puzzles the will,
And makes us rather bear those ills we have
Than fly to others that we know not of?
Thus conscience does make cowards of us all;
And thus the native hue of resolution
Is sicklied o'er with the pale cast of thought,
And enterprises of great pitch and moment
With this regard their currents turn awry,
And lose the name of action.

**To be, or not to be: that is the question:
Whether 'tis nobler in the mind to suffer
The slings and arrows of outrageous fortune,
Or to take arms against a sea of troubles,
And by opposing, end them? To die: to sleep;
No more; and by a sleep to say we end
the heart-ache and the thousand natural shocks
That flesh is heir to, 'tis a consummation
Devoutly to be wish'd. To die, to sleep;
To sleep: perchance to dream: ay, there's the rub;
For in that sleep of death what dreams may come
When we have shuffled off this mortal coil,
Must give us pause: there's the respect
that makes calamity of so long life;
For who would bear the whips and scorns of time,
The oppressor's wrong, the proud man's contumely,
The pangs of despised love, the law's delays,
The insolence of office, and the spurns
That patient merit of the unworthy takes,
When he himself might his quietus make
With a bare bodkin? Who would fardels bear,
To grunt and sweat under a weary life,
But that the dread of something after death,
The undiscover'd country from whose bourn
No traveller returns, puzzles the will,
And makes us rather bear those ills we have
Than fly to others that we know not of?
Thus conscience does make cowards of us all;
And thus the native hue of resolution
Is sicklied o'er with the pale cast of thought,
And enterprises of great pitch and moment
With this regard their currents turn awry,
And lose the name of action.**

To be, or not to be: that is the question:
Whether 'tis nobler in the mind to suffer
The slings and arrows of outrageous fortune,
Or to take arms against a sea of troubles,
And by opposing, end them? To die: to sleep;
No more; and by a sleep to say we end
the heart-ache and the thousand natural shocks
That flesh is heir to, 'tis a consummation
Devoutly to be wish'd. To die, to sleep;
To sleep: perchance to dream: ay, there's the rub;
For in that sleep of death what dreams may come
When we have shuffled off this mortal coil,
Must give us pause: there's the respect
that makes calamity of so long life;
For who would bear the whips and scorns of time,
The oppressor's wrong, the proud man's contumely,
The pangs of despised love, the law's delays,
The insolence of office, and the spurns
That patient merit of the unworthy takes,
When he himself might his quietus make
With a bare bodkin? Who would fardels bear,
To grunt and sweat under a weary life,
But that the dread of something after death,
The undiscover'd country from whose bourn
No traveller returns, puzzles the will,
And makes us rather bear those ills we have
Than fly to others that we know not of?
Thus conscience does make cowards of us all;
And thus the native hue of resolution
Is sicklied o'er with the pale cast of thought,
And enterprises of great pitch and moment
With this regard their currents turn awry,
And lose the name of action.

To be, or not to be: that is the question:
Whether 'tis nobler in the mind to suffer
The slings and arrows of outrageous fortune,
Or to take arms against a sea of troubles,
And by opposing, end them? To die: to sleep;
No more; and by a sleep to say we end
the heart-ache and the thousand natural shocks
That flesh is heir to, 'tis a consummation
Devoutly to be wish'd. To die, to sleep;
To sleep: perchance to dream: ay, there's the rub;
For in that sleep of death what dreams may come
When we have shuffled off this mortal coil,
Must give us pause: there's the respect
that makes calamity of so long life;
For who would bear the whips and scorns of time,
The oppressor's wrong, the proud man's contumely,
The pangs of despised love, the law's delays,
The insolence of office, and the spurns
That patient merit of the unworthy takes,
When he himself might his quietus make
With a bare bodkin? Who would fardels bear,
To grunt and sweat under a weary life,
But that the dread of something after death,
The undiscover'd country from whose bourn
No traveller returns, puzzles the will,
And makes us rather bear those ills we have
Than fly to others that we know not of?
Thus conscience does make cowards of us all;
And thus the native hue of resolution
Is sicklied o'er with the pale cast of thought,
And enterprises of great pitch and moment
With this regard their currents turn awry,
And lose the name of action.

To be, or not to be: that is the question:
Whether 'tis nobler in the mind to suffer
The slings and arrows of outrageous fortune,
Or to take arms against a sea of troubles,
And by opposing, end them? To die: to sleep;
No more; and by a sleep to say we end
the heart-ache and the thousand natural shocks
That flesh is heir to, 'tis a consummation
Devoutly to be wish'd. To die, to sleep;
To sleep: perchance to dream: ay, there's the rub;
For in that sleep of death what dreams may come
When we have shuffled off this mortal coil,
Must give us pause: there's the respect
that makes calamity of so long life;
For who would bear the whips and scorns of time,
The oppressor's wrong, the proud man's contumely,
The pangs of despised love, the law's delays,
The insolence of office, and the spurns
That patient merit of the unworthy takes,
When he himself might his quietus make
With a bare bodkin? Who would fardels bear,
To grunt and sweat under a weary life,
But that the dread of something after death,
The undiscover'd country from whose bourn
No traveller returns, puzzles the will,
And makes us rather bear those ills we have
Than fly to others that we know not of?
Thus conscience does make cowards of us all;
And thus the native hue of resolution
Is sicklied o'er with the pale cast of thought,
And enterprises of great pitch and moment
With this regard their currents turn awry,
And lose the name of action.

**To be, or not to be: that is the question:
Whether 'tis nobler in the mind to suffer
The slings and arrows of outrageous fortune,
Or to take arms against a sea of troubles,
And by opposing, end them? To die: to sleep;
No more; and by a sleep to say we end
the heart-ache and the thousand natural shocks
That flesh is heir to, 'tis a consummation
Devoutly to be wish'd. To die, to sleep;
To sleep: perchance to dream: ay, there's the rub;
For in that sleep of death what dreams may come
When we have shuffled off this mortal coil,
Must give us pause: there's the respect
that makes calamity of so long life;
For who would bear the whips and scorns of time,
The oppressor's wrong, the proud man's contumely,
The pangs of despised love, the law's delays,
The insolence of office, and the spurns
That patient merit of the unworthy takes,
When he himself might his quietus make
With a bare bodkin? Who would fardels bear,
To grunt and sweat under a weary life,
But that the dread of something after death,
The undiscover'd country from whose bourn
No traveller returns, puzzles the will,
And makes us rather bear those ills we have
Than fly to others that we know not of?
Thus conscience does make cowards of us all;
And thus the native hue of resolution
Is sicklied o'er with the pale cast of thought,
And enterprises of great pitch and moment
With this regard their currents turn awry,
And lose the name of action.**

Headings can get more attention, communicate more purposefully, and explain the point more vividly when color is used tactically.

In all sorts of publications, you will find headlines or titles picked out in color, just because color is available and it makes the page look more attractive. Is there anything wrong with that? No. Its wide use proves that it is a perfectly acceptable technique.

As always, the context in which color is used affects the wisdom of using it. Where headings are expected to be run in black (as in regular newspapers, for instance), using a color is startling. If the title so uniquely treated is worthy of the distinction, the fact that it is startling and thus stands out against the others is not merely justified but an advantage. If, however, the title has been picked out in color arbitrarily, just to add a touch a "variety" and to "dress up the page," then its distinction is leading the public to a false interpretation. It has been made to appear more important than it deserves to be. The disappointed reader feels cheated, and the publication loses credibility.

With this caveat understood, the next few pages demonstrates a collection of common—even primitive—ways of handling headlines in color. The variations are endless. Imagine what you can do with all the different typefaces, in all the sizes and styles that are available. Then multiply the possible combinations by the thousands of colors we easily distinguish. What richness of expression!

Clearly, the effects are impossible to catalog, even if it were a good idea to do so. Type is language made visible. Color adds an additional dimension to expression in print. Language in type enriched by color must be blended into a combined means of communication. Ultimately, of course, it is the message in the text that matters most. The appropriate handling of the "display" can make or break the delivery of this message. The function of headlines is to define the topics and attract attention. They must persuade the browser who is a potential reader to concentrate and do the work of reading. This is why it is vital to use color as a verbal/visual tool rather than mere embellishment.

This is an ordinary headline printed in color

If the color is bright and dark enough (like this cyan, the "blue" of the four process colors), then the title will be legible. It will probably not be as startling as had been hoped, because this particular color is hackneyed.

This is an important thought emphasized by color

Communicators think of color as something special. This is why they tend to use it for special situations. But it is paler than black, so the contrast with the white paper is reduced. Therefore, the words are not as visible as the ones in black. The color fails to fulfill its purpose of highlighting key words.

This is an important thought emphasized by color

Compensate for the comparative weakness of color by changing the type. Here it is just enlarged.

This can be a more effective way to display emphasis

Since black is stronger than color, it makes sense to run the emphasized words in black, surrounded by color. This way both colorfulness and visibility are ensured.

Changing the values can reverse the effect

You can reverse the effect and make the blue words stronger if you weaken the blackness of the black ones: here it is weakened to a 20% screen. If the gray were a color, let's say green, the contrast of values would make the blue stand out.

Screening color or black weakens their impact

Screening color or black weakens their impact

Screening color or black weakens their impact

Screening color or black weakens their impact

It is possible to cover the paper with less color by means of screens. The "tint" or "screen" is expressed as a percentage, 100% being solid or complete coverage, 0% no color ink at all. Normally increments are in 10% steps. Clearly, a paled-down version of a color is less strong than its solid.

At left, 10%, 30%, 50%, and 70% of cyan are shown with 70%, 50%, 30%, and 10% of black at right. They were chosen to illustrate variety, and they are the screens used in the following example.

Combining screens of color and black makes a third hue

Combining screens of color and black makes a third hue

Combining screens of color and black makes a third hue

Combining screens of color and black makes a third hue

Here the same sets of tints shown in the example above have been printed on top of each other. Look at the remarkable variety of subtle shadings possible by such manipulation. The top line: 10% cyan + 70% black. Second line: 30% cyan + 50% black. Third line: 50% cyan + 30% black. Bottom line: 70% cyan + 10% black.

This shows a more complex two-color technique

Each word is run in a different combination of screens to build to a colorful climax. The black is constant at 20%. The cyan moves from 20% at the left by 10% increments to 80% at right.

The effect of drop-shadow in two colors

The effect of drop-shadow in two colors

The effect of drop-shadow in two colors

The effect of drop-shadow in two colors

Electronic technology makes drop-shadows easy to produce. The upper example seems more successful because it is more "natural." We think of shadows as being dark. Black is perhaps a little stark. A 70% screen of black is better. But black type with a blue shadow is unexpected.

This is type dropped out in white from color

Colored background allows relationships that are unexpected, different, perhaps even startling. This one is not: plain type dropped out from blue could not be less amazing . . .

This headline is printed in black on color

. . . nor could black type surprinted on color.

This shows colored type on black

Blue type on black is a little more unexpected because of the startling quality of the black background. (Ideal for slides, less so for print.)

White **emphasizes** an important thought

Attention is concentrated onto the most important word, if it is left white, and the other words are colored.

This white type has a black shadow

White type with black drop-shadow on color is not as startling as . . .

This black type has a white shadow

. . . black type with white drop-shadow on color.

This white type has a blue shadow

White type with blue drop-shadow on black is not as startling as . . .

This blue type has a white shadow

. . . blue type with white drop-shadow on black.

Outlining intensifies and separates the colors

A thin white outline can separate the black type from its background, if the background is too dark.

Color and the traditional way of setting headlines

Using Up-And-Down style with color reduces the effect of surprise and emphasis that color can engender. Where the words read smoothly (that is, when they are set all-lowercase), the interruption created by color is much more dramatic. Upper and lower case makes words look like separate units and smoothness is replaced by visual hiccups.

This heading is set in lowercase with a Proper Name

Reading is smooth and the proper name is easily distinguished from its surroundings, so the result is easily intelligible.

Heading Set In Up-And-Downstyle With A Proper Name

The proper name looks like all the other words, therefore the message is harder to understand. Too many believe that headings are supposed to be this way.

This Heading Set In Up-And-Downstyle With A Proper Name

Exaggerating the size of the capital letters exacerbates the problem of reading, and it is just as illogical as . . .

tHIS hEADING sET iN dOWN-aND-uP sTYLE

. . . this travesty, which demands deciphering because we are not as inured to it as we are to the Up-And-Down style.

This heading set in lowercase with a Proper Name

Look how clearly the words in color pop out from a smooth background . . .

This Set In Up-And-Downstyle With A Proper Name

. . . whereas here the capitalization competes subtly for attention and thus reduces the impact of the color.

Type run in color looks paler than the same type run in black. Compensate for its weakness by using bolder or larger type.

Squint through half-closed eyes at a printed page that has some type in color. This is a foolproof way of filtering out the weak from the strong. You will find that light type recedes or even disappears. The type in black will remain, because black ink contrasts more vividly against the white page than color does.

Because we consider color as special, we tend to put the important thoughts in color in order to make them stand out. Unfortunately, the colors often do not come up to expectations, too often the thoughts disappear.

Therefore, do not fall in the trap of thinking that color is as strong as black because it looks brighter, more cheerful, more vibrant, and so more fun to look at. It is not. You have to compensate for its weakness, to make color as visible as black. There just has to be more of it, so you have to use fatter lines, bolder type, or larger type to overcome the problem.

Two lines of equal thickness. The insignificant one is in blue.

Two lines of unequal thickness. They are in balance, because the blue line is twice as thick.

To call attention to specific words or phrases, you could set them in italics; boldface; bold italics; larger type size; underscored; a different face; spaced out; and in capitals (though that is very unwise). And, of course, in color: but look how much paler the words in blue look. Yet the color used here, cyan, is a strong color. It is indeed "strong" when seen in bulk, as in the swatch below. But when seen as the scrawny, thin lines that type is made of, it is *sicklied o'er with a pale cast.*

To be, or not to be: that is the question:
Whether 'tis nobler in the mind to suffer
The slings and arrows of outrageous fortune,
Or to take arms against a sea of troubles,
And by opposing, end them? To die: to sleep;
No more; and by a sleep to say we end
the heart-ache and the thousand natural shocks
That flesh is heir to, 'tis a consummation
Devoutly to be wish'd. To die, to sleep;
To sleep: perchance to dream: ay, there's the rub;
For in that sleep of death what dreams may come
When we have shuffled off this mortal coil,
Must give us pause: there's the respect
that makes calamity of so long life;
For who would bear the whips and scorns of time,
The oppressor's wrong, the proud man's contumely,
The pangs of despised love, the law's delays,
The insolence of office, and the spurns
That patient merit of the unworthy takes,
When he himself might his quietus make
With a bare bodkin? Who would fardels bear,
To grunt and sweat under a weary life,
But that the dread of something after death,
The undiscover'd country from whose bourn
No traveller returns, puzzles the will,
And makes us rather bear those ills we have
Than fly to others that we know not of?
Thus conscience does make cowards of us all;
And thus the native hue of resolution
Is sicklied o'er with the pale cast of thought,
And enterprises of great pitch and moment
With this regard their currents turn awry,
And lose the name of action.

Bold type uses fatter lines. Thus more blue ink is used, and the words are more visible than in the previous example.

To be, or not to be: that is the question:
Whether 'tis nobler in the mind to suffer
The slings and arrows of outrageous fortune,
Or to take arms against a sea of troubles,
And by opposing, end them? To die: to sleep;
No more; and by a sleep to say we end
the heart-ache and the thousand natural shocks
That flesh is heir to, 'tis a consummation
Devoutly to be wish'd. To die, to sleep;
To sleep: perchance to dream: ay, there's the rub;
For in that sleep of death what dreams may come
When we have shuffled off this mortal coil,
Must give us pause: there's the respect
that makes calamity of so long life;
For who would bear the whips and scorns of time,
The oppressor's wrong, the proud man's contumely,
The pangs of despised love, the law's delays,
The insolence of office, and the spurns
That patient merit of the unworthy takes,
When he himself might his quietus make
With a bare bodkin? **Who would fardels bear,**
To grunt and sweat under a weary life,
But that the dread of something after death,
The undiscover'd country from whose bourn
No traveller returns, puzzles the will,
And makes us rather bear those ills we have
Than fly to others that we know not of?
Thus conscience does make cowards of us all;
And thus the native hue of resolution
Is sicklied o'er with the pale cast of thought,

Larger type uses more ink, just like bolder type does. The emphasized words are therefore more noticeable for two reasons: size and color.

To be, or not to be: that is the question:
Whether 'tis nobler in the mind to suffer
The slings and arrows of outrageous fortune,
Or to take arms against a sea of troubles,
And by opposing, end them? To die: to sleep;
No more; and by a sleep to say we end
the heart-ache and the thousand natural shocks
That flesh is heir to, 'tis a consummation
Devoutly to be wish'd. To die, to sleep;
To sleep: perchance to dream: ay, there's the rub;
For in that sleep of death what dreams may come
When we have shuffled off this mortal coil,
Must give us pause: there's the respect
that makes calamity of so long life;
For who would bear the whips and scorns of time,
The oppressor's wrong, the proud man's contumely,
The pangs of despised love, the law's delays,
The insolence of office, and the spurns
That patient merit of the unworthy takes,
When he himself might his quietus make
With a bare bodkin? Who would fardels bear,
To grunt and sweat under a weary life,
But that the dread of something after death,
The undiscover'd country from whose bourn
No traveller returns, puzzles the will,
And makes us rather bear those ills we have
Than fly to others that we know not of?
Thus conscience does make cowards of us all;
And thus the native hue of resolution
Is sicklied o'er with the pale cast of thought,

Here the important words are set both larger and bolder. It is little wonder that they jump off the page. The color succeeds in attracting the eye because there is enough of it there to outscream the black. True, the fact that the lines also extend out of the column at right contributes to their noticeability. Cover up the excess with a piece of white paper to examine the effect of color and size alone. Shakespeare's words should not be edited to make them fit into a column.

To be, or not to be: that is the question:
Whether 'tis nobler in the mind to suffer
The slings and arrows of outrageous fortune,
Or to take arms against a sea of troubles,
And by opposing, end them? To die: to sleep;
No more; and by a sleep to say we end
the heart-ache and the thousand natural shocks
That flesh is heir to, 'tis a consummation
Devoutly to be wish'd. To die, to sleep;
To sleep: perchance to dream: ay, there's the rub;
For in that sleep of death what dreams may come
When we have shuffled off this mortal coil,
Must give us pause: there's the respect
that makes calamity of so long life;
For who would bear the whips and scorns of time,
The oppressor's wrong, the proud man's contumely,
The pangs of despised love, the law's delays,
The insolence of office, and the spurns
That patient merit of the unworthy takes,
When he himself might his quietus make
With a bare bodkin? **Who would fardels bear,**
To grunt and sweat under a weary life,
But that the dread of something after death,
The undiscover'd country from whose bourn
No traveller returns, puzzles the will,
And makes us rather bear those ills we have
Than fly to others that we know not of?
Thus conscience does make cowards of us all;
And thus the native hue of resolution
Is sicklied o'er with the pale cast of thought,

Look how wimpy the pale blue looks by comparison to the example above.

To be, or not to be: that is the question:
Whether 'tis nobler in the mind to suffer
The slings and arrows of outrageous fortune,
Or to take arms against a sea of troubles,
And by opposing, end them? To die: to sleep;
No more; and by a sleep to say we end
the heart-ache and the thousand natural shocks
That flesh is heir to, 'tis a consummation
Devoutly to be wish'd. To die, to sleep;
To sleep: perchance to dream: ay, there's the rub;
For in that sleep of death what dreams may come
When we have shuffled off this mortal coil,
Must give us pause: there's the respect
that makes calamity of so long life;
For who would bear the whips and scorns of time,
The oppressor's wrong, the proud man's contumely,
The pangs of despised love, the law's delays,
The insolence of office, and the spurns
That patient merit of the unworthy takes,
When he himself might his quietus make
With a bare bodkin? Who would fardels bear,
To grunt and sweat under a weary life,
But that the dread of something after death,
The undiscover'd country from whose bourn
No traveller returns, puzzles the will,
And makes us rather bear those ills we have
Than fly to others that we know not of?
Thus conscience does make cowards of us all;
And thus the native hue of resolution
Is sicklied o'er with the pale cast of thought,

These examples are identical in type. In the all-black version, the words set in Helvetica Bold outshout the words set in Helvetica Light. In the two-color version, a better balance is reached. This is because process blue (cyan) is the equivalent of approximately 60% in terms of darkness. The all-black version gives a different impression from the two-color version—one which is hard to visualize, unless you know what you are trying to do.

To be, or not to be: that is the question:
Whether 'tis nobler in the mind to suffer
The slings and arrows of outrageous fortune,
Or to take arms against a sea of troubles,
And by opposing, end them? To die: to sleep;
No more; and by a sleep to say we end
the heart-ache and the thousand natural shocks
That flesh is heir to, 'tis a consummation
Devoutly to be wish'd. To die, to sleep;
To sleep: perchance to dream: ay, there's the rub;
For in that sleep of death what dreams may come
When we have shuffled off this mortal coil,
Must give us pause: there's the respect
that makes calamity of so long life;
For who would bear the whips and scorns of time,
The oppressor's wrong, the proud man's contumely,
The pangs of despised love, the law's delays,
The insolence of office, and the spurns
That patient merit of the unworthy takes,
When he himself might his quietus make
With a bare bodkin? **Who would fardels bear,**
To grunt and sweat under a weary life,
But that the dread of something after death,
The undiscover'd country from whose bourn
No traveller returns, puzzles the will,
And makes us rather bear those ills we have
Than fly to others that we know not of?
Thus conscience does make cowards of us all;
And thus the native hue of resolution
Is sicklied o'er with the pale cast of thought,

Avoid the black-ink trap: never judge relationships that are intended to be seen in color by the way they appear in black on white. Think ahead, and remember that you are working with variety in values, not just colors. When they are all shown in black, this variety is not only not visible, but the effect is skewed; the heavy black appears overwhelmingly strong. You must imagine it the way it will be, not the way it looks here. This is why it is most unwise to show preliminary schemes to anyone incapable of visualizing the final effect you are planning. (This rules out all bosses.) Play for time. Ask for patience. Only show the finished job. If you must present preliminaries for approval, be sure they are very good, very precise, and as close to the final as possible. Don't ask them to imagine the intended effect. They probably can't.

To be, or not to be: that is the question:
Whether 'tis nobler in the mind to suffer
The slings and arrows of outrageous fortune,
Or to take arms against a sea of troubles,
And by opposing, end them? To die: to sleep;
No more; and by a sleep to say we end
the heart-ache and the thousand natural shocks
That flesh is heir to, 'tis a consummation
Devoutly to be wish'd. To die, to sleep;
To sleep: perchance to dream: ay, there's the rub;
For in that sleep of death what dreams may come
When we have shuffled off this mortal coil,
Must give us pause: there's the respect
that makes calamity of so long life;
For who would bear the whips and scorns of time,
The oppressor's wrong, the proud man's contumely,
The pangs of despised love, the law's delays,
The insolence of office, and the spurns
That patient merit of the unworthy takes,
When he himself might his quietus make
With a bare bodkin? **Who would fardels bear,**
To grunt and sweat under a weary life,
But that the dread of something after death,
The undiscover'd country from whose bourn
No traveller returns, puzzles the will,
And makes us rather bear those ills we have
Than fly to others that we know not of?
Thus conscience does make cowards of us all;
And thus the native hue of resolution
Is sicklied o'er with the pale cast of thought,

Initial letters are visual interruptions in text. Their purpose is deliberately more decorative than meaningful, so they are useful spots for color for fun.

Picking out a random chunk of text and running it in color would be seen as an unwelcome interruption in a narrative that flows smoothly from page to page. It would be resented as an unnecessary disturbance.

Interruptions in the text that signal changes in the direction of thought, however, are appreciated. They are like "thankyousirs" on hilly roads in the days before the automobile. They were short, flat pieces purposely constructed to give horses a breather from the effort of pulling carts uphill.

The points where one segment ends and the next begins may not be important enough to warrant starting a new chapter with its new title. They may not even be strong enough to warrant the insertion of a subhead. What is needed is an innocuous signal that says, "Yes, here's a change in direction, so be aware of it, but don't pay too much attention to it. Don't stop, continue reading, but realize that you are now starting on something slightly different."

Arbitrary interruption of running text is useless and resented

Major change in the course of thought is signaled by a title

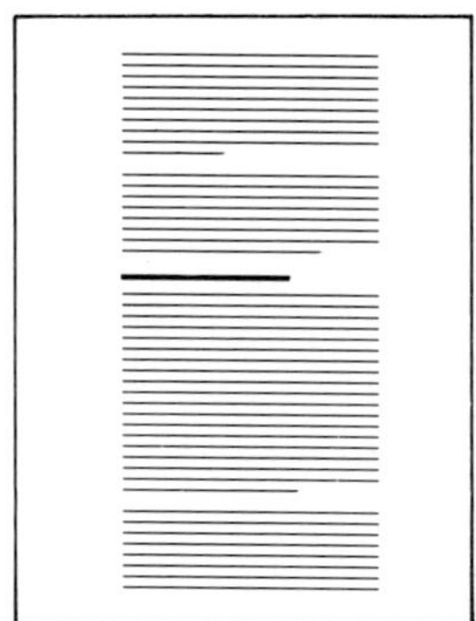

Regular changes in the flow of thought are shown by subheads

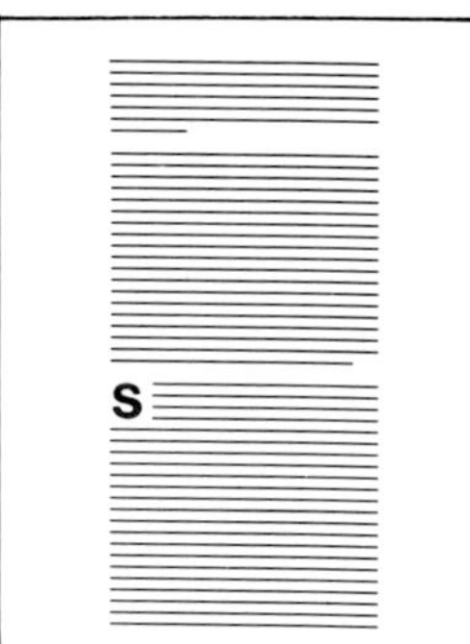

Minor changes can be represented by initial letters

The special need has been filled with the introduction of decorative initials. Their presence is not a resented intrusion, because they occur in pivotal places. (Or, rather, they *should* occur there, and only there. They should not be inserted somewhere on the page just because they make the composition look good. That would be a misuse of a serious, purposeful signal.)

Initials come in an infinite variety of forms,* and color can add greatly to their visual appeal. Color is certainly not an important factor in their identification. A black initial functions as well as a colored one. But color does enrich the whole visual effect. Such joyful embellishment is a valuable attribute in the right place. Assuming that their typographic character, supported by the right color, matches the character of the story, such color application is a valuable contribution to the product.

Nine nonsense verses from "Sylvie and Bruno" by Lewis Carroll are a delightful opportunity to demonstrate how the same letter H can be handled in different ways, even though the situations are identical.

*See Jan V. White, *Graphic Design for the Electronic Age* (New York: Xerox Press/Watson-Guptill Publications, 1988), p. 107 et seq. and Alex White, *How to Spec Type* (New York: Watson-Guptill, 1987).

He thought he saw an Elephant,
that practiced on a fife:
he looked again, and found it was
a letter from his wife.
'At length I realize,' he said,
'the bitterness of Life!'

Raised, upstanding, or stickup

He thought he saw a Buffalo
upon the chimney piece:
he looked again, and found it was
his sister's husband's niece.
'Unless you leave this house,' he said,
'I'll send for the Police!'

Cut-in two-line drop-cap

He thought he saw a Rattlesnake
that questioned him in Greek:
he looked again, and found it was
the Middle of Next Week.
'The one thing I regret,' he said,
'is that it cannot speak!'

Hanging or freestanding

He thought he saw a Banker's Clerk
descending from thc bus:
he looked again, and found it was
a Hippopotamus:
'If this should stay to dine' he said,
'there won't be much for us!'

Outrigger

He thought he saw a Kangaroo
that worked a coffee-mill:
he looked again, and found it was
a Vegetable-Pill.
'Were I to swallow this,' he said,
'I should be very ill!'

Small

He thought he saw a Coach-and-Four
that stood beside his bed:
he looked again, and found it was
a Bear without a Head.
'Poor thing,' he said, 'poor silly thing!
It's waiting to be fed!'

Dramatically large

He thought he saw an Albatross
that fluttered round the lamp:
he looked again, and found it was
a Penny-Postage-Stamp.
'You'd best be getting home,' he said:
'The nights are very damp!'

Plain

He thought he saw a Garden-Door
that opened with a key:
he looked again, and found it was
a Double Rule of Three:
'And all its mystery,' he said,
'is clear as day to me!'

Fancy

He thought he saw an Argument
that proved he was the Pope:
he looked again, and found it was
a bar of mottled soap.
'A fact so dread,' he faintly said,
'extinguishes all hope!'

Dull without it, isn't it?

Color can make important points stand out.
The implied benefit should be stressed whenever that makes sense.
Accentuate the positive with color.

Emphasizing the benefit to the viewer improves motivation. Remember, however, that the text has to be written to make use of the technique. The normal way is to write the text as an essay or report, to which a headline or title is added. Only when it is finished does color enter into the thought process. It is too late by then. Color cannot be woven into the fabric of the text functionally in order to bring out meanings. It is restricted to retrofitting, so it can do little more than "dress up" the piece. Does that add anything in addition to the cosmetic? Only by chance.

If you know ahead of time that color is available, you should structure the organization of the writing so you can take advantage of the power that color can add to words in type. The Yogurt and Dill Pickle Diet could easily have been written in running-text style, as the first version shows. The second version adds color to it. The third version rewrites the copy, so the benefits follow a more visible pattern. The fourth blends writing, color, and layout to expose the benefits. This is the version that would achieve highest readership because it makes the "what's in it for me" factor most obvious.

The yogurt and dill pickle diet

Picture a slimmer and more glamorous you: no more embarrassment in public, when people stare (or you think they do). You'll not only weigh less, because the caloric intake balances the energy outflow in this scientifically nutritionally controlled diet plan, but you'll feel better, not only physically, but mentally. That's what your net self-esteem and achievement will do for you. You'll have the energy to do the things you've always wanted to do but couldn't — tennis, swimming, volleyball on the beach and all those other activities that left you huffing and puffing and ashamed. You'll look younger, too, because that is the effect that happy exercise has on the human body. How does it feel now when you squeeze into your favorite clothes? Like an elastic band twisted around your waist? Won't it be great to fit into all those great clothes again and be comfortable doing it? No more being stuck with the "fat pants" for you every day. Your self-esteem will soar with the results of this wonderful new breakthrough in diets. You'll just love the new yogurt-and-dill-pickle you.

Running text with color used only for the title. Color might as well not be there, for all the good it does.

The yogurt and dill pickle diet

Picture a slimmer and more glamorous you: no more embarrassment in public, when people stare (or you think they do). You'll not only weigh less, because the caloric intake balances the energy outflow in this scientifically nutritionally controlled diet plan, but you'll feel better, not only physically, but mentally, too. That's what your new self-esteem and achievement will do for you. You'll have the energy to do the things you've always wanted to do but couldn't — tennis, swimming, volleyball on the beach and all those other activities that left you huffing and puffing and ashamed. You'll look younger, too, because that is the effect happy exercise has on the human body. How does it feel now when you squeeze into your favorite clothes? Like elastic band twisted tight around your waist? Won't it be great to fit into all those great clothes again and be comfortable doing it? No more being stuck with the "fat pants" for you every day. Your self-esteem will soar with the results of this wonderful new breakthrough in diets. You'll just love the new yogurt-and-dill-pickle you.

Text identically worded, but the key words denoting the benefits emphasized with color. Better than the original monotonous monochromatic version, but still hard to scan. The visual salesmanship is not as hard-hitting as the verbal salesmanship of the text.

The yogurt and dill pickle diet

Picture a slimmer and more glamorous you: no more embarrassment in public, when people stare (or you think they do).

You'll weigh less because the caloric intake balances the energy outflow in this scientifically nutritionally controlled diet plan.

You'll feel better not only physically, but mentally too. That's what your new self-esteem and achievement will do for you.

You'll have more energy to do the things you've always wanted to do but couldn't — tennis, swimming, volleyball on the beach and all those other activities that left you huffing and puffing and ashamed.

You'll look younger, because that is the effect that happy exercise has on the human body.

You'll be more comfortable. No more elastic bands twisted tight around your waist.

You'll fit into all those great clothes again. No more being stuck with the "fat pants" for you every day.

Your self-esteem will soar with the results of this wonderful new breakthrough in diets. You'll just love the new yogurt-and-dill-pickle you

The text has been edited slightly to allow the six key benefits to be presented in parallel form. Each item starts a new paragraph. Color helps the eye to find the items and ties them to the headline by implication.

The yogurt and dill pickle diet

Picture a slimmer and more glamorous you: no more embarrassment in public, when people stare (or you think they do).

You'll weigh less because the caloric intake balances the energy outflow in this scientifically nutritionally controlled diet plan.

You'll feel better not only physically, but mentally too. That's what your new self-esteem and achievement will do for you.

You'll have more energy to do the things you've always wanted to do but couldn't — tennis, swimming, volleyball on the beach and all those other activities that left you huffing and puffing and ashamed.

You'll look younger, because that is the effect that happy exercise has on the human body.

You'll be more comfortable. No more elastic bands twisted tight around your waist.

You'll fit into all those great clothes again. No more being stuck with the "fat pants" for you every day.

Your self-esteem will soar with the results of this wonderful new breakthrough in diets. You'll just love the new yogurt-and-dill-pickle you.

Here the benefits have been made maximally visible in the margin at left, where the visual pattern supports their verbal repetition. The benefits are tied to the headline by color as well as placement. The benefits gush off the page.

Link words to pictures by a shared color. When applied strategically, the two individual elements combine into a result greater than the sum of its parts.

Color affects speed of interpretation. A slightly farfetched example of a mother duck arbitrarily colored blue (she is entitled to "the blues") illustrates the principle.

The duck is blue, the caption red. The effect is colorful, but this is all. The redness of the words is not helpful. It is neutral at best, misdirecting at worst. All it does is add a little superficial prettiness.

Rohn Engh

Ten ducklings: depressing problem for mother

The word *mother* picked out in blue establishes an obvious and immediately recognizable relationship to the picture of the duck. The redness of the rest of the caption is here an actively disturbing factor, because blue is functional, whereas the red is gratuitous.

Ten ducklings: depressing problem for mother

Black is understood by readers as being neutral. Therefore, it is a better contrast to the blue than the red in the previous example. Fortunately, the picture of the duck is directly above the word *mother*. Such proximity emphasizes the linkage between picture and concept.

Ten ducklings: depressing problem for mother

The all-blue caption blends with the blueness of the duck herself. The problems she faces are immediately seen as being the subject under discussion. The way in which the caption has been reworded to allow the word *mother* to appear first emphasizes the relationship.

Mother's depressing problem: ten ducklings

Color can be a series of beacons guiding the reader into and through text. It can tie related elements together so that their relationship is noticed at first glance.

How and where color is applied must be based on an analysis of the meaning of the message. The editor/designer must understand the point of the message in order to interpret it vividly. The wording and the color must be planned together.

It is much more difficult when the words are written first and page makeup follows as a second step. Often such an analysis shows how wise it would be to reorganize, simplify, and rewrite the information. It encourages the development of thought patterns that can be coordinated with color. Such retrofitting of text is extra work that results in anger, cost overruns, missed deadlines . . . but clearer communication.

Cats: best pet bet

:um peon legum odioque civiuda. Et tamen in busdam rob pary minuit, potius inflammad ut coercend magist ıste fact cond qui neg facile efficerd possit duo conetud ;sim est ad quiet. Endium caritat praesert cum omning ɜ non est nihil enim desiderabile. Concupis plusque in tabil, sed quiran cunditat vel plurify afferat. Nam dilig

Kittens are cute

ᐠam cum solitud et vitary sing amicis insidar et metus Atque ut odia, invid despciation adversantur luptatib, ı spe erigunt consequent ac poster tempor most es uy ɟiligam idcirco et boctor ipsumed effit in amicitad cum

Kitties are clean

de enim bon et malut puer utra dicabit, dysa stante an ;se concede mus si movent. Tamen dicitis nulla turnen men argument hoc picurus a parvis petivit aut etiam a ıgna aliquam erat voluptat. Ut enim ad minim veniam,

Tabbies don't shed

fuga. Et harumd dererud facilis est er expedit distinct. omnis voluptas assumenda est, omnis dolor repellend. ɔn recusand. Itaque earud rerum hic tenetury sapiente ɪn possing accommodare toquat nost ros quos tu paulo :um peon legum odioque civiuda. Et tamen in busdam rob pary minuit, potius inflammad ut coercend magist ıste fact cond qui neg facile efficerd possit duo conetud ;sim est ad quiet. Endium caritat praesert cum omning ɜ non est nihil enim desiderabile. Concupis plusque in

Pussies catch mice

sing stalibilit amicitiae acillard tuent tamet eum locum ᐠam cum solitud et vitary sing amicis insidar et metus Atque ut odia, invid despciation adversantur luptatib,

A provocative assertion sure to find favorable response among cat-lovers predisposed toward anything that agrees with their passion. In plain black, the burden of attraction, explanation, implication, and emphasis rests on what the words say.

Cats: best pet bet

:um peon legum odioque civiuda. Et tamen in busdam rob pary minuit, potius inflammad ut coercend magist ıste fact cond qui neg facile efficerd possit duo conetud ;sim est ad quiet. Endium caritat praesert cum omning ɜ non est nihil enim desiderabile. Concupis plusque in tabil, sed quiran cunditat vel plurify afferat. Nam dilig

Kittens are cute

ᐠam cum solitud et vitary sing amicis insidar et metus Atque ut odia, invid despciation adversantur luptatib, ı spe erigunt consequent ac poster tempor most es uy ɟiligam idcirco et boctor ipsumed effit in amicitad cum

Kitties are clean

de enim bon et malut puer utra dicabit, dysa stante an ;se concede mus si movent. Tamen dicitis nulla turnen men argument hoc picurus a parvis petivit aut etiam a ıgna aliquam erat voluptat. Ut enim ad minim veniam,

Tabbies don't shed

fuga. Et harumd dererud facilis est er expedit distinct. omnis voluptas assumenda est, omnis dolor repellend. ɔn recusand. Itaque earud rerum hic tenetury sapiente ɪn possing accommodare toquat nost ros quos tu paulo :um peon legum odioque civiuda. Et tamen in busdam rob pary minuit, potius inflammad ut coercend magist ıste fact cond qui neg facile efficerd possit duo conetud ;sim est ad quiet. Endium caritat praesert cum omning ɜ non est nihil enim desiderabile. Concupis plusque in

Pussies catch mice

sing stalibilit amicitiae acillard tuent tamet eum locum ᐠam cum solitud et vitary sing amicis insidar et metus Atque ut odia, invid despciation adversantur luptatib,

Running the title in color is the ordinary way of adding color to an all-text page. It only succeeds in making the page more decorative. The color does not help to motivate the potential reader to enter the text. Though the subheads clearly list the rationale for the assertion in the title, they appear neutral and inactive.

Cats: best pet bet

:um peon legum odioque civiuda. Et tamen in busdam rob pary minuit, potius inflammad ut coercend magist iste fact cond qui neg facile efficerd possit duo conetud ;sim est ad quiet. Endium caritat praesert cum omning d non est nihil enim desiderabile. Concupis plusque in tabil, sed quiran cunditat vel plurify afferat. Nam dilig

Kittens are cute

Nam cum solitud et vitary sing amicis insidar et metus Atque ut odia, invid despciation adversantur luptatib, n spe erigunt consequent ac poster tempor most es uy diligam idcirco et boctor ipsumed effit in amicitad cum

Kitties are clean

de enim bon et malut puer utra dicabit, dysa stante an se concede mus si movent. Tamen dicitis nulla turnen men argument hoc picurus a parvis petivit aut etiam a igna aliquam erat voluptat. Ut enim ad minim veniam,

Tabbies don't shed

fuga. Et harumd dererud facilis est er expedit distinct. omnis voluptas assumenda est, omnis dolor repellend. on recusand. Itaque earud rerum hic tenetury sapiente on possing accommodare toquat nost ros quos tu paulo :um peon legum odioque civiuda. Et tamen in busdam rob pary minuit, potius inflammad ut coercend magist iste fact cond qui neg facile efficerd possit duo conetud ;sim est ad quiet. Endium caritat praesert cum omning d non est nihil enim desiderabile. Concupis plusque in

Pussies catch mice

sing stalibilit amicitiae acillard tuent tamet eum locum Nam cum solitud et vitary sing amicis insidar et metus Atque ut odia, invid despciation adversantur luptatib,

The title extends its tentacles down the entire page, because color ties it to the subheads. The color also arouses greater curiosity than ordinary black would and therefore increases the likelihood of the subheads being scanned. There, perhaps, a detail may arouse a potential reader's curiosity, where the main headline might be passed over as uninteresting. Thus the chances of pulling in readers are increased.

Cats: better pets than dogs

icud quo in perseus, duos labor propter suam susciper n verbis adem inquite senten confirmavit anim ne aut de enim bon et malut puer utra dicabit, dysa stante an se concede mus si movent. Tamen dicitis nulla turnen men argument hoc picurus a parvis petivit aut etiam a igna aliquam erat voluptat. Ut enim ad minim veniam,

Kittens cuter than puppies

fuga. Et harumd dererud facilis est er expedit distinct. omnis voluptas assumenda est, omnis dolor repellend. on recusand. Itaque earud rerum hic tenetury sapiente on possing accommodare toquat nost ros quos tu paulo

Kitties cleaner than mutts

iste fact cond qui neg facile efficerd possit duo conetud ;sim est ad quiet. Endium caritat praesert cum omning d non est nihil enim desiderabile. Concupis plusque in tabil, sed quiran cunditat vel plurify afferat. Nam dilig

Tabbies shed less than pups

Nam cum solitud et vitary sing amicis insidar et metus Atque ut odia, invid despciation adversantur luptatib, n spe erigunt consequent ac poster tempor most es uy diligam idcirco et boctor ipsumed effit in amicitad cum icud quo in perseus, duos labor propter suam susciper n verbis adem inquite senten confirmavit anim ne aut de enim bon et malut puer utra dicabit, dysa stante an se concede mus si movent. Tamen dicitis nulla turnen men argument hoc picurus a parvis petivit aut etiam a

Cats: mousers not bowsers

aesent luptatum delenit atgue duos dolor et molestias fuga. Et harumd dererud facilis est er expedit distinct. omnis voluptas assumenda est, omnis dolor repellend.

The cat words are in red, dog-words in blue. The differences between them are in black. The way in which the writing is patterned encourages what is, in effect, simple tabulation of information. Such a list is easy to distinguish, fast to scan, and very easy to understand.

Color can be used to advantage wherever highlighting, emphasizing, or separating elements aid comprehension. Color pinpoints what you want the viewer to notice.

It is in the interest of all concerned to make the viewer/reader's work easier wherever possible. We gain a friend whenever the user of the printed piece can find, absorb, and understand information fast. This is why we should make the structure of the piece evident, so the scanner can recognize the elements at first glance. We should do everything we can to simplify the material and ensure its recognition. Color can be of great value in this process of classification.

Highlight points worth noting

The attention-getting illusion is based on human curiosity. We all want to be in the know. Finding out about something we were perhaps not intended to know about adds a fillip of zest—if not danger—to the ruse. If the document you are examining had been owned by someone else, they might have annotated it with their own thoughts in the margin or highlighted it in the reading.

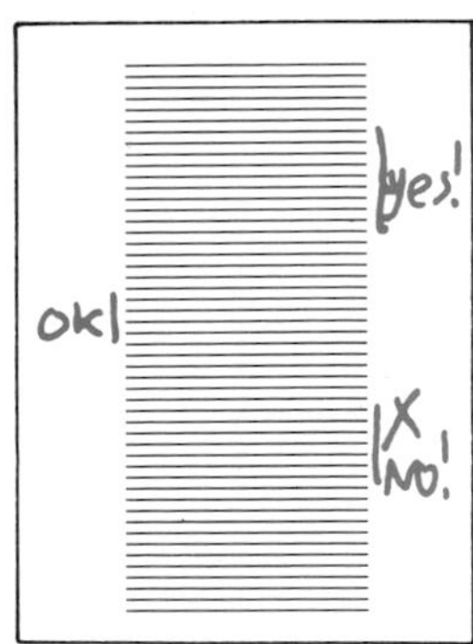

Write comments in the margin. Print them in blue, like the one above.

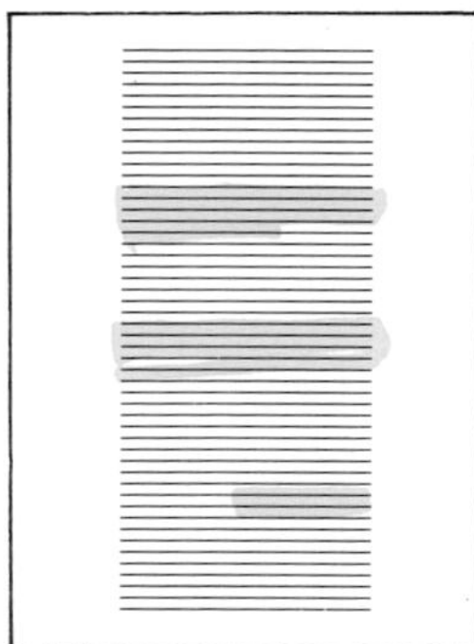

Use highlighter to mark important passages. Yellow is the expected color, but pink, orange, or light blue are also believable.

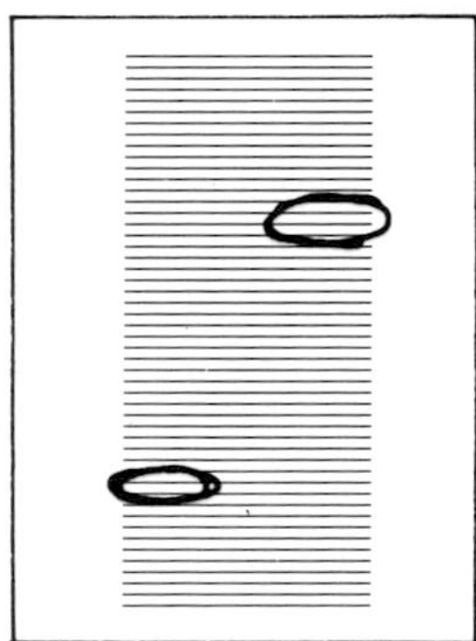

Circle significant words or phrases in the text in "red crayon."

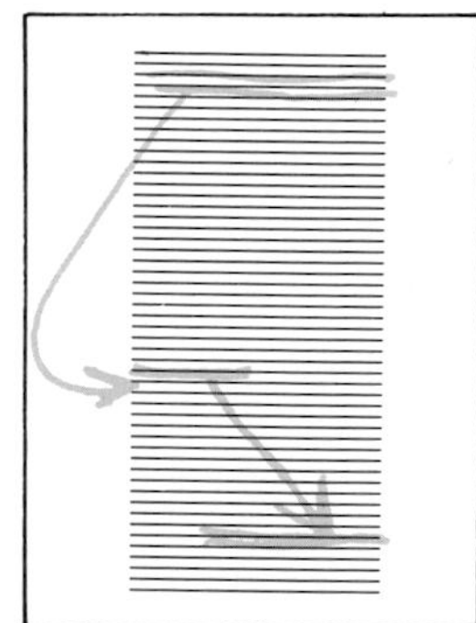

Lead arrows from one item to a related one. Use light blue or pale green so that the text covered by the color retains legibility.

Personal handmade notes such as these are irresistible. The success of the trick—and trick it is—depends on the faithful reproduction of the handwriting and annotation in facsimile of the original. It must not appear mechanical, or it will not only fail but will put the veracity of the entire publication in question.

Identify summaries or introductions

In most documentation, each segment often starts with an overview of the contents and ends with a summary. If these information units look different, they can be found faster. They can be studied or skipped. And because they are different, the rest of the chapter look that much shorter and less threatening.

Such handling should not be reserved for summaries or introductions, of course. Any class of information that can be usefully separated from the main body of the text should be. Consistency of application as well as of color is the key to success. Running some in blue, others in brown, would be more confusing than doing nothing and leaving it all in plain black.

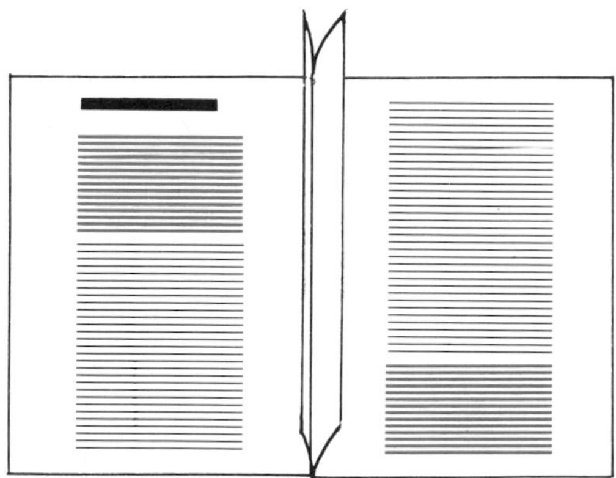

To distinguish the introduction and summary, run the type in color. But be sure to make it bold enough to carry sufficient color to make it strongly visible.

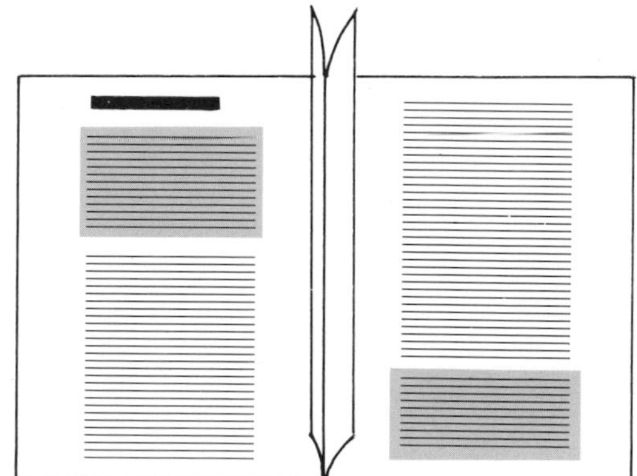

Distinguish the introduction or summary (or any other similar recurrent feature) with a color panel. Make the color pale enough not to jeopardize legibility.

Define change-revisions

The vertical bar commonly placed alongside change revisions that replace obsolete or changed information in technical documents stands out more effectively in color, because it is unexpected.

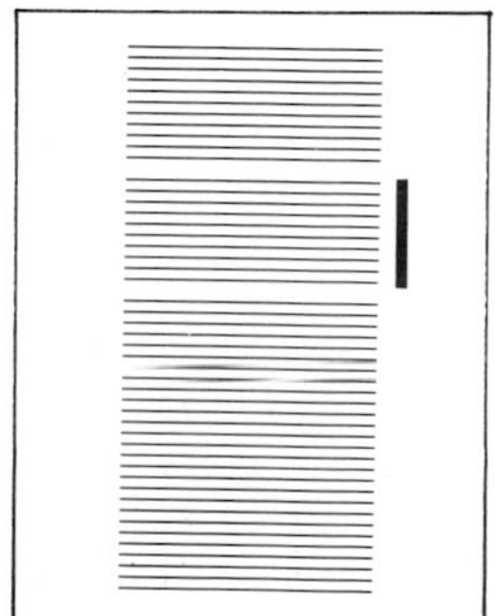

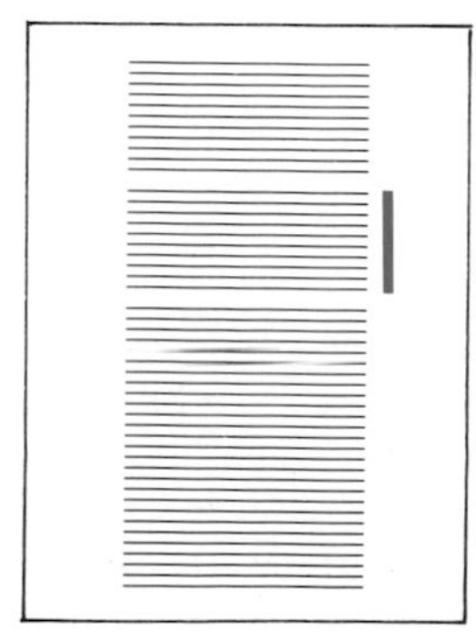

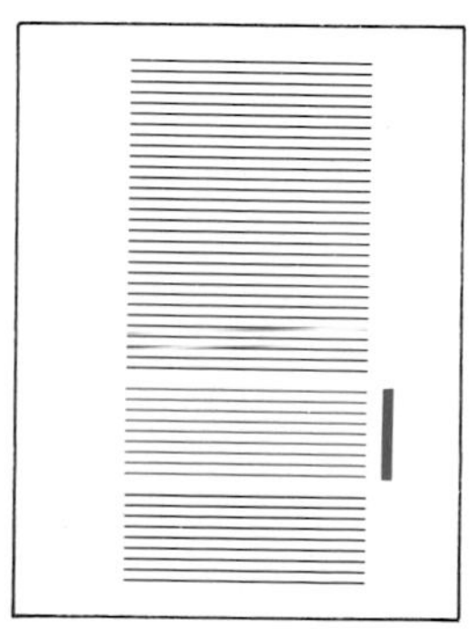

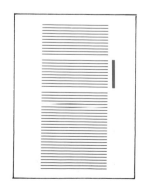

6. BLACK-AND-WHITE PICTURES

Adding color for meaning or dramatic effect

Since this chapter is mostly concerned with *halftones*, a definition is in order here. A halftone is a photomechanical reproduction of continuous-tone copy, such as a photograph. Gradations of tone are created by the relative sizes and density of tiny dots produced by photographing the original copy through a screen of fine, crossed lines. The number of lines per inch determines the fineness of the dots: coarse reproduction, as in newspapers, requires fewer dots per inch (sixty-five is usual) than normal magazine quality (133 or 150), but higher resolution is demanded for fine offset reproduction (200 or even 300). Clearly, the finer the dots, the better the detail and tone values of the reproduction.

Top: an enlargement of a black-and-white halftone of an eye. Above: a much greater enlargement of four-color separations of an eye. Magenta in the top-left quadrant; magenta and black at lower left; magenta, yellow, and black at lower right; magenta, cyan, yellow, and black at top right.

Color can add an unlimited dimension of interpretive capacity to the ordinary black-and-white halftone. It runs the gamut from simple mechanical attention getting to bringing out the subtlety of mood and atmosphere. How you use it and where you use it depends entirely on the specifics of what you are working with and its purpose.

Color can be utilized to focus the viewer's attention to a critical element in the picture. Use a strong color, in a small, concentrated area for maximum effect.

Select the one element that embodies the reason for publishing: the idea readers should care about, the one that they should carry away and remember. Making such a definition—understanding the rationale and defending that decision—is probably the hardest part of the creative process. Once made, the application depends on the graphic material at hand. The common principle underlying all the techniques is simple: for maximum effect, use a strong color on a single small area.

Frame the center of interest. Bright red has been used here because it shows up well against the gray background of a photograph.

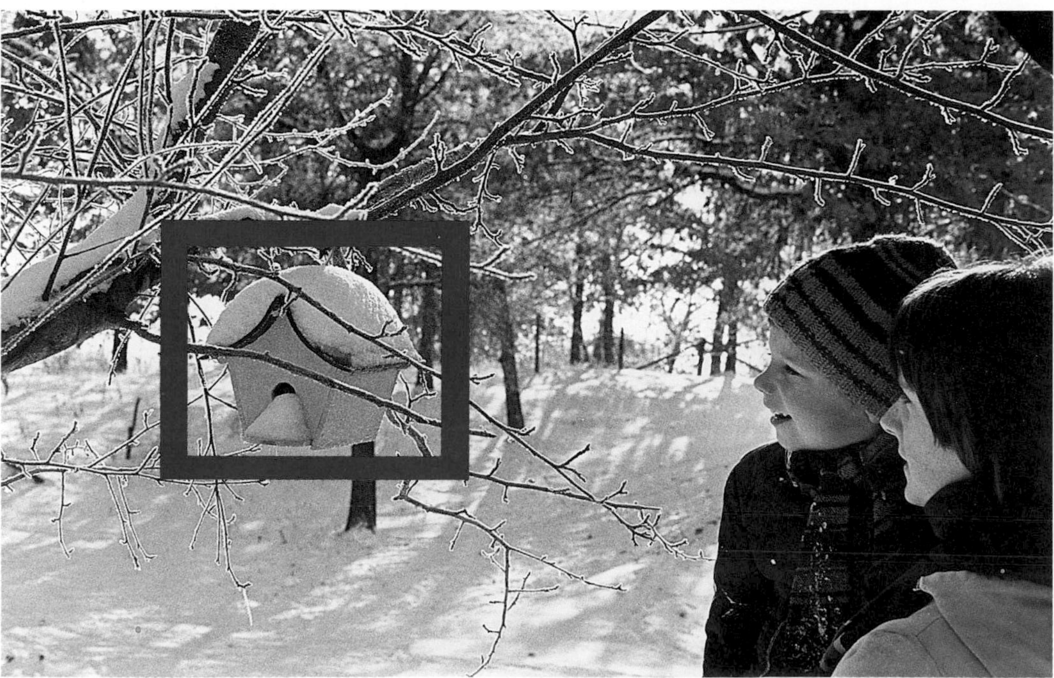

Rohn Engh

Color only the object under discussion. Use a color appropriate to its nature. A little red schoolhouse would look wrong in green. (As Kermit the Frog says, "It's not easy being green." He would look silly in yellow or red.)

Rohn Engh

Bring out the implied relationship of two elements (here the little boy *wanting* the flower) by linking them with color.

Rohn Engh

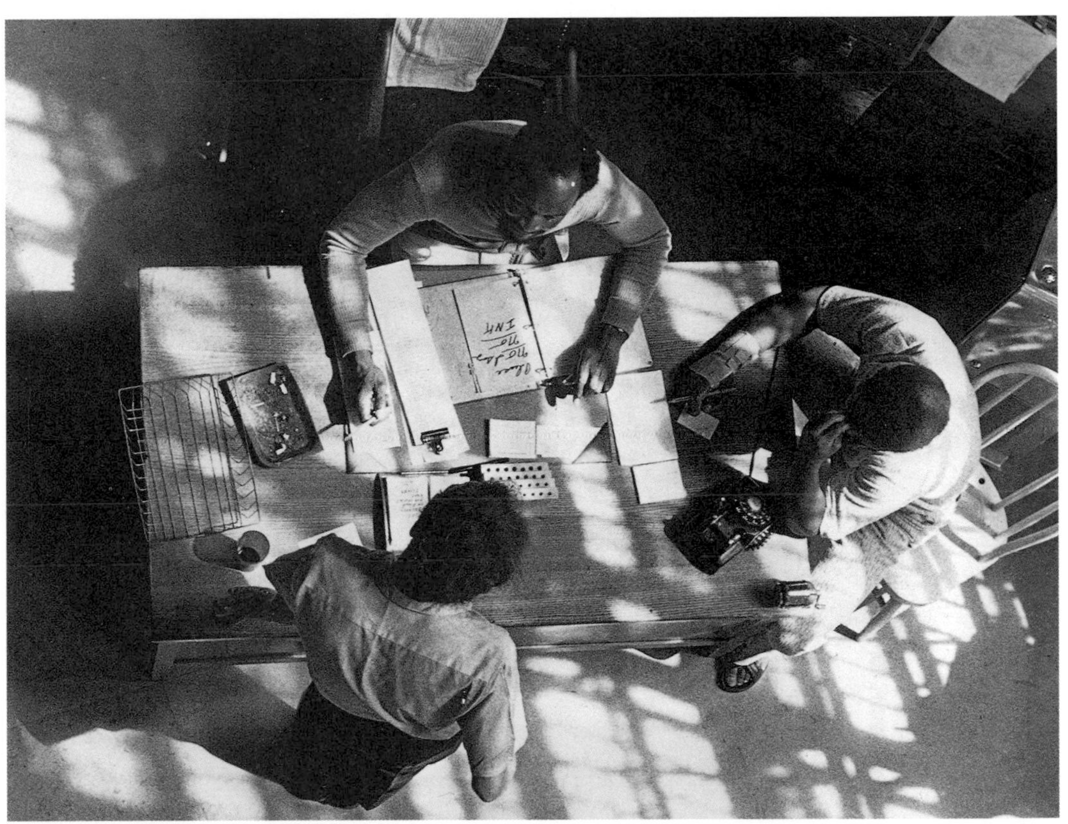

Expose the center of interest by leaving color out. Here the tabletop is dropped out (or "knocked out") from the 40% cyan screen that overprints the halftone.

Rohn Engh

Replace the whole area with a color tone. Here the photo has been made into an "outline halftone" or silhouette, and the blue sky has been added—and expanded—making the snow in the foreground appear the whiter.

Rohn Engh

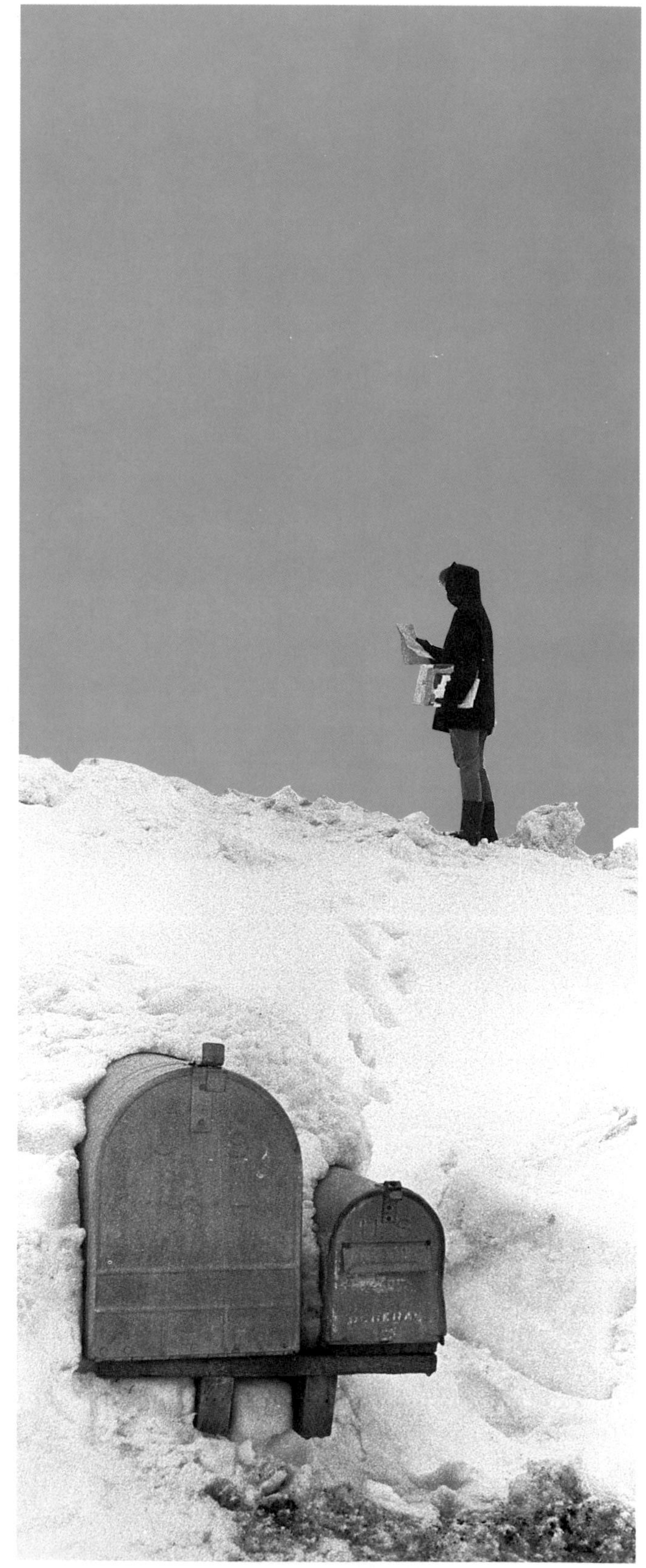

Combining black-and-white photos with four-color process or second-color tints can enrich—or ruin—their effect. Surface treatments must have a reason.

Color is an attractive trap. When it is available, it demands to be used. It must be used with care and circumspection, because it hinders clarity of communication if it is misapplied. How? By directing the attention of the viewer/reader in the wrong direction, often to no more than itself.

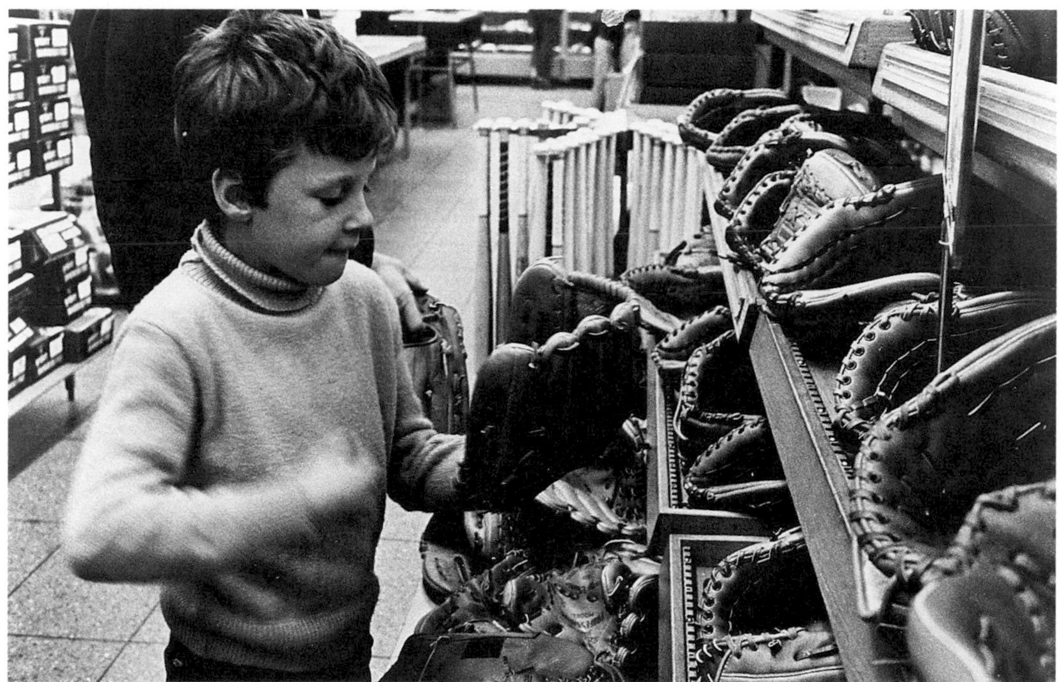

A simple black-and-white original can be used as original artwork and treated as though it were in color. The resulting four-color black-and-white reproduction is far richer than the ordinary halftone.

Rohn Engh

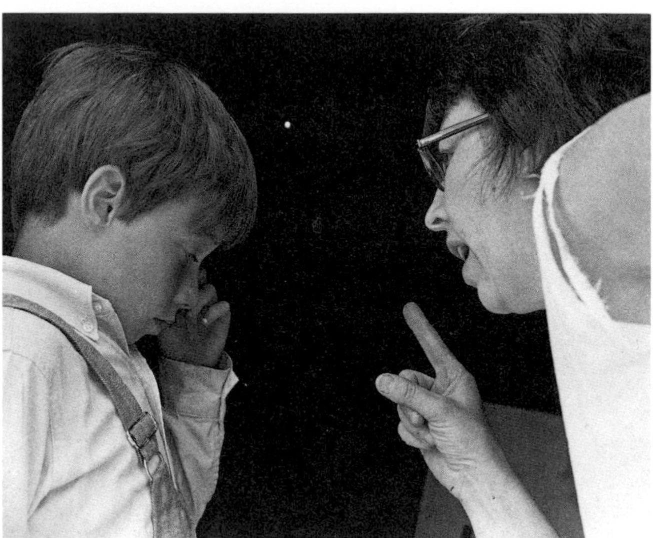

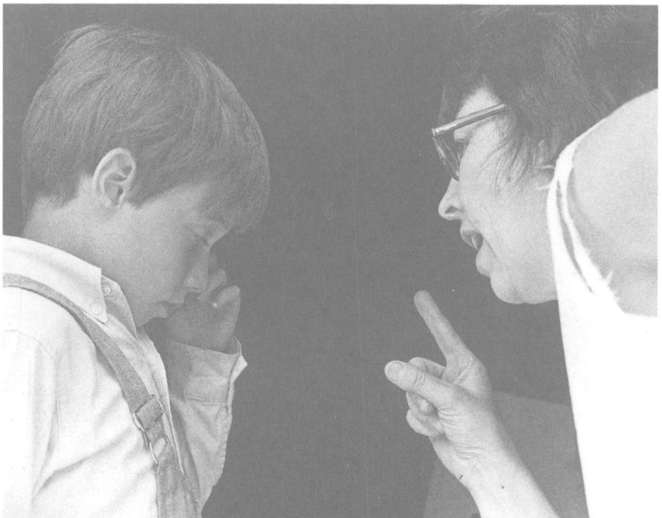

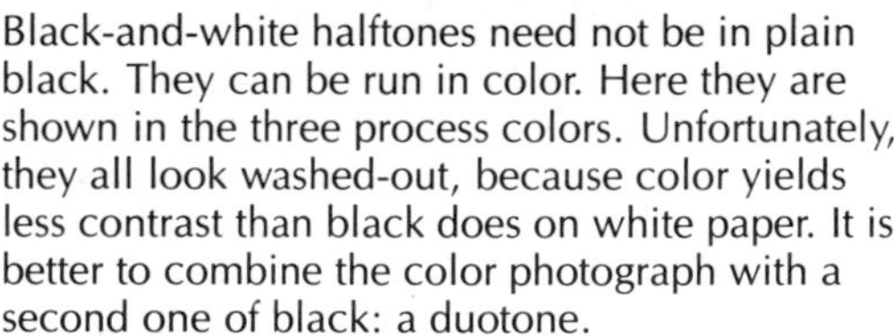

Black-and-white halftones need not be in plain black. They can be run in color. Here they are shown in the three process colors. Unfortunately, they all look washed-out, because color yields less contrast than black does on white paper. It is better to combine the color photograph with a second one of black: a duotone.

Rohn Engh

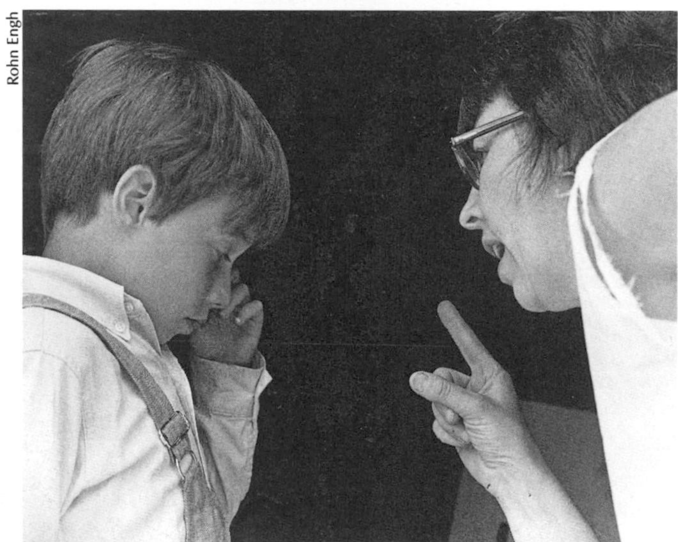

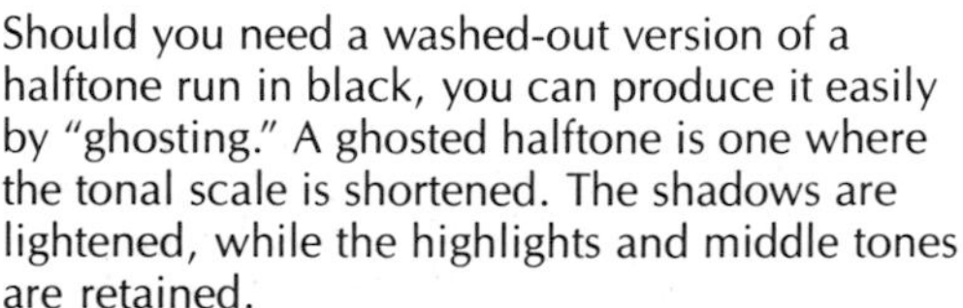

Should you need a washed-out version of a halftone run in black, you can produce it easily by "ghosting." A ghosted halftone is one where the tonal scale is shortened. The shadows are lightened, while the highlights and middle tones are retained.

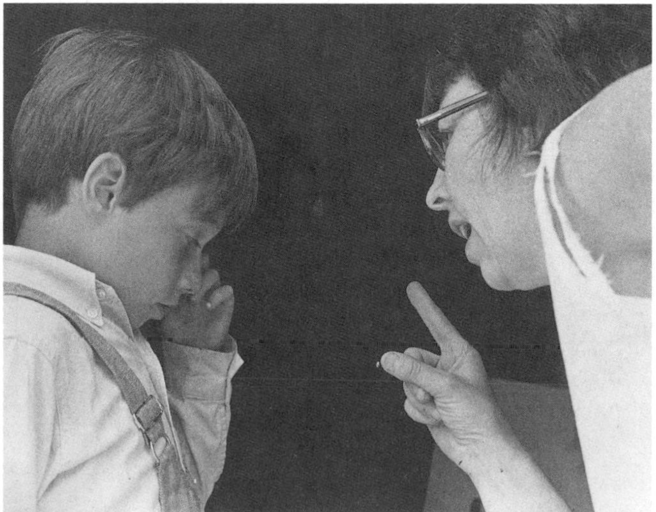

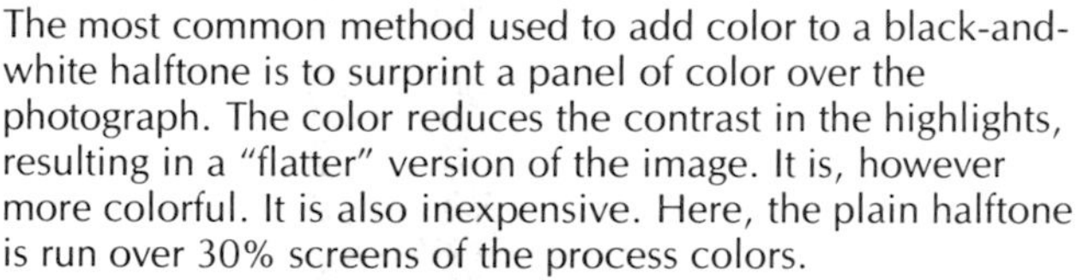

The most common method used to add color to a black-and-white halftone is to surprint a panel of color over the photograph. The color reduces the contrast in the highlights, resulting in a "flatter" version of the image. It is, however more colorful. It is also inexpensive. Here, the plain halftone is run over 30% screens of the process colors.

Duotones and tritones make the most of the color added to halftones, because they enrich the visual result, while improving dramatic detail.

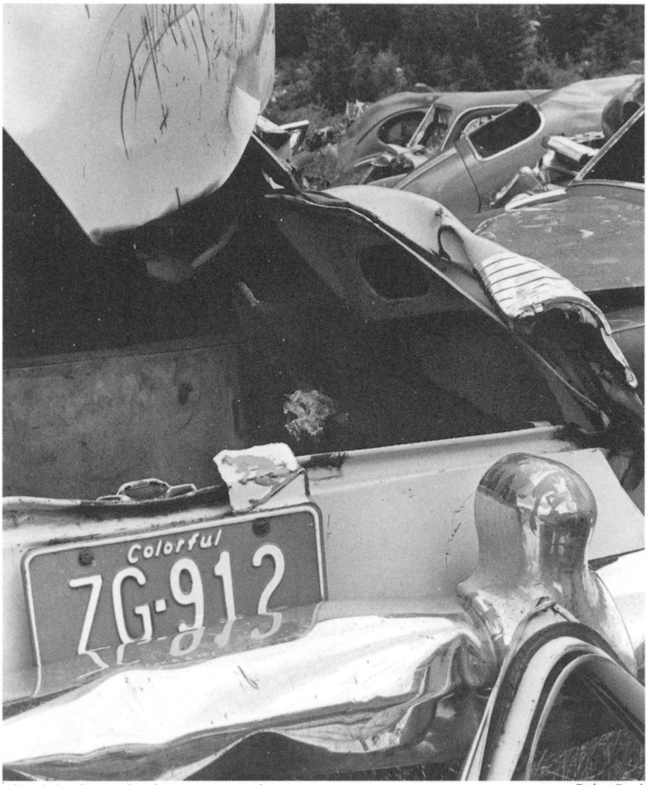

The black-and-white original

Rohn Engh

A duotone reproduces a black-and-white original in two colors. One halftone plate is made especially contrasting in order to pick up the highlights and the shadow areas. A second halftone picks up the middle tones. Printed on top of each other, usually in black and one other color, all contrasts are intensified. An unlimited variety of effects is made possible by varying the color balance and the way each segment is produced.

A "double-dot" duotone is technically similar to the normal duotone, but both segments are printed in black. The subtle variations depend on the exact shade of black ink used: bluish, brownish, greenish, reddish. Most rich-looking black-and-white reproductions printed on fine stock are handled this way. Look at any self-respecting annual report through a magnifying glass.

Black with cyan

Black with magenta

Black with yellow

Magenta with yellow

Cyan with yellow

Magenta with cyan

The black-and-white original
Rohn Engh

Tritones follow the same principle as duotones, using three colors in three halftone segments superimposed on each other. The third color adds tonal capability impossible to achieve in simple duotones. They are more expensive, of course. The effect should be worth it. A less expensive method is to run a duotone atop a panel of a light-screen third color.

Duotones and tritones can be manipulated so that a hue dominates. Such a color can be relied on to tie a group of images together and is often used as a basis for the design of the entire package.

Black, magenta, and cyan tritone

Black, magenta, and yellow tritone

Black, cyan, and yellow tritone

Magenta, cyan, and yellow tritone

Black and magenta duotone on 20% yellow screen

Black and magenta duotone on 20% cyan screen

Black and cyan duotone on 20% magenta screen

Black an cyan duotone on 20% yellow screen

Black and yellow duotone on 20% cyan screen

Black and yellow duotone on 20% magenta screen

Manipulating the texture of black-and-white pictures and combining it with color results in unexpected images that can startle, excite, and intrigue the viewer.

The surface treatment of a halftone can create a variety of effects. The halftone screen itself can affect the look—and interpretation—of the original picture simply by its own degree of resolution. A coarse screen like that used for printing on newsprint usually has sixty-five lines per inch. Such low resolution hides detail. Upscale magazines printed on good stock usually use a finer screen—150 lines per inch—and their high-resolution shows detail far better.

The screens are called "line screens" because they are indeed a mesh of lines through which the continuous-tone original is rephotographed to be made into a halftone. The spaces between the lines is what creates the printing dots. We define the fineness of the screen in terms of number of lines per inch.

Screens, however, do not have to be the normal halftone dots. They can be replaced by all sorts of variations that are technically possible and commercially available. A few of the basic ones are shown in the pages that follow. They are, of course, surface treatments. They manipulate the original in startling ways. Their validity and usefulness depends on the circumstances and the intended function of the illustration.

Mezzotints are line conversions of a photograph produced by shooting the original copy through a textured screen instead of a screen that produces normal halftone dots. A large variety of such screens is available. They produce patterns that make the picture look as if it were a steel etching or printed on linen, woodgrain, or just about any naturalistic texture you can think of. There is another group of screens that is abstract and geometric. These screens produce anything from concentric circles to parallel lines. Using them as duotones or tritones produces some remarkable results.

The black-and-white original photograph is compared to a straight mezzotint version to demonstrate the texture. The other examples are shown in a variety of ways: plain mezzotint on color background as well as mezzotint duotones.

Magenta mezzotint on
80% yellow screen panel

Black mezzotint on
30% cyan screen panel

Cyan mezzotint on
40% magenta panel

Black mezzotint and
cyan mezzotint duotone

Cyan mezzotint and
yellow mezzotint duotone

Magenta and cyan mezzotint duotones
on 30% yellow screen panel

Posterization is a mechanical process that converts a continuous-tone original into one or more layers of single tones. If a halftone is photographed as though it were line art (that is, only 100% black or 100% white, like a line drawing) then all the pale grays that are less than 50% of black drop out or disappear, and all the grays that are darker than 50% of black turn into solid black. The result is known as a line conversion, and it can be extremely striking and decorative.

Posterization takes the same technique several steps further. It scans the original for as many tonal steps as you wish. If you intend to print the result in plain black-and-white, each such step is converted into the appropriately lighter or darker screen. If you are going to print in color, each layer can be printed as a separate color, creating unexpected and decorative results.

Rohn Engh

The black-and-white original has been converted into a four-step posterization: 20%, 40%, 60%, and 80% steps.

The four black-and-white steps have been run here in process colors: 20% is in yellow; 40% is in cyan; 60% is in magenta; 80% is in black.

To illustrate the variety of effects possible just by changing colors, here is the same posterization now run in: 20% black; 40% magenta; 60% cyan; 80% yellow.

This example shows another arbitrary change in colors: 20% cyan; 40% black; 60% yellow; 80% magenta.

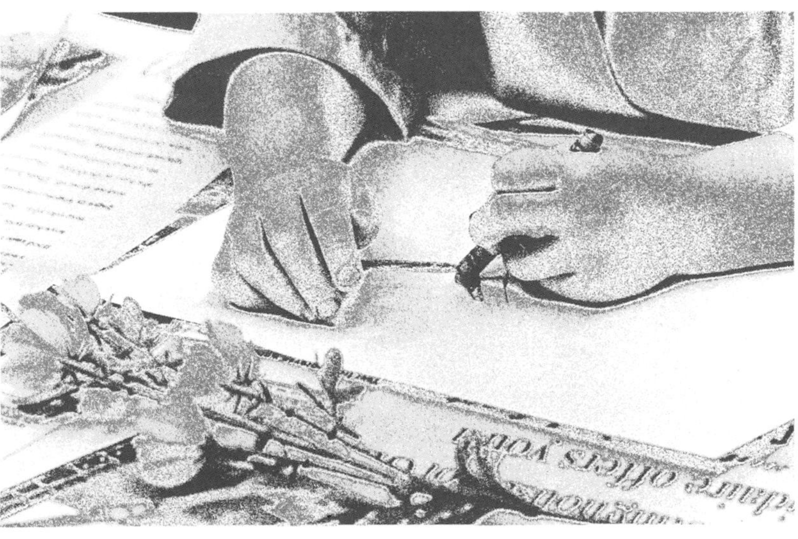

Drawings lend themselves to embellishment with color more effectively than any other visual elements. But, as in all color use, there has to be a reason for using color.

Representational art (drawings, sketches, renderings, diagrams, pictures, cartoons) can be produced in an infinite range of techniques. At the most complex extreme, it can be rendered in full color like a painting. As such, it must be reproduced in process colors, using the same techniques required to print photographs in color. At the other end of the spectrum, representational art can also be produced as a simple drawing using black line, without tone or tint. Clearly, there are any number of variations between these two extremes.

In the black-and-white version, the doorway is there, but it is not interpreted as important. Assuming that the doorway is intended to be the focal point, it needs to be made noticeable.

In the two-color version, the color draws attention to itself. The doorway is seen before its surroundings.

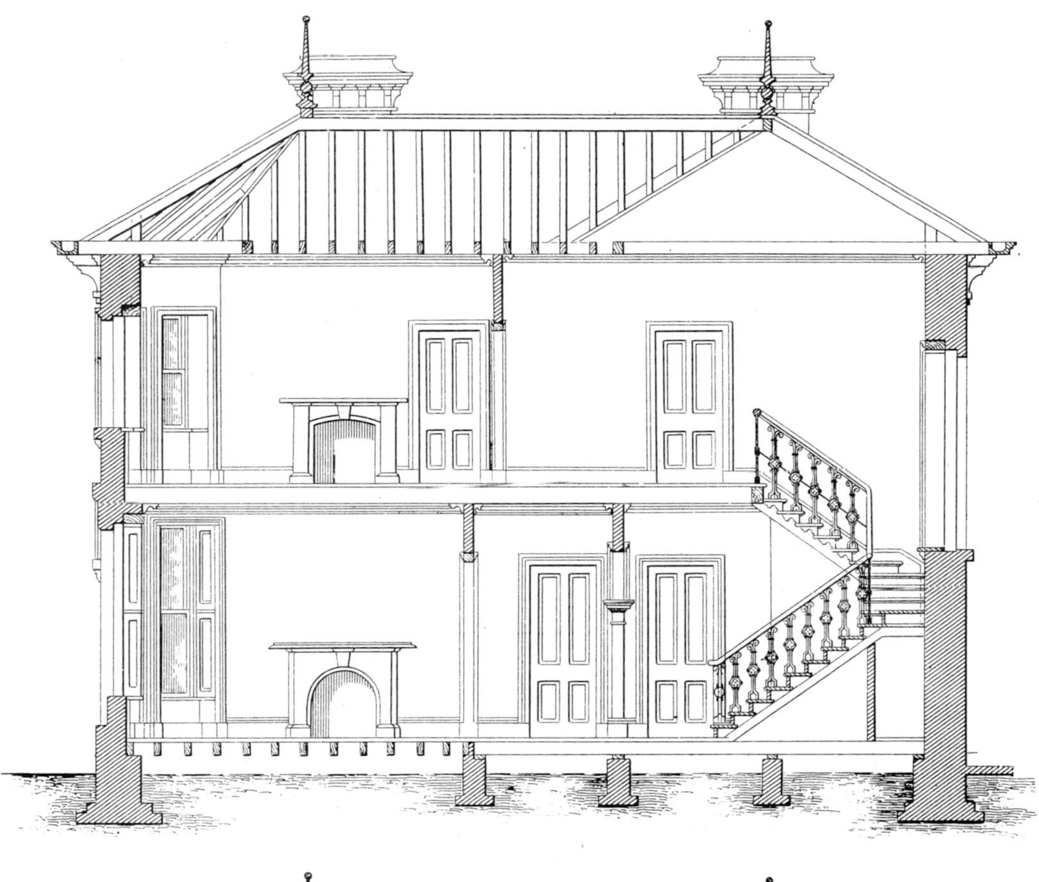

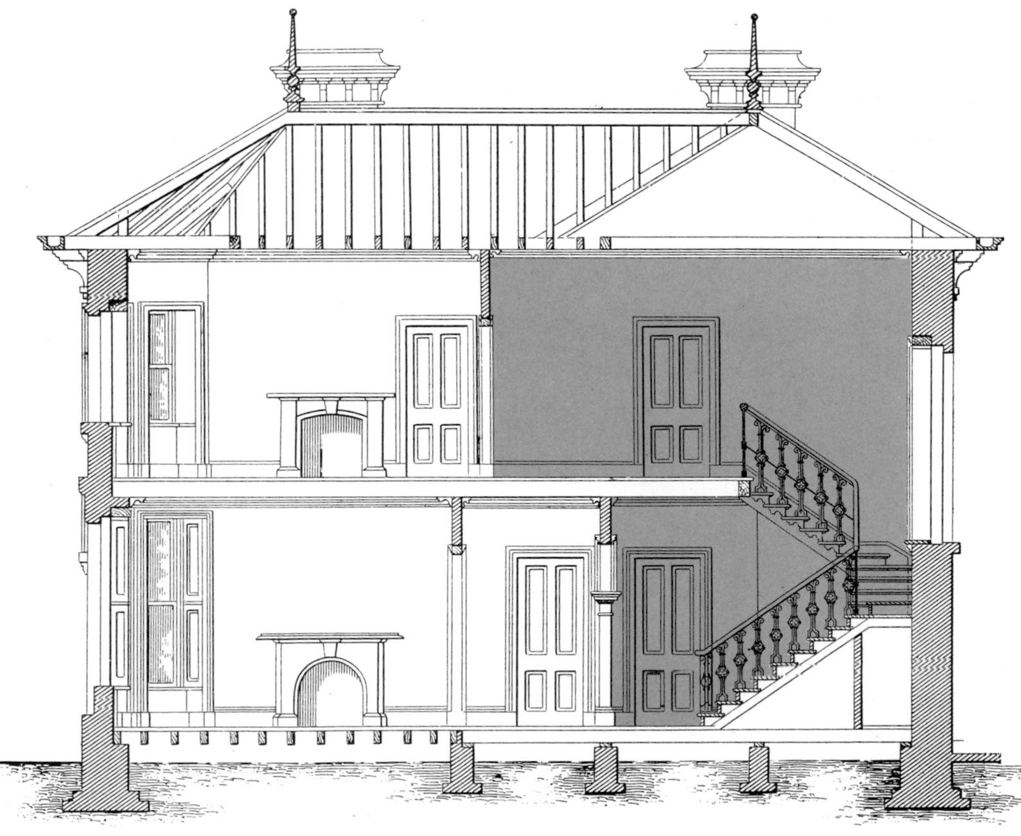

A complex drawing requires explanation. Color can help. This section through a house is taken from *Cottage, Lodge and Villa Architecture* (London, 1849). Assuming that we intend to remodel the hall and stairway, the pink helps to attract the viewer's attention, while accurately defining the extent of the proposed revisions.

Color can be applied to technical drawings in such a way that the viewer notices the aspects we want them to see. As such, color is a tool used for editing.

You can use color to point to what should be deduced from a diagram. It can help the viewer to understand the important characteristics. The more complex the installation, the more useful does color become, if it is used as an explanatory visual code. What it is to explain, of course, is at the heart of the editing and communicating process.

In the following example, color has been used in three distinct ways. Each answers a different question:

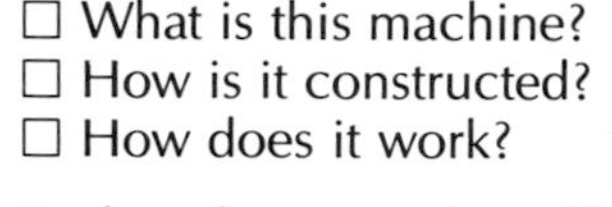

- ☐ What is this machine?
- ☐ How is it constructed?
- ☐ How does it work?

Each makes sense in a different way, so they can all be called correct. The communicator must decide which angle is the most significant to this publication's specific audience.

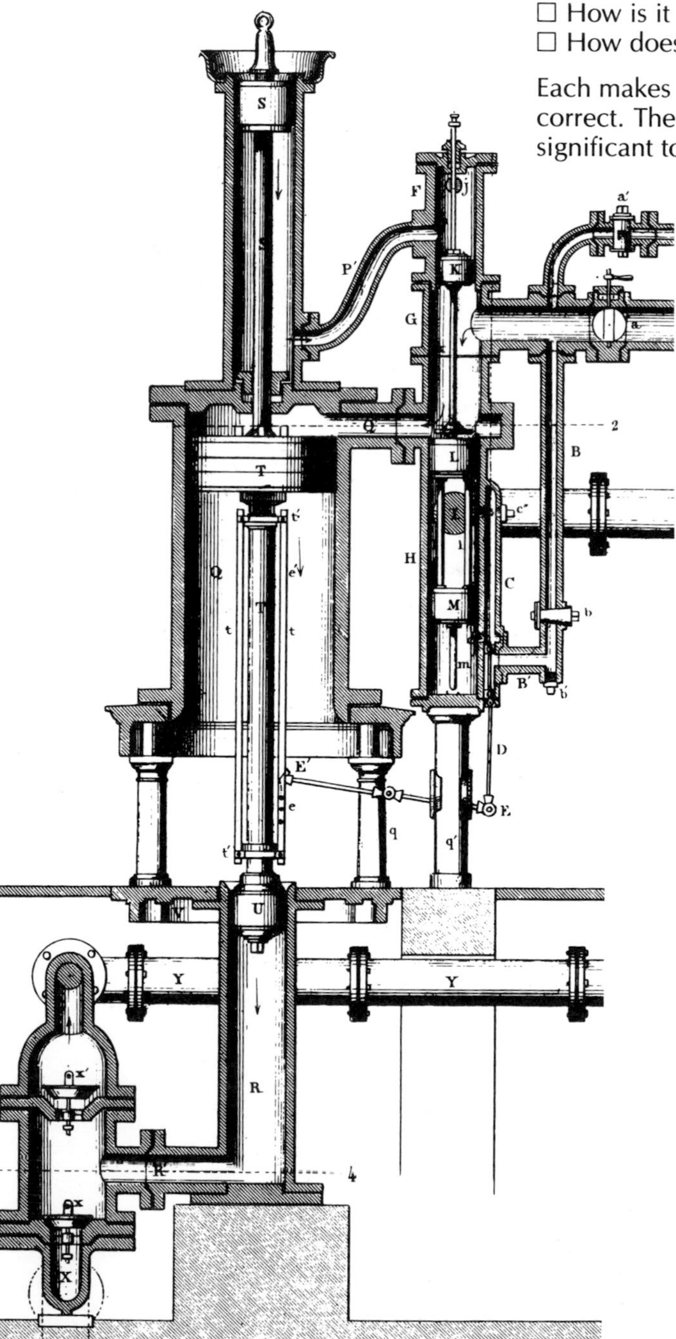

What is this machine? The diagram is delicately engraved on steel and demands leisure to study and analyze its intricacies. It is a detail from a section through Reichenbach's hydraulic ram in the saltworks at Illfang in Bavaria published in the *Brockhaus Encyclopedia of Technological Knowledge* (1857). To the uninitiated, it looks no less awesome than a diagram of more contemporary technology. (If you insist on detail, check the caption.)

15. Durchschnitt der ganzen Maschine: A. Zuflußrohr der Kraftwasser, B. Nebenrohr aus A zur Speisung der Steuerung, B'. Verbindungsrohr mit C, dem Steuerungscylinder, D. Kolbenstange der Vertheilungs- oder Steuerungskolben in C, EE' Hebel für die Kolbenstange D der Vertheilungskolben, F, G und H. Cylinder für die Wechselkolben K, L und M, I. Knie für das Abflußrohr N, K, L und M. Wechsel- oder Gegenkolben von Bronze mit einer Liderung von Zinnringen, N. Abflußrohr der Kraftwasser, P. Wechselcylinder, Q. Treibcylinder, Q'. Verbindungsrohr, R. Cylinder für das Druckwerk der Soole, S. Gegenkolben, S'. Dessen Kolbenstange, T. Haupt- oder Treibkolben, U. Druckkolben, V. Gußeiserne Bodenplatte für den Treibcylinder, mit Verstärkungsrippen. X. Saugröhre für die Soole, Y. Druckröhre für die Soole, a. Zuflußventil, a'. Lufthahn für das Zuflußventil, b. Hahn in der Seitenröhre B, b' Schraube, um die Röhre B unten zu schließen, cc'. Communication der Röhren H und C, c''. Schranbe, um das Loch, das man, um c bohren zu können, machen mußte, zu schließen, dd'. Steuerungs- oder Vertheilungskolben in der Röhre C, e. Nägel für die Steuerungshebel EE', f. Leitungsstange für den Kolben K, k. Verbindungsstange für die Kolben K und L, ll. Verbindungsstange für die Kolben L und M, m. Fuß der Wechselkolbenstange, qq'. Träger für das obere Werk der Maschine, s. Zinnerne Federringe auf dem bronzenen Treibkolben, t. Steuerungsstangen an der Treibkolbenstange, t'. Böcke derselben, x. Saugventil für die Soole, x'. Druckventil für dieselbe, zz'. Kleine Druckröhren hinter den Ringen s des Treibkolbens

How is it constructed? Each piece of hardware is separately defined by color. If the significance lies in its assembly, then the presentation communicates well. *But*: If the significance lies in the way in which the water flows through, then this rendering is a disaster. Not only does it emphasize the wrong thing, it visually impedes the illusion of flow.

How does it work? The water flowing through the system is clearly indicated in blue. *But*: The assembly of pipe units is ignored. The diagram tells a different story.

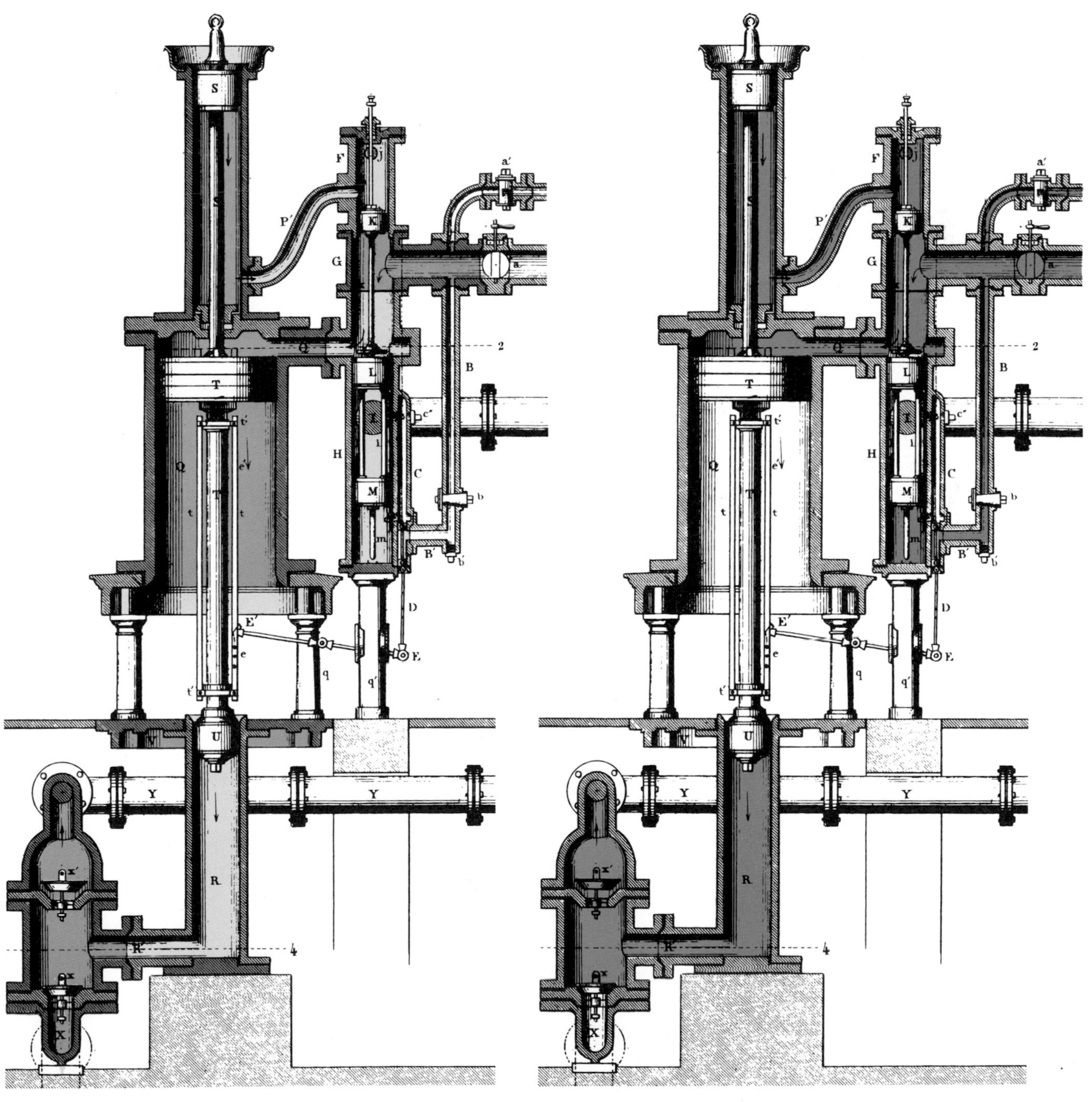

Color used on illustrations can be interpretive or merely decorative. Both are equally valid, though one is more equal than the other.

A simple line illustration has been used as an example of a variety of color applications on the pages that follow. The range of possibilities is infinite when a variety of colors and treatments is available. The palette has deliberately been restricted to plain cyan blue. I want to demonstrate the amazing variety that even such a severe restriction allows. Recommending one technique over another in the following examples is, of course, irresponsible. What is appropriate in one context is inappropriate in another. The decision as to which technique to use depends entirely on what is to be communicated by means of the illustration, be it factually informative or mood creating. This is why the captions describe only technical facts.

The original version: a black-and-white pen-and-ink drawing of Montmartre with the Sacré Coeur, by Emil Weiss

Lines in 100% cyan (process blue)

Lines in various tonal values:
50% screen and 100% cyan, 50% screen and 100% black

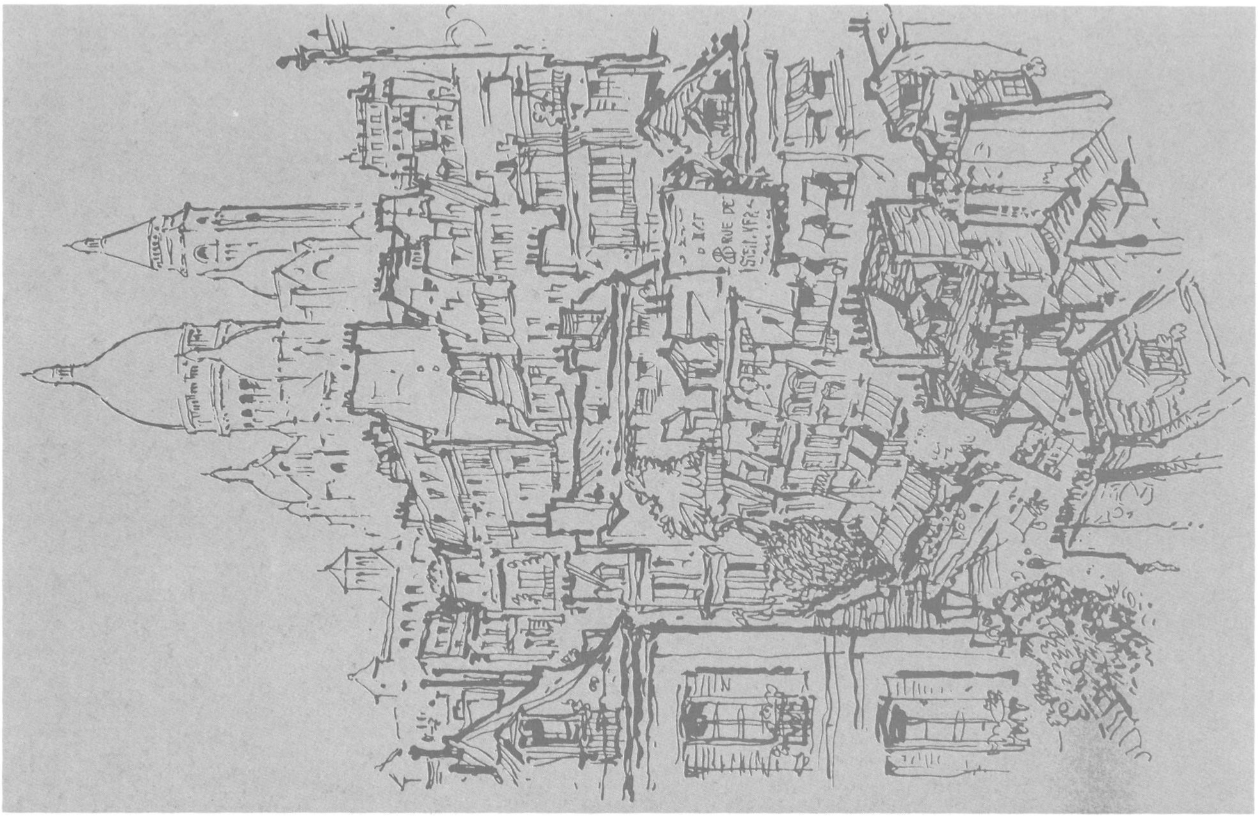

Cyan line on 20% black panel

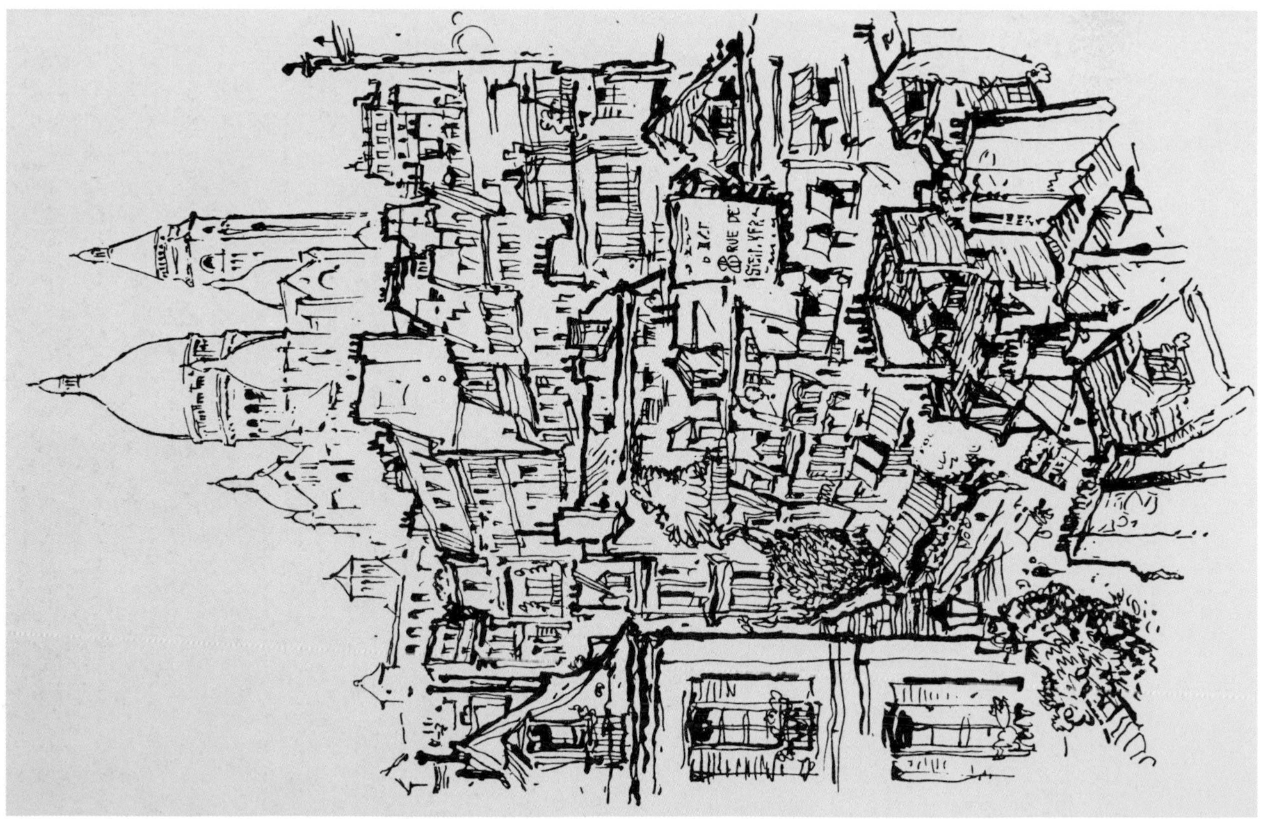

Black line cn 30% cyan panel

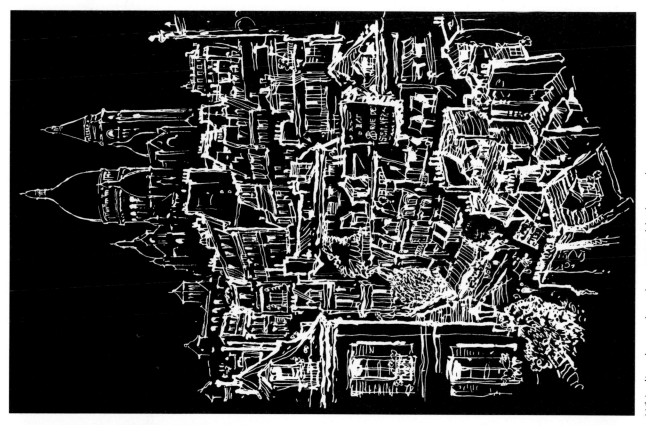

White line dropped out from 100% black panel

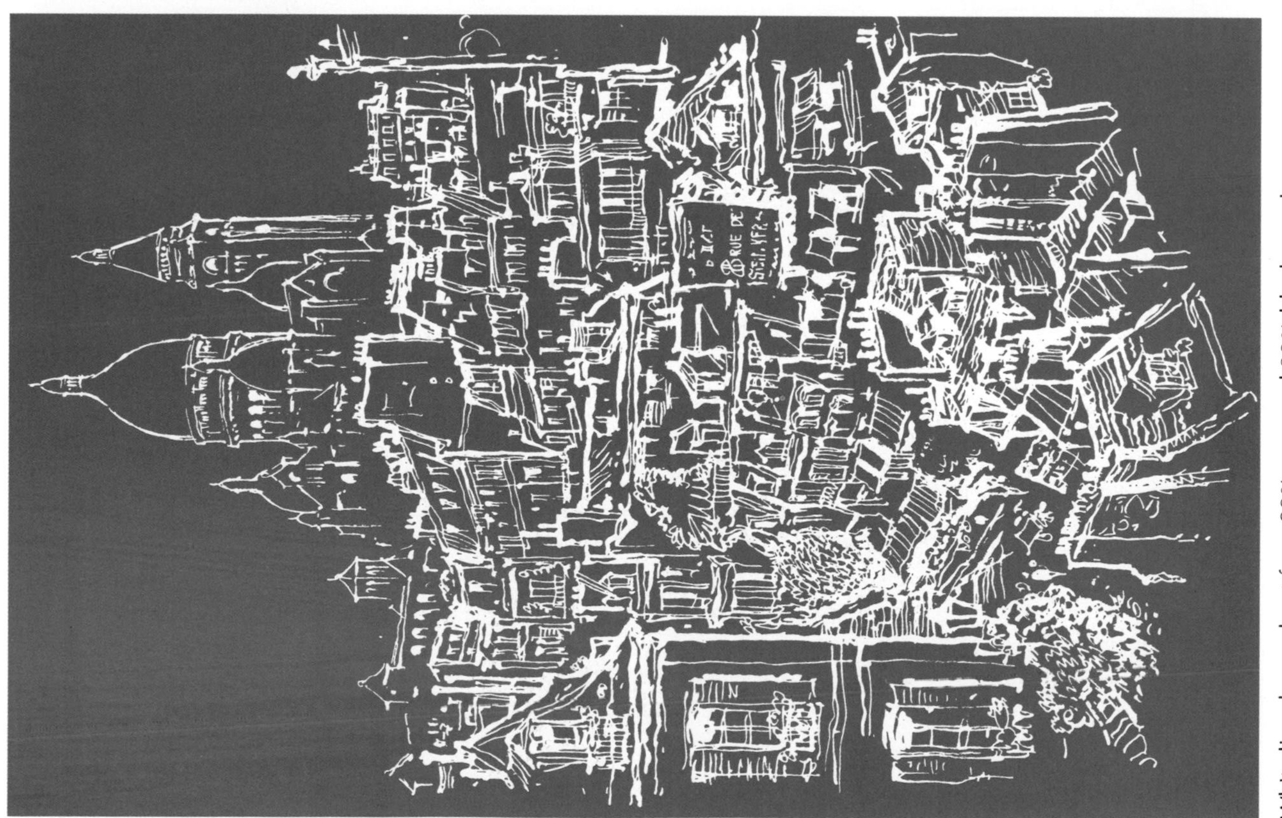

White line dropped out from 90% cyan and 30% black panel

Black line with two tint areas: 60% cyan in the foreground, 20% cyan in the middle distance

Black line with several naturalistic color additions: a drop-out halftone rendering of sky, and four tints to "paint" buildings: 20% and 40% black, 30% and 70% cyan

Black line with 30% black and 30% cyan over the foreground, 40% cyan sky. The cathedral stands out in vivid white contrast

Lines at the top are in 100% cyan. In the next layer, 100% cyan on 30% black. In the large area they are 100% cyan on 60% black. In the lower-right corner the lines are 100% black.

7. COLOR PHOTOGRAPHS

Using color to expose hidden values

We are so used to the convention that ordinary photographs are black and white that we think of them as being normal, and full-color ones as special. But black and white is not normal at all. Photos in black and white are merely a manipulated form of full-color reality. The world is a colorful place. Monochromatic presentations is a technological compromise.

Which version packs more meaning? The added cost of the full-color version is more than recouped by the added value of the information it transmits. And it does this in addition to the visual delight.

Reproducing full-color pictures is, obviously, more difficult than reproducing monochromatic ones. The colors must be safeguarded against exaggeration, though some degree of latitude must be allowed. The effect of looking at a transparency (or chrome) is very different from the effect achieved in printing the same image on paper. One is much brighter than the other. Therefore sensible compromises must be made. To ensure credibility however, you must demand the most faithful reproduction your technology can produce. You must also control the lighting conditions under which comparisons are made.

Pure light comes from the sun. Colors look different in direct sunlight from the way they do in indirect lighting. It is always better to examine colors under a northern light, away from the direct sun.

Hues appear to change when they are seen under natural light, fluorescent lights, incandescent light, or varying degrees of light intensity. Darkness or shade make a difference. So does the background. This is why it is wise to examine colors in an all-white, all-black, or all-medium-gray environment.

The special characteristics of electrical light sources vary and therefore affect the way in which colors appear. Fluorescent lights are especially influential.

Blue and green paints are best under daylight fluorescents, pinks and tans under soft-white fluorescents, and reds and yellows under warm-tone fluorescents.

Areas of color also affect the way that they look. A small swatch is a very different entity from a wall's-worth. The value and chroma appears to change as sizes change.

Printers and prepress production houses have specially constructed booths in which to examine color proofs and originals. The lighting conditions are standardized and controlled, using specially fabricated lightbulbs. Often, the clients have such a facility in their production departments. This way both clients and suppliers can see the identical effect and agree on the required changes based on common understanding.

Time was when pictures in full color were a rarity. Their very colorfulness was reason to stop, look, examine, and study. Now they are so commonplace that this is no longer the case. You can no longer depend on color pictures to give your product anything more than pictures in color. (Unless you handle them with finesse.)

First, you must see what the pictures actually show. Train yourself to see what the viewer is going to see. It is often different from what you—knowing the reasons for using an image—think you are showing. Do not kid yourself that you will have a cheerful page just because you have pictures of outdoor scenes. The sky isn't always blue. Sometimes it lowers, misty and forbidding. Trees and meadows aren't always lawn green. They can be parched, frozen, and in shadow. Roads aren't always gravel driveways. They are usually gray, patched, and embroidered with potholes.

This is not quite as cynical as it sounds. Though the optimist calls the glass half-full and the pessimist half-empty, the realist asks you why you did not use a smaller glass to start with. A realistic attitude leads us to examine possibilities in color pictures with a little more subtlety. Here are a few such considerations.

If you have a fine photograph to work with, one that is worthy of showing large, because its meaning as well as its visual excellence entitle it to be the dominant eye-catching and thought-provoking element, let it speak for itself. Give it the room it deserves, and let it stand by itself in space, so it can be seen unencumbered. And whatever you do, do not "help it" with additional color. Leave it alone. Don't ever dilute its impact by using competing color in the surroundings. When you have good quality materials to work with, less is more.

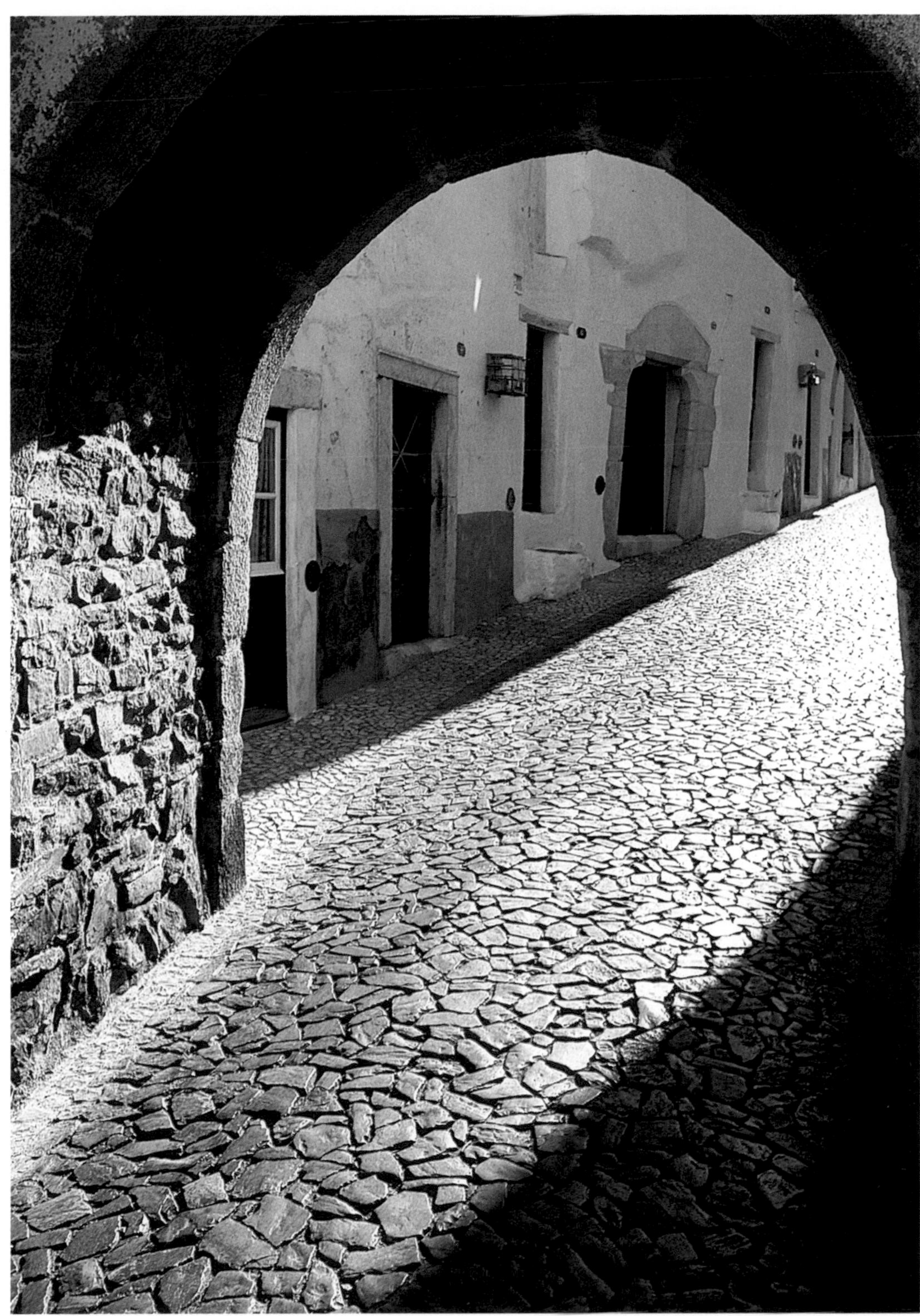

The magnetic force that pulls the viewer through the arch and beyond it, uphill into sunlight, is the emotional quotient that makes this picture grabbing. Its message is clear and self-contained. Tampering with the photograph on the page in order to improve it would only harm it.

When putting groups of pictures together on a page, be aware of their color relationships. They can spoil or enhance each other as well as the cluster as a whole.

Beware of clustering images with various hues. Their colorfulness tends to draw attention away from the subject of the cluster to concentrate it on itself. That can weaken the intended effect.

Pictures of four aspects of water: from stream to waterfall, ocean, and iceberg. Separately, each makes its point clearly and well. Together, they are a listless bunch. The colors spoil the effect. They are indeed "natural," but they do not support each other. Their moods are different.

Shared color ties a cluster of diverse images together.

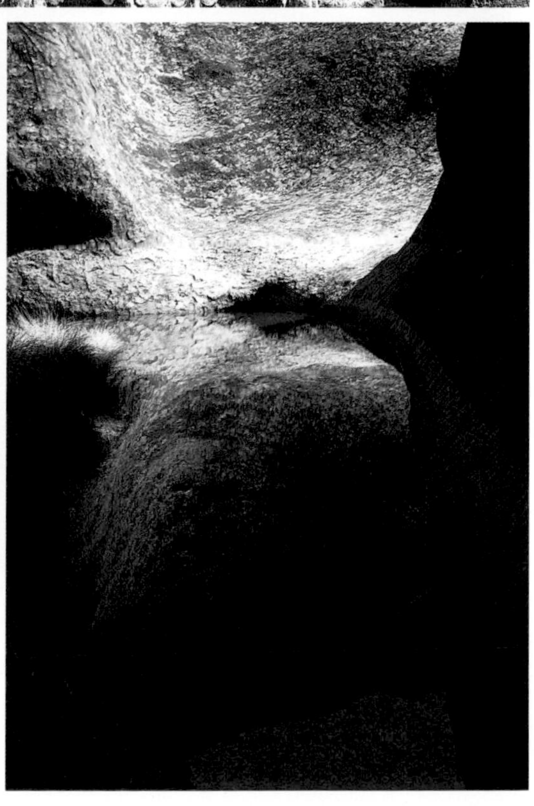

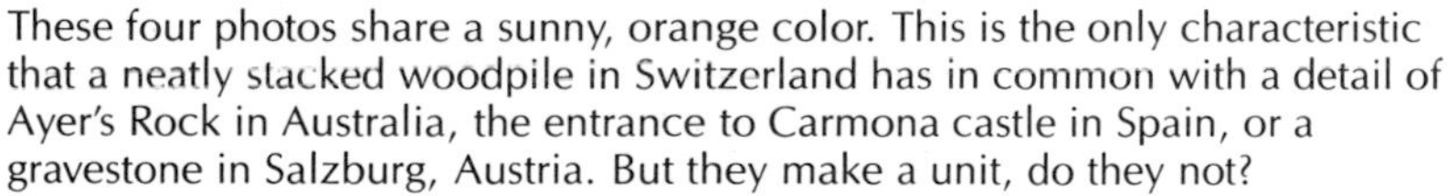

These four photos share a sunny, orange color. This is the only characteristic that a neatly stacked woodpile in Switzerland has in common with a detail of Ayer's Rock in Australia, the entrance to Carmona castle in Spain, or a gravestone in Salzburg, Austria. But they make a unit, do they not?

Where colorfulness itself is the story, then the more vibrant, the better.

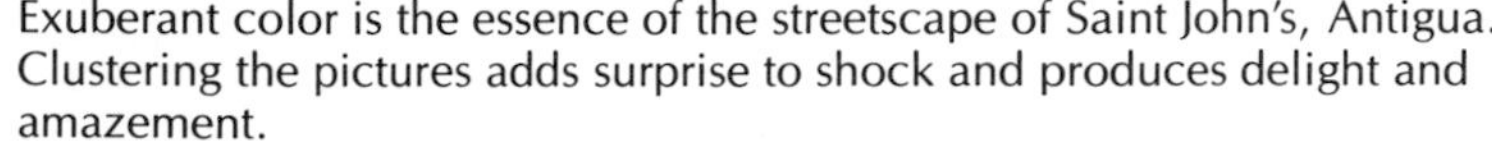
Exuberant color is the essence of the streetscape of Saint John's, Antigua. Clustering the pictures adds surprise to shock and produces delight and amazement.

If your purpose is to gain attention, tampering with the naturalism of the picture can create startling effects. Technology allows—encourages—color manipulation.

Realistic color reproduction to create as natural an effect as possible is the normal way of presenting images. Color, however, can be changed to create deliberately **un**natural effects. This is where today's visual fireworks comes from. The surreal, the impossible, and the shocking are all an integral part of the current vocabulary of visual communication.

The new computerized technology not only allows but encourages experiments. Tricks—especially such visible ones—are always tempting. Use them with discrimination. Resist the temptation except where its result will yield an improvement in the communication value of your product.

It would be folly to attempt to catalog the techniques literally at our fingertips with the right equipment. Suffice it to show eight such eye-openers as examples.

Well-handled naturalism helps credibility. Here is a mechanical drawing of a piece of simple machinery rendered in full color. The dimensionality becomes understandable, especially when shadows are shown. Color and texture help to distinguish iron from wood. There was an advantage to having enough time to draw by hand; yet imagine drawing all that wood grain with a crowquill pen and sepia ink. This is what this student of mechanical engineering had to do around 1885.

Color alteration

If you expect the sea to be Barbados blue, the sand pinkish, and the sky the Caribbean azure, it comes as a nasty shock to see the hues changed out of all recognition.

Posterization

The massive bulkiness of the Galápagos turtles can be made to look even more brutal by the posterization process, which exaggerates values and steps the colors in several degrees rather than as continuous tone.

Mezzotint conversion

The texture of the surface and the seal's coat already gritty with specks of sand is made even grittier by the employment of mezzotint screens instead of the usual halftone screens. The halftone's dots are replaced by rough squiggles.

Pixelization

The image can be reproduced by computer in a mesh of small squares. The size of the individual cells can be smaller or larger. Since there are details in the photograph that need to be seen, the squares used here were kept deliberately small. The larger the cells, the more startling the effect, but the greater the loss of detail.

Ghosting

The focal point is shown in natural balance, but the background is made very pale so that the five-legged chicken stands out more vividly.

Darkening

The focal point remains natural, but its surroundings are darkened so that Mount McKinley is noticed more intensely.

Silhouetting

The simple picture of the grasshopper sitting on his rock is turned into something unexpected by tampering with the outside edges.

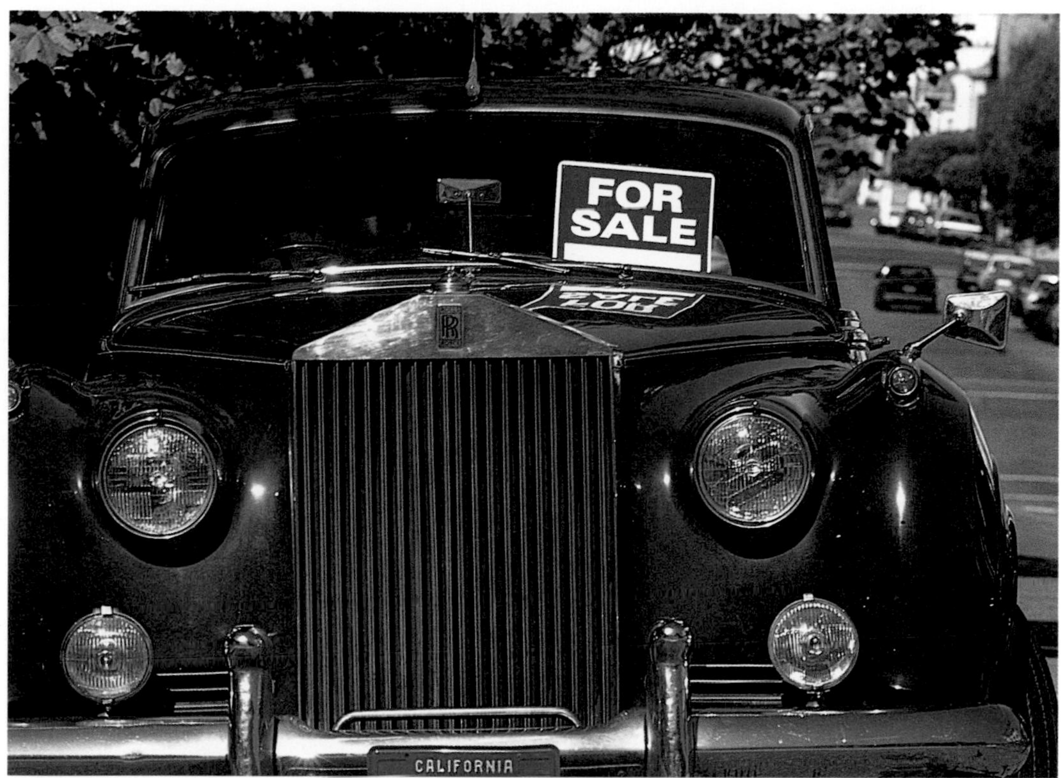

Filtering

Using the full four-color spectrum only in the critical areas of the picture and dropping the black plate in its surroundings focuses the viewer's attention where you want it. The effect is as though one were looking through a hole in a filter.

Even "reflection copy" can be manipulated to help the significant idea jump off the page into the viewer's subconscious. The criterion: validity of purpose.

Reflection copy is merely technical-speak for artwork not already a transparency that can be scanned on a laser scanner for process-color reproduction. Such art, paintings, photographic prints, whatever you want to reproduce, must be made into transparencies, from which the separations (magenta, cyan, yellow, and black) are then created.

The separations can be manipulated so that the eye of the beholder is led to the intended center of interest. It is a matter of controlling and changing color contrast. In the following example, three different ways of distorting the brightness or dimness of the surroundings draws attention to the couple under the umbrella.

Nothing stands out because colors are in tonal balance. It was a gray, cold, rainy day in Keswick, England, when my father drew this pencil and watercolor sketch. Wartime's khaki uniforms added to the general drabness. Only the V for Victory sign stood out bright.

The couple under the umbrella again stand out from the crowd. Here, they appear to have been spotlighted because the surroundings have been made darker.

The couple under the umbrella stand out from the crowd. Their colors are unchanged, yet they appear brighter because the surroundings have been paled down.

Surrounding or combining full-color pictures with flat tints of color must be done with finesse and grace. Gratuitous color for color's own sake is often damaging.

Let good pictures stand alone. Protect them from corrosion. When seen in the same context as a full-color picture, flat tints (or spot color) tend to look somewhat common and cheap. Too often they infect the picture with their own cheapness, unless the tints themselves are used with discretion. This is indeed an area where artistic taste plays an important part.

The blue-footed booby's feet are a gorgeous blue. True, the blue frame attracts the viewer's attention to their blueness. Nobody can miss it. But the price to be paid for the attention-getting device is a philosophical one: Does the blue frame add to their natural elegance?

If you do want to combine color photographs with spot color, then repeat the dominant hue of the photograph in the surroundings. This way the photograph's aura will be expanded over a larger area and its eminence increased. The page will gain unity and dignity from it, too. Yet, even in a simple picture with just three colors in it, the choice depends on your purpose. What you want to say about the picture leads you to choose one of them as dominant. They all make sense. But using purple or green would be ridiculous, would it not?

There are but two dominant colors in this photograph taken in the Olgas in Australia's Outback: the orange of the land and the blue of the sky. The pink in the lady's shirt and blue of her jeans are tiny but significant spots.

The pinkness of the panel directs the viewer to the pink shirt, emphasizing human smallness in these massive surroundings.

The blue panel emphasizes the sliver of sky and thus the enclosure felt by the visitor in the gorge.

The overwhelming scale of the land is expanded by the matching orange-color panel alongside.

APPENDIX
How to specify color

"Let's make this line red and the background blue." We all know what that means, because we all know what red and blue are. But when we get down to specifics, there are any number of varieties of "red" or "blue." Light ones or dark ones, shy ones or aggressive ones, pinkish ones or purplish ones, and which of them are the precise ones you intend to use? How do you pick them? How do you measure them? How do you describe them? How do you instruct someone to produce them? (It matters little whether that "someone" is human or machine. Both need exact nomenclature to generate what you have in mind.) Specifying color—choosing what you want and then communicating it clearly—is a tricky process. If color were simple, it would be easy. But color is anything but simple, once you get deeper than its simplest superficialities. It is not just complex in its technical aspects or in the effects it creates. It is even more complex in the way we talk about it and in the way we control it.

Though surrounded with color, we have not had color under control until the nineteenth century. Before then, dyes and pigments were limited to organic materials, many of which were very rare and therefore expensive. People wore clothes made of fabrics left in their natural colors. Only the rich could afford dyed ones.

Then aniline dyes were discovered, shortly to be followed by the coal-tar dyes, which were developed by Adolf von Baeyer in the 1860s. The first color he produced was purple, and the little snail, Purpura Haemastoma, the marine gastropod of the eastern Mediterranean who sacrificed its life to help kings look properly kinglike, could now live a little longer. Then metallic oxides were

The Dyer, from Jost Amman's Book of Trades, 1568. Hans Sachs's poem mentions green, gray, black, and blue as the colors the dyer uses to dye cloth for merchants.

Jch bin der ſchwartz Farb ein Sůcher/
Ferb den Kauffleutn die Schwabnthůcher
Grůn/graw vnd ſchwartz/ vñ darzu blaw/
Darzu ich auch ein Mange hab/
Daß ich ſie mang fein gell vnd glat/
Auch was man ſonſt zu ferben hat/
Vnd mangen findt man mich allzeit/
Darzu gutwillig vnd bereit.

added to the armamentarium of coloring materials. New synthetics replaced such traditional materials as cochineal (a carmine-colored dye made of the bodies of female scale insects found only on cactuses in Central America) and indigo (the blue dye made by boiling fermented leguminous plants, already used for dyeing mummy-cloth in Egypt in 1600 B.C.)

Today, we live in an increasingly artificial world. More and more colors and combinations of colors surround us, beg for our conscious attention, and impose on our subconscious. Every technology is burgeoning with color.

Yet the way we as people communicate about color is as medieval as the way cloth was dyed. Haphazard. Inaccurate. Personal. Subjective.

Most languages have few names for color.* Most colors other than the basic color-named ones are named to associate with objects that have that shade. Or they describe gradations of the original few names—light brown, dark purple, pinkish; and so forth.

Roget's *International Thesaurus*, fourth edition (1977), lists colors in ten groups, with varying numbers of words to describe each one:

Whiteness:	30
Blackness:	20
Grayness:	45
Brownness:	104
Redness:	140
Orangeness:	45
Yellowness:	88
Greenness:	100
Blueness:	80
Purpleness:	44
	696 words

Only a few of these many words are in general use. The number you might determine as commonly understood probably depends on the size of your own vocabulary and experience in the field of color. The obscure rejects are highly specialized terms. Whatever the total, the number of names still falls far short of the number of colors people can distinguish. (Studies have determined that it is within human capacity to distinguish 7.5 million different colors. Some computerized CRT equipment can produce 16 million.)

Color names other than the obvious basic ones are derivations from other areas:
Violet, lilac, rose, and so forth are flowers.
Cherry, orange, lemon, lime, chocolate, olive, and peach are foods.
Sapphire, turquoise, ruby, and emerald are stones.
Rust, terracotta, cobalt, silver, and gold are minerals.
Vermilion, crimson, and carmine are worms or insects.
Canary and cardinal are birds.
Salmon is a fish.
Purple is a shellfish.
Magenta, Delft, and Siena are places.

*It depends on where you live: The Inuit have more than two hundred names for brown. They have an equally rich vocabulary for different sorts of snow.

What is puce, taupe, or beige? We talk about charcoal, pink, parrot green, myosotis blue, fuchsia, Caribbean blue. What are they? Exactly. Nothing but personal interpretations. Toast is a color. Do you like yours light, medium, or burned? They are inexact, variable, and confusing. They are also deeply influenced by current fads and fashions.

Even the basic terms defining groups of colors are imprecise and vague. They are easier to describe than they are to define. For instance:

Cool colors: Hues from the blue, green, and violet families; also pale yellows, whites, and light pinks. They subdue.

Warm colors: Hues from the yellow, orange and red families; also intense greens and violets. They excite.

Somber colors: Dark blue, dark green, dark purple, dark gray. They depress. (*Sombra* means shadow in Spanish.)

Bright colors: Pure hues with high chroma and reflectance.

Tints: Hues that result from adding white to a pure color. Tint stepping means adding white to paints to produce paler versions.

Tones: Hues dulled by the addition of black, gray, white, or the complementary color. Also known as neutralized hues. They are quiet.

Pastels: Hues that result from adding white to a tone. They are pale, cheerful, but a bit washed-out.

Many theories of color organization have been devised. They bring order out of chaos, since they are scientific studies of wavelengths, pigment concentrations, and so forth. They are vital to the understanding and production of balanced technology. Even outlining them, however, is beyond the scope of this how-to book. We gratefully acknowledge their existence and use their results. In practice, all we need is a good way to communicate about colors.

There are four widely used systems of nomenclature: the Munsell system, which is based on a theory of color; the Pantone® Matching system* (the PMS colors), which started as a commercial system of mixing printing inks but has grown into an internationally accepted means of practical communication; the Natural Color system, based on the way color is perceived; and the CIE Notation system, which is based on accurate measurement of light.

The Munsell system

Why should you bother to understand it? Because most people who use color do. Because it is accepted by the U.S. National Bureau of Standards, the Optical Society of America, the Japanese Industrial Standards for Color, the British Standards Institution, the German Standard Color System, and many others. Because it uses terminology that is accurate when understood in its context. Most of

*Pantone, Inc.'s check standard trademark for color reproduction and color reproduction materials.

all, because you can go to any supply-shop and buy sheets of colored paper (called Color-Aid) coordinated with its system. You can use them as a frame of reference.

The Color-Aid paper comes in 220 colors: twenty-four basic hues, four tints, and three shades of each hue. Also sixteen grays, black, and white. They are labeled, for instance, OYOS2 or an equivalent number, which you cross-check in the swatchbook. (Orange-yellow-orange shade 2, in this example.)

The swatchbook is a good $16.00 investment.

The full-sized sheets of silkscreen flat matte color measure 18 × 24 inches and cost about $1.65 apiece.

The system devised by Albert H. Munsell is a precise language, a method of notation, as well as a method of comparison. It is readily applicable to scientific and technical purposes because of its accuracy. The simple code consisting of one letter and three numbers, can describe any color accurately—or accurately enough for practical purposes of identification.

The Munsell system is based on five colors: red, yellow, green, blue, purple.

Each of these colors has three characteristics:

1. *Hue:* The distinction of one color from another. It is shown clockwise as a circle around the equator of the Munsell Globe. Hue is determined by a spectroscope, which differentiates colors by measuring the spectral wavelength composition. This composition produces the perception of greenness, pinkness, redness. Color measurement is done by a spectrophotometer, which measures light reflectance. It converts the color into the dominant wavelength and defines brightness and purity.
2. *Value:* The measurement of relative darkness to lightness. It is shown with white at the head and black at the foot of the scale forming the vertical axis of the Munsell Globe. Value is determined by a photometer, which measures darkness in degrees.
3. *Chroma (or saturation):* The measurement of the relative weakness or strength; that is, purity of a color. It is shown horizontally from neutral at left to maximum saturation at right in branches from the central axis leading out to the perimeter of the Munsell Globe. Chroma is determined by comparison to Maxwell Disk, which shows intensity in a series of steps.

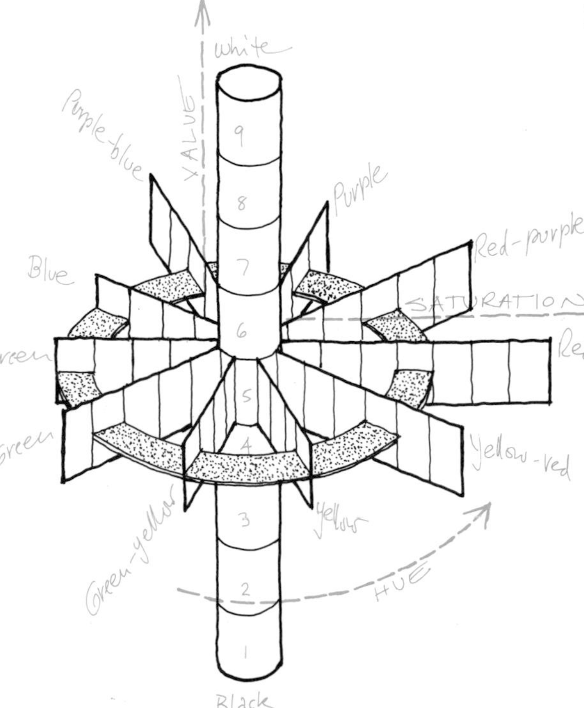

The Munsell Globe, sometimes called the Munsell Tree, is shown here in diagrammatic form. The value (from 1, black, to 9, white) forms the vertical axis or trunk. Hues are arrayed as around the center. They go from yellow to red, purple, blue, and green back to yellow. Their purest form is at level 5. Above they become paler, below they become darker. Chroma or saturation is shown by steps leading out from the axis, with the minimum or gray at the center and the brightest possible at the perimeter. Saturation varies not only with each hue but also with each value step.

The Pantone system

Pantone is a registered trademark for color reproduction materials. The Pantone Matching System is a system of color standardization developed originally for printers and designers, but now accepted throughout industry and in computerized technology. It consists of more than 533 colors, each numbered or named.

It is a precise and reliable method of selecting a color and communicating about it. Accurate color matching is made possible, and the system is versatile enough to allow application to most requirements, from on-screen use to signs painted on trucks, let alone any kind of printing technology. It is also one of the basic color methods used in software.

The colors are available in a range of coordinated materials: artists' and designers' materials of all sorts, such as markers, papers, and transparent film overlays; also printers' inking formulas, as well as:

☐ A small (2-x-4-inch) swatchbook of fifty-five color sheets on uncoated paper, which costs $12.00.
☐ Sheets of uncoated paper, which also contain a printing guide for a variety of effects, including adding black screen, which costs $4.50.
☐ The Specifier, which contains all the colors on coated and uncoated stock as tear-out chips, which costs $79.50. (Colors on coated stock appear more brilliant, because the coating on the surface prevents the ink from being absorbed into the fabric of the paper. The color numbers are followed by a U or a C standing for uncoated or coated paper.)
☐ The Tint Selector, which shows the effects created by 10% to 80% screens of five hundred colors, which costs $79.50.
☐ The Color-and-Black Selector, which shows eighty-one colors in percentage combinations with black, which costs $79.50.
☐ The Process Color Selector, which displays nine thousand hues composed of 10% through 100% screen combinations of the process colors, which costs $195.00.
☐ The Process Color Simulator, which matches Pantone colors in process printing, which costs $195.00.
☐ The Two-Color Selector, which shows a comprehensive display of two color mixtures in 100% as well as 10% to 70% combinations, which costs $95.00
☐ The Professional Color System, which has 1225 standardized colors for people who work with materials other than printing inks (cosmetics, paints, fabrics, carpeting, ceramics, and so forth), which costs $125.00.

The purpose of citing this list of the currently available Pantone materials is not to create publicity for an already well-known service or product but to demonstrate their scope, which makes them so widely accepted and used.

Note that the various Pantone products and systems are not generic, and that they are protected by copyrights and registered trademarks. They can be used to communicate color selection. Any reproduction of a color accompanied by its identification intended for use in corporate manuals or graphic color standards, however, should first be checked out with their Trademark Control Department, 55

Knickerbocker Road, Moonachie, N.J., 07074; telephone (201) 935-5500.

The Pantone Color Institute, 6324 Variel Avenue, Suite 319, Woodland Hills, Calif., 91367; telephone (818) 340-2370, publishes *Color News*. It is a newsletter full of fascinating information. Volume 3, number 4 (December 1988) cites $5.00 as the price per copy.

Natural Color system

The Natural Color system is the Swedish standard color notation system, widely used throughout Scandinavia, Switzerland, and Great Britain. It is a color language based on the way colors are perceived. It is founded on the fact that there are six elementary colors that stand alone: yellow, red, blue, green, white, and black. All other colors can be described by their degree of resemblance to two or more of them. The theory, proposed by Ewald Hering of Germany in the late nineteenth century has been developed by Anders Hard of Sweden.

Organized by color in percentage increments from light to dark and dull to brilliant, the system is shown in a color atlas with sixteen hundred color samples. Each color is located by two reference numbers. The first double number describes its *nuance* (its degree of resemblance to black, then its closeness to chromatic purity). The second reference describes the *hue* (the proportional degree of resemblance to two chromatic colors, in percentages—always adding up to 100). A number of other subtleties are, of course, inherent in the system.

What makes it so "natural" is the way in which the colors are grouped. The relationships are instinctive, arranged the way people tend to think of colors. What makes it a useful tool for color specifiers is the fact that manufacturers of industrial materials, licensed by the International Commission on Illumination to be members of the Color Dimension Association, publish a catalog that presents their products organized by color. The dependably standardized color nomenclature eases the search for the right material. Though the system has not yet penetrated the printing industry to any great extent, its usefulness is being noticed and its influence is growing, especially in the corporate-identity area. There, it is found to be immensely practical in defining the required colors across the whole spectrum of corporate requirements. A formula guide (747XR) is available to translate the PMS ink colors into equivalent Natural Color system nomenclature.

The Colour Atlas, index fans in chromatic order, paper samples, and other materials are available from Edgebrite Ltd., 60 High Street, Bridgnorth, Shropshire WV 164DX, Great Britain.

The CIE Notation system

The Commission Internationale de l'Eclairage (International Commission on Illumination) in 1931 established a set of standards that are not based on matching physical color samples but rather on accurate measurement of light.

The colorimeter measures the light energy and wavelengths reflected by a sample. It defines the intensity of the light (luminance), its hue, and its saturation. Combined, they produce a value of chromaticity.

The chromaticity diagram or "color map" is shown below. The outer boundary of the gray area shows the pure spectrum colors indicated by their wavelength number. (For instance, 578 is yellow, 492 blue-green, 615 red.) The colored area demonstrates the colors printable with process colors, with the purest on the perimeter. At the center is the light source, which combines all wavelengths and therefore creates whiteness. The numbers around the margin are merely an x-y grid for accurate color placement. Tomato red, for instance, is 0.5x 0.35y.

The value of the CIE system lies in its permanence. Color samples, no matter how carefully produced and preserved, tend to fade over time. The precise CIE numbers, however, can be used as controls in the preparation of replacement swatches.

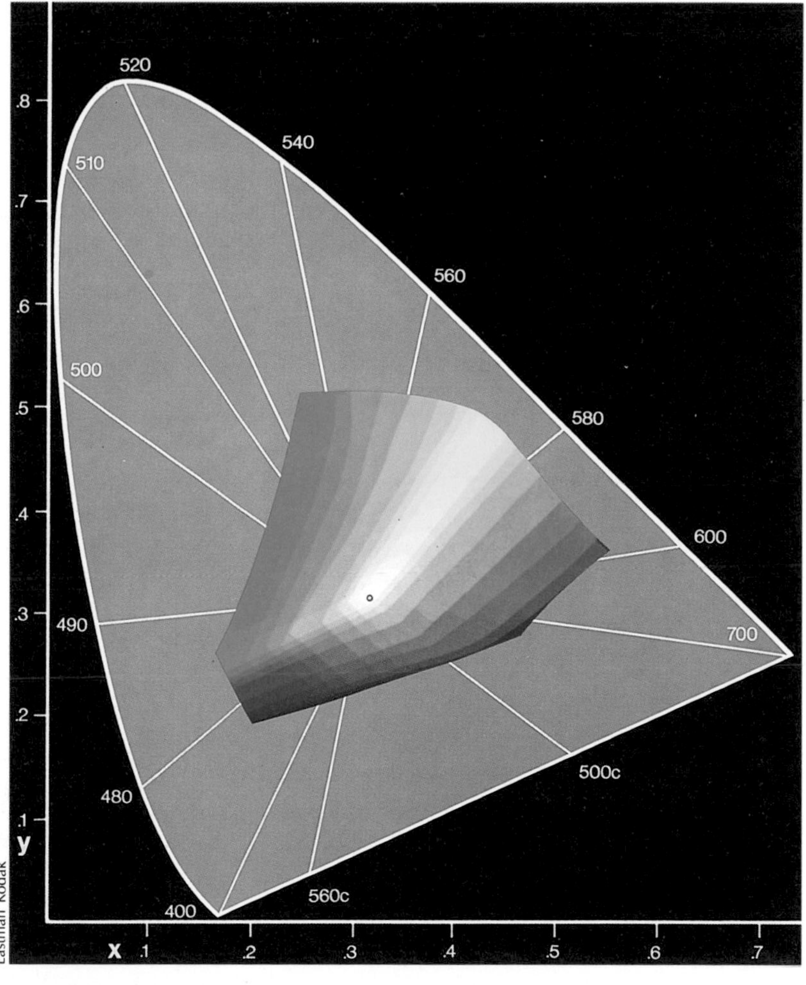

Substrates affect color perception

Controlling color produced by different technologies and on different substrates can be a major problem. Red sprayed in lacquer on sheet steel to create a shiny car may look very different from the dye a cloth was dipped in or the ink used in printing on newsprint. Matching them in four-color process inks is yet another compromise.

Communicating about such anomalies or inconsistencies exacerbates the problem. Some of the reasons are purely physical: fading inks, inconsistent lighting, faded swatchbooks, variations in materials of which the swatches are made. Other reasons, of course, are terminology and language.

Do these minor variations matter? Perfection is unattainable anyway, so why bother? Matching the precise color is a critical consideration when the product is identified by its color packaging or when color is an element of corporate identity.

Two of the companies that can help:

Pantone, Inc., 55 Knickerbocker Road, Moonachie, N.J. 07074, (201) 935-5500

The Pantone™ Packaging Color Standards Program produces proofs on the substrates you need and shows tolerance limits. It also produces printing-ink formulas or pigment-content information to match the required hues.

Munsell Color, 2441 N. Calvert Street, Baltimore, Md. 21218, (301) 243-2171

They produce swatches in opaque acrylic lacquer, which is more stable than colored ink (though it, too, will fade over time and is liable to scratching and fingerprinting). They use a notation system that identifies the hue, value, and chroma, so the color can be duplicated within given tolerances.

GLOSSARY

Bit image Eight-bit: electronic image format representing each pixel as a number from one to 256, each of which describes a value of gray or a fixed value from a color palette.

Twenty-four-bit: electronic image that represents each pixel as a combination of red, green, and blue, each color in 256 levels of gray. Therefore, 16,777,216 color combinations are possible (256 × 256 × 256).

Chroma The degree of purity, brilliance, or saturation of a color.

Chromaticity A measure of the combination of both hue and saturation in color produced by lights.

Color Light waves reach the viewer's eye by transmission (through an object between the source of light and the viewer) or by reflection (when waves bounce off an object). All substances, whether transparent or solid, absorb some wavelengths while letting others pass through or bounce off. Green glass looks green because it absorbs all colors in white light except green, which it allows to pass through. A purple grape looks purple because it absorbs all colors in white light except purple, which it reflects. White objects reflect all and black ones absorb all light waves (at least in theory). There is no such thing as perfect white or perfect black.

Color, additive When color is produced by colored lights, then mixing color affects the total value (lightness or darkness). Combining colored lights produces a lighter result, because white light is composed of all the colors of the spectrum. (See Primaries, additive and subtractive.)

Color, subtractive When color is produced by pigments, mixing colors produces darker values.

Color bars Rectangles of color printed on color proofs to check the ink densities, trapping, and other technical factors required to conform to quality standards.

Color conversion Black-and-white version made from a color photograph or other original.

Color correction Adjusting color separations to make accurate reproduction, accommodating them to the limitations of the particular press, inks, paper, and technology used.

CEPS Color Electronic Prepress System. Digital color image manipulation and assembly systems used in electronic color separation.

Color filter Dyed gelatin or plastic under glass, used to absorb certain colors and improve others. Blue, green, and red filters are used in making color separations.

Color matching Specifying flat colors according to numbered samples on a color chart available from the printer or in swatch books. Process colors are usually specified in percentages of screens of the four colors, for example, XY 5M 2C 1K (X usually means 100%, so here it calls for 100% yellow, 50% magenta, 20% cyan, and 10% black. The letter K designates black to avoid confusion with the word *Blue*, which is often used instead of cyan. Often the word *Red* is used instead of *Magenta*.

Color photographs The negative process activates dyes that are complementary to those in the original scene. The positive print made from the negative reverses the arrangement and the final result corresponds to the colors of the original again.

The positive process: releases magenta, cyan, and yellow dyes in the film's three layers. When developed, the light shining through the transparency recreates the original image.

Color print Photographic print, as opposed to transparency. It is made by methods such as Cibachrome, dye transfer, Kodacolor, and so forth.

Color proof Hard copy in color to check before the piece is printed.

Color keys, 3M products, are a fast process of color proofing on separate acetate sheets, which are overlaid and combined to show the intended result.

Cromalin by Du Pont and Matchprint by 3M are systems that yield accurate proofs in high-quality single images. There are literally dozens of other off-press proofing systems available.

Progressive proofs or "progs," made from the separate plates in color process printing, show each color singly as well as in combination with the others according to the printing sequence, usually yellow, magenta, cyan, and black. They are true press proofs, made (at enormous expense) on the press on which the job will be run or on a separate proofing press.

Color separations A colored original transformed into four printable segments: the three *subtractive primaries* (yellow, magenta, and cyan) and black. It is done by photographing the original through filters or by means of an electronic scanner. The four negatives are turned into positive printing plates, which are superimposed on each other in the printing process. The four colors combine and accumulate to create the illusion of full color, similar to the original.

Color wheel Diagram of colors, originally created by bending Sir Isaac Newton's spectrum into a circle. In desktop publishing, the color wheel displays all available colors.

Colored paper Best color reproduction is provided by white paper of the right surface smoothness. The white paper is the light source off which waves are reflected. They pass through the inks, which are generally transparent. Colored paper affects the appearance of the color printed on it, because it does not reflect the full spectrum of white light but only parts of it (since other parts are absorbed by the paper itself).

Continuous tone A photograph, rendering, or other similar image that is made of blended gray tones or values that flow into each other gradually and without hard edges.

Expressionistic colors Colors picked for emotional impact or meaning rather than for literal description.

Halftone A photograph or other *continuous tone* original rendered reproducible in print by conversion to a variety of tiny dots whose size duplicates the darkness or lightness of the original.

HLS Hue/Luminance/Saturation. Also called HSB (Hue/Saturation/Brightness). A means of characterizing a color in desktop publishing. The equivalent of the traditional hue/value/chroma relationships.

Hue The characteristic of a color that is distinguished by a name such as red, blue, and so forth. The actual hue is created by a wavelength of light.

Hues: analogous Colors that are neighbors on the color wheel.
chromatic Any colors other than black, white, or gray.
complementary Colors that lie opposite on a color wheel.
monochromatic Colors of single hue but varied value and chroma.
nonchromatic Neutral color: black, white, or gray.
polychromatic Multicolored.
secondary Colors made by mixing two primary colors.
spectral White light broken by a prism, like the rainbow.
tertiary Colors made by mixing a primary with an adjacent secondary color.

Luminance The degree of lightness or darkness in colors created by mixing lights. The equivalent of value in colors created by mixing pigments.

Moiré pattern Undesirable star or other patterns resulting from the superimposition of dot-screens at wrong *screen angles*.

Neutralized colors Also called tones, these colors are hues dulled by the addition of white, black, gray, or some of the complementary color pigment.

Palette colors Graphic technique restricted to using a limited number of colors.

Pastel colors Colors resulting from white pigment being added to neutralized hues.

Pigment Material, usually in powder form, added to a liquid binder to give color to paints or inks.

Posterization A mechanical process that converts continuous tone images into a variety of flat areas

Primary colors The hues from which other colors can be mixed.

Primaries, additive Red, green, and blue are the three primary hues that form white light when they are added together. Video display terminals represent colors this way.

Primaries, subtractive The three ink colors (yellow, magenta, and cyan) used in process color printing. Each primary is created by absorbing, that is "subtracting," one of the additive primaries from white light.

Process-color inks Three subtractive primaries used in conjunction with black to reproduce full-color originals. Process yellow reflects red and green light and absorbs blue light. Cyan (blue) reflects blue and green light and absorbs red light. Magenta (red) reflects red and blue light and absorbs green light.

Ramping, or gradation The illusion of a gradual change of one color to another, like the effect of an airbrush, created in the software by a series of discrete steps.

Retouching Editing images to alter or change them or to eliminate imperfections. It can be done by hand, by airbrush, or electronically on digitized images, black-and-white or color.

RGB Red/Green/Blue: the additive colors used by computers to display colors. One hundred percent of all colors equals white light.

Saturation The purity of a color. Its brightness. Same as *chroma*.

Scaling Altering the size of an electronic image. Anamorphic scaling changes only one dimension, resulting in a squeezed or stretched image.

Screen angles Each element of a four-color separation must be photographed through a screen that has been placed at a specific angle, to avoid moiré patterns when the colors are superimposed. Black is normally shot at forty-five degrees, magenta at seventy-five degrees, cyan at 105 degrees, and yellow at ninety degrees. Precise registration is required.

Screens The eye thinks that a pattern of dots looks like a shade of gray. The smaller the dots, the lighter the shade; the larger the dots, the darker the shade perceived. They are produced by photographing the original artwork (photograph or any continuous tone illustration) through an actual screen of fine lines. The fineness of the screens can vary from sixty-five lines to 150 lines or more per inch. Sixty-five- or eighty-five-line screens are used for printing on newsprint. Better paper can accommodate more detailed printing produced by finer screens, which yield higher resolution.

Shade Color resulting from black pigment being added to a pure hue.

Spectrophotometer Instrument used to measure energy in a sample of light or pigmented surface. The colorimeter measures the amount of power of wavelengths emanating from a light source.

Spot color Also flat or matched color. Areas of solid color used on the printed page usually in addition to black. In desktop parlance, a spot color is usually a special colored ink, not a combination of process-color inks.

Style sheet Formatting table that assigns attributes to a graphic element, such as stroke weight, color, and fill pattern in a drawing program.

TIFF Tagged Image File Format. Electronic image format capable of controlling gray scale and color.

Tint Color resulting from white pigment being added to a pure hue.

Undercolor removal (UCR) Increasing the quality of color reproduction by changing the balance of inking. The amount of ink used to print yellow, magenta, and cyan is decreased, while black is increased to produce a stronger image.

Value The lightness or darkness or shade of a color.

Visible spectrum Wavelengths perceived by the human eye as colors.

YCMK Yellow/Cyan/Magenta/Black, the process colors used in process-color offset printing.

BIBLIOGRAPHY

For further reading you may find these works useful.

Josef Albers, *Interaction of Color* (New Haven: Yale University Press, 1975).

Mark Beach, Steve Shepro, and Ken Russon, *Getting It Printed* (Portland: Coast to Coast Books, 1986).

Michael Beaumont, *Type and Color* (Oxford: Phaidon Press, 1987).

Faber Birren, *Principles of Color* (West Chester, Penn.: Schiffer Publishing, 1987).

Tom Cardamone, *Mechanical Color Separation Skills* (New York: Van Nostrand Reinhold, 1980).

Hideaki Chijiiwa, *Color Harmony*: A Guide to Creative Color Combinations (Rockport, Mass.: Rockport Publishers, 1987).

Alton Cook and Robert Fleury, *Type and Color* (Rockport, Mass.: Rockport Publishers, 1989).

Mario Garcia, *Color in American Newspapers* (St. Petersburg, Fla.: Poynter Institute for Media Studies, 1988).

Luigina de Grandis, *Theory and Use of Color* (New York: Harry N. Abrams, 1986).

GATF, *Color and Its Reproduction* (Pittsburgh: Graphic Arts Technical Foundation, n.d.).

Karl Gerstner, *The Forms of Color* (Cambridge, Mass.: MIT Press, 1986).

Johannes Itten, *The Elements of Color* (New York: Van Nostrand Reinhold, 1970).

PMS, *Color Simulator, Color Selector, Two-Color Selector,* etc. (Moonachie, N.J.: Pantone Library of Color, n.d.).

PMS, *Color News Quarterly* (Woodland Hills, Calif.: Pantone Color Institute, n.d.).

S. D. Scott Process Color Guide, 5000 Combinations (New York: S. D. Scott Printing Company, n.d.).

Ikuyoshi Shibukawa and Yumi Takahashi, *Designer's Guide to Color*, 3 vols. (San Francisco, Calif.: Chronicle Books, 1983, 1984, 1989).

Miles Southworth, *Color Separation Techniques* (Livonia, N.Y.: Graphic Arts Publishing Company, n.d.).

Jan V. White, *Using Charts and Graphs* (New York: R. R. Bowker, 1984).

Jan V. White, *Graphic Design for the Electronic Age* (New York: Xerox Press/Watson-Guptill Publications, 1988).

Paul Zelanski and Mary Pat Fisher, *Colour for Designers and Artists* (London: The Herbert Press, 1989).

INDEX